10/₂ $5⁰⁰

"Robin Casarjian elevates the concept of forgiveness to a new level. Like a rose giving off its fragrance, this book radiates immense love, compassion and caring."
  —Larry Dossey, M.D.,
    author of *Meaning & Medicine* and *Recovering the Soul*

"A gentle, compassionate and powerful guide, full of useful exercises for deep self-healing and psychospiritual growth."
  —Harold H. Bloomfield, M.D.,
    author of *Making Peace with Your Parents* and *Making Peace with Yourself*

"Robin Casarjian's book *Forgiveness* can help us find our path out of guilt, fault, blame, resentment and rage. . . . Forgiveness will heal your life and the lives of those you touch and your true potential can then manifest itself."
  —Bernie S. Siegel, M.D.,
    author of *Love, Medicine & Miracles* and *Peace, Love & Healing*

"If my patients read this book, it will make my work much easier and their healing more joyous and more complete."
  —O. Carl Simonton, M.D.,
    author of *Getting Well Again* and *The Healing Journey*

"Robin Casarjian helps us reclaim the sacred healing power of forgiveness that lives within every human heart. If you absorb its message, this book will change your life."
  —Jacquelyn Small,
    author of *Becoming Naturally Therapeutic* and *Awakening in Time*

FORGIVENESS

A
Bold Choice
for A
Peaceful Heart

ROBIN CASARJIAN

BANTAM BOOKS
NEW YORK · TORONTO · LONDON · SYDNEY · AUCKLAND

FORGIVENESS

A Bantam Book/September 1992

All rights reserved.

Copyright © 1992 by Robin Casarjian.
Cover design copyright © 1992 by Kathy Saksa Design.
No part of this book may be reproduced or transmitted
in any form or by any means, electronic or mechanical,
including photocopying, recording, or by any information
storage and retrieval system, without permission in
writing from the publisher.
For information address: Bantam Books.

Library of Congress Cataloging-in-Publication Data

Casarjian, Robin.
  Forgiveness : a bold choice for a peaceful heart / by Robin Casarjian.
     p.   cm.
  Includes bibliographical references.
  ISBN 0-553-35236-9
  1. Forgiveness.   I. Title.
BF637.F67C37   1992
158'.2—dc20   92-7239
                  CIP

Published simultaneously in the United States and Canada

_____

Bantam Books are published by Bantam Books, a division of Bantam
Doubleday Dell Publishing Group, Inc. Its trademark, consisting of the
words ''Bantam Books'' and the portrayal of a rooster, is Registered in
U.S. Patent and Trademark Office and in other countries. Marca
Registrada. Bantam Books, 666 Fifth Avenue, New York, New York
10103.

_____

PRINTED IN THE UNITED STATES OF AMERICA

FFG   0 9 8 7 6 5 4 3 2 1

CONTENTS

Nearly a decade ago, I attended a wellness conference as a guest lecturer, speaking on the physiology and psychology of the bodymind. I was heading back to my office with the single-mindedness of a resolute swimmer bent on outdistancing a surging tide of paperwork, when I heard a welcoming voice call my name. I turned around and recognized Robin Casarjian from one or two previous encounters. Since she taught a stress-management course at the Harvard Community Health Plan, an HMO in the Boston area, and I ran a clinic at a nearby hospital for people with stress-related disorders, we had overlapping professional interests. Something about the warmth of Robin's greeting and her *presence*— Robin is one of those people who really is present when she talks to you—made me forget the beckoning mounds of paperwork. I decided to stay and attend the lecture she was about to give, even though the topic seemed unusual for a health conference. It was a lecture on forgiveness.

"Forgiveness?" I thought as we waited for the lecture to begin. "What does forgiveness contribute to healing?" As my mind reran a recent phone conversation with my mother, my body responded with tightened muscles, a spasming gut and a racing heart. Having installed my buttons to begin with, she knew exactly where they were. Our relationship was stuck in a repeating dance of button pushing, hurt, anger, defensiveness and guilt. Years of therapy and personal growth work had given me a lot of insight into our relationship, but I still felt stuck. Something was missing in the healing of our relationship. That something clearly affected my stress levels and my physical health. As I sat in contemplative silence waiting for Robin to begin her lecture, the deepest wisdom of my heart told me that the missing element was forgiveness— and that forgiveness might just be the most critical key to healing.

As I began to think about what it would actually mean to forgive both my mother and myself, a number of mental walls began to go up and seal off the wisdom in my heart. Would forgiving my mother mean that she was right and I was wrong? Would it mean that I would have to keep swallowing the intense anger I often felt toward her? That I had to turn the other cheek and pretend that she couldn't hurt me?

Robin interrupted my reverie at this point with an invitation: "Close your eyes and take a few letting-go breaths." She smiled. "Then reach into your head and gently pull out all the ideas you have about forgiveness." I felt reassured when she told us that we could temporarily store these concepts under our chair and were free to pick them up again any time we liked. My own concepts about forgiveness have long since composted under that chair.

In the years that have passed since I first heard Robin speak, I have learned at both a personal and a professional level that forgiveness is both a sign of healing and a key to it. All the insight in the world is worth very little if we still rise up in resentment every time the action of a stranger reminds us of our own unhealed relationships. What use is self-knowledge if we use it to fuel the self-hatred and guilt that tell us that in spite of all our efforts we will never be enough, do enough, care enough or help enough to be worthy of our own love.

Robin's teaching about forgiveness is clear, sensible and eminently practical. Forgiveness entails the authentic acceptance of our own worthiness as human beings, the understanding that mistakes are opportunities for growth, awareness and the cultivation of compassion, and the realization that the extension of love to ourselves and others is the glue that holds the universe together. Forgiveness, as she explains it, is not a set of behaviors, but an attitude. When our choices are informed by our core sense of Self, rather than through the many voices of fear and doubt we've learned along the way, we can trust ourselves to act in a way that affirms and encourages the light within us all.

In a concise and thoughtful manner, Robin traces how the voices of our past keep us from being present to the Now. And just as importantly, she leads the reader through a series of simple yet transformative exercises that free us from the past and help us re-own the peace and power of our own essential nature.

For those of us who have been troubled by fear, doubt, anger, self-hatred, and guilt—in other words, almost everyone who is human—this book is a real and rare treasure. In the years that I've had the pleasure of knowing Robin and referring clients to her for therapy, I've been amazed at the transformation she catalyzes. The reason for this is simple. Robin *is* what she teaches. When you are in the presence of a teacher who is unafraid to delve into the darkest of emotions, but never loses sight of the light, you feel safe. When you sense that a person sees to the very core of your worthiness as a human being, you cannot help but feel worthy.

I've heard Robin speak the words in this book many times, and I've experienced being led through some of her exercises—both in person and via her excellent audiocassette tapes. Each time I experience her work, a deeper level of healing is possible. Of the many people I've had the pleasure to work with and learn from, Robin shines like a beacon. I am absolutely delighted that through this book, so many people can be touched by this exceptional teacher.

Joan Borysenko, Ph.D.,
author of *Minding the Body, Mending the Mind* and
Guilt Is the Teacher, Love Is the Lesson

This book is dedicated in loving memory to my mother,
Alice Casarjian

INTRODUCTION

I was initially drawn to teaching about forgiveness because as a therapist I saw that this essential key to healing was little understood or encouraged. I spoke with many colleagues and found that the real necessity and value of forgiving was, for the most part, like a blind spot in their awareness. Yet it was clear to me that people who forgave were able to go beyond just coping to a deeper healing and to truly enjoying their lives. It was also clear that those who got lost in anger, resentment, guilt, and shame became emotionally stuck and disempowered. As a stress-management trainer and consultant, I saw the negative impact of hostility and guilt on people's stress levels and on their physical health.

It became apparent that if I was to help myself and others heal, grow, and love life, forgiveness had to be an integral part of that process.

A number of influences have taught me a great deal about forgiving. Among them have been people who inspired me by example; the study of *A Course in Miracles* (a three-volume work that focuses on healing oneself and relationships through forgiveness); the practice of meditation, which has been invaluable in helping me to cultivate awareness and insight; those people and circumstances that have triggered anger and judgments in me, giving me the opportunity to forgive again and again; and the many challenges of forgiving myself.

Although I didn't know it then, my mother was my first teacher of forgiveness. I am one of those rare individuals who grew up in a loving, joyful home with a mother who lived forgiveness in its most expanded sense. She was consistently loving, nurturing, generous, encouraging, and affectionate. She skillfully balanced the limits she set by encouraging independence. I always felt accepted and respected. When I brought home mediocre grades from school I was encouraged to try harder while assured that it was understood that I was already making an effort. I felt a love that wove a feeling of acceptance and safety into the fabric of my life. Even if she disagreed with me or got angry, her heart was always open.

Despite having lived through the Armenian massacres in Turkey where one of her brothers starved to death and her family suffered great trials, despite having lost an eye as a young girl (which was considered quite an aesthetic handicap when she was young), despite having lived most of her life with financial insecurity and hardship, despite having had many other experiences that would have made it easy for her to justify being angry and resentful, she always seemed to be able to see beyond rejection, fear, anger, judgments, and pettiness to bring love, clarity, and goodwill to places and people that would have been easy to pass over as undeserving of a kind response. I'm sure she didn't consciously practice forgiveness, nor was she religious. She just instinctively believed in the basic goodness and value of others.

Yet even a loving, secure home environment couldn't protect me from the trials and challenges of growing up in the world at large. My home environment gave me a firm foundation, but, like everyone, I've had and have my share of forgiving to do.

Part of self-forgiveness is moving beyond confining judgments and perceptions of ourselves that keep us limited and insecure. Through years of negative experiences in public school I internalized a static concept of myself as uncreative. In order to get to

the point where I would take the risk of expressing myself creatively and even write this book, I had to face my fears and move
beyond many old limiting self-perceptions.

Like everyone, I've had my share of forgiving to do in personal
relationships, especially in my most primary and intimate ones.
Over the years, I've had long-term intimate relationships with
lovers who have cheated, lied, and left me unexpectedly.

I have also had personal traumas that particularly challenged
my willingness to forgive. One of my most difficult experiences
was a rape when I was a twenty-one-year-old college student. The
rapist was threatening, hostile, and towered over me in size. The
rape was an extreme violation of my personal freedom, and an
assault upon my body and emotions. At first my overwhelming
feeling was anger and fear, but with the passage of time I came
to forgive. As you will read throughout the book, forgiving never
means condoning behaviors that are unacceptable or abusive.
There is no way in the world that I could or would condone what
happened to me. Yet there is no question that at this point in my
life I have forgiven; and because of the choice to forgive, the
experience hasn't hardened my heart. By forgiving, I released myself from the burden of remaining a victim forever, and freed myself
to fully enjoy my life now.

Sometimes forgiving was easy for me; sometimes forgiving was
a very bold choice. Whatever kind of choice it was, it always led
me to a more peaceful heart. It always left me happier and free to
move on to create healthier relationships with others and with
myself.

Since I started facilitating workshops and lecturing on the subject
of forgiveness nine years ago, I have had the privilege of learning
so much about forgiveness from others. My audiences have in-
cluded groups of both men and women in prison, incarcerated for
serious crimes; groups gathered to share and be supported in their
journey beyond addiction; mothers living in shelters for the homeless with their children; groups in the corporate, health-care, and
lay communities seeking ways to deal with the stress of everyday
living, to investigate the subject of forgiveness, and to gain skills
to be more effective in their personal lives and professional roles.

In these groups I've seen numbed faces expressing the pain and powerlessness of despair. I've seen these same faces transformed in the process of opening up and forgiving. I've felt the palpable anguish of mothers suffering guilt about letting their children down. I've seen the same women begin to unburden their shame and transform it through forgiveness into self-acceptance. I've seen couples stuck in noncommunication struggling together in their mutual isolation. I've seen these same couples learn through forgiveness how to let an open, loving relationship emerge.

I don't think anyone really wants to live with anger, resentment, shame, and guilt. Yet most of us haven't known forgiveness as a workable option. We haven't been taught how to forgive ourselves or others. Too few, if any, traditional training programs for health-care providers offer the opportunity to explore the healing of such critical issues as anger and guilt through the practice of forgiveness.

Until recently, Twelve Step programs such as Alcoholics Anonymous have been among the only places outside of religion that have explicitly declared the value and necessity of forgiveness for healing. In modern Western culture, forgiveness has been left for too long to the almost sole responsibility of religious institutions. And, as I see it, even here it has been too often misunderstood.

One of the reasons forgiveness has been so well received is that it makes sense. It appeals to one's reason, guts, and heart. In the following pages it is my intent to take forgiveness out of the realm of a lofty ideal and bring it down to a practical skill that we can all fully integrate as our own.

SOME SUGGESTIONS FOR USING THIS BOOK

As you read through the following pages you will notice that in addition to the general text there are a variety of self-reflective exercises.

Sections set off by the directions to "Pause and Reflect" are usually a series of questions to ask yourself. You may answer them in your mind, or you may find it helpful to write your answers down.

From time to time you will see "seed thoughts" boxed and set in bold type. Seed thoughts are germinal ideas that can serve to inspire new insight and awareness. You are encouraged to write each seed thought on a card or piece of paper, and carry it with you or put it in a place where you will see it often. Whenever you notice it, pause for a few moments and think about its meaning.

There are also longer exercises and visualizations. Visualizations are best done by listening to the prerecorded audiotapes listed on page 244, by prerecording the visualizations yourself, or by having them read aloud by a friend. It is important to find yourself a comfortable position where you aren't likely to be disturbed, then allow yourself to freely imagine the scenes that are described.

Set apart from the main text you will also find personal accounts of forgiveness in the form of stories and letters. These were shared primarily by clients, workshop participants, and friends. Their names and some biographical details have been changed to insure anonymity. These stories of forgiveness in action illustrate the practical power of forgiveness to heal even in very difficult situations.

Although certain chapters focus on forgiving particular people or groups, you will find that most of the concepts can be generalized to forgiving anyone. Even if you feel very loving toward the particular people that the chapter focuses on, I encourage you to read it anyway.

CHOOSING
FORGIVENESS

I

A college friend from whom I hadn't heard in eight years called me recently at 7:15 A.M., having lain restlessly awake for hours before daring to call so early. The incessant movement of her mind filled with imaginary explaining, yelling, and conversing with an old boyfriend who was long gone; the empty pit in her stomach; and the anger and pain of feeling like the deserted lover long after the desertion was over—all felt like too much to bear.

The night before she called she heard that I was writing a book on forgiveness. She said that from the moment that she heard "forgiveness," she felt compelled to call me, to hear more. She described how angry she had been for months, yet how some part of her had known that only if she could forgive was there the promise of finding some peace and resolution. After talking for about an hour, we made plans to meet later that week for coffee and talk more about how forgiving might work for her.

Many times when I give a workshop on forgiveness, I start by asking the participants what prompted them to come. What promise did forgiveness hold for them?

Each person, like my friend, tells their own story of anger and pain, but the common thread that runs through all their responses is that forgiveness holds the promise of freedom and relief.

For my friend it was the promise of resting her head quietly upon her pillow at night, of stopping the ache in her stomach, of healing the sadness in her heart. For others it is the promise of reconciliation after years of estrangement from parents or siblings. It is the promise of more harmony at work and empowerment with co-workers. It is the promise of letting go of relationships that are over and finding the freedom to move on unencumbered. It is the promise of having a more loving and joyful relationship with an intimate partner. It is the promise of ending a longtime battle with oneself and living with greater compassion and self-respect.

Regardless of our unique story, forgiveness holds the promise that we will find the peace that we all really want. It promises our release from the hold that another's attitudes and actions have over us. It reawakens us to the truth of our own goodness and lovableness. It holds the sure promise that we will be able to increasingly unburden ourselves from emotional turmoil and move on feeling better and better about ourselves and about life.

Theologian and philosopher Paul Tillich wrote, "Forgiveness is an answer, the divine answer implied in our existence." Forgiveness is the means for taking what is broken and making it whole. It takes our broken hearts and mends them. It takes our trapped hearts and frees them. It takes our hearts blemished with shame and guilt and returns them to their unspoiled state once again. Forgiveness restores our hearts to the innocence that we once knew—an innocence that allowed us the freedom to love.

When we forgive and are forgiven, our lives are always transformed. The sweet promises of forgiveness are kept. And we are actually given a fresh start with ourselves and the world.

CHAPTER ONE

THE CHALLENGE OF FORGIVENESS

Just say the word "forgive" and for some the response is immediate: "Are you kidding?" or "Never" or "Not after what she's done!" or even "I wish I could." Sometimes the mere thought of actually forgiving someone may result in intensified feelings of anger and rage. At other times it may immediately bring relief.

Take a few minutes and notice what the suggestion of forgiving someone evokes for you. Allow an individual to come to mind whom you feel has been the source of personal pain. How do you feel about forgiving that person? What does it mean to you to forgive him or her? What would you have to do in order to forgive?

We each have a set of preconceived ideas of what forgiveness means, accompanied by feelings that help to keep these ideas anchored in place. Your concept of forgiveness can either hinder you and limit your capacity for clarity and joy, or it can uplift you, giving you a way to release the past and be free to live with greater peace and happiness.

For instance, if you believe that forgiving someone means you condone their behavior and must accept whatever they did, then you may write off a lot of people as unforgivable and hold onto resentment forever. This seems like a very reasonable and sane response, for who would condone the behavior of an abuser, a manipulator, or anyone insensitive to the basic rights of another?

The beliefs that you hold about forgiveness open or close possibilities for you, determine your willingness to forgive, and, as a result, profoundly influence the emotional tone of your life.

AN INVITATION

Because some of your current concepts of forgiveness may limit what is possible for you, I invite you to do the following:

Before you read further, stop reading for a few minutes—take a few deep breaths, breathing in a longer, slower breath than usual. As you breathe out, feel yourself releasing tension and relaxing. Let your shoulders relax . . . . Then, in your imagination, gently put your hands to your head, go into your mind, and gently, very gently, take out all the ideas that you currently hold about what forgiveness means. Now place these ideas somewhere safe where you can retrieve them after reading this book (or even sooner), should you feel you would like them again.

I invite you to be open to a whole new way of defining forgiveness and working with it in your everyday life. By suspending familiar ideas, you will create an openness that will allow you to engage most powerfully and fully with the magnificent possibilities of forgiveness.

Let's clear up some misconceptions first by starting with what forgiveness is not.

WHAT FORGIVENESS IS NOT

Forgiveness is *not* condoning negative, inappropriate behavior— your own or someone else's. Abuse, violence, aggression, betrayal, and dishonesty are just some of the behaviors that may be completely unacceptable. You may feel that firm and decisive action— divorce, litigation, or leaving a relationship—are called for or even required to prevent the behavior from happening again. Forgiveness does not mean you approve or support the behavior that has caused you pain, nor does it preclude taking action to change a situation or protect your rights. For instance, the thought of forgiving a rapist, as I described in the introduction, may disturb or even outrage you. It may seem impossible to forgive someone who so blatantly violated someone else; it is only impossible if one is required to accept the behavior in order to forgive.

Forgiveness is *not* pretending everything is just fine when you feel it isn't. Sometimes the distinction between being truly forgiving and denying or repressing anger and hurt can be deceptive and confusing. Because being angry is frequently considered unacceptable (especially if you express your anger), many people learn early in life to replace genuine feelings with more acceptable feelings and behaviors that won't result in punishment and abandonment.

Reflect on your childhood for a few moments. Think of times when you expressed anger. Were your parents, teachers, and others understanding? Did they listen? Or did you get sent out of the room, reprimanded, ridiculed, yelled at, or ignored? What messages, directly or indirectly, were you given about being angry? Were you told "Don't talk back," "Nice girls don't yell," "What will the neighbors think?" "Don't be disrespectful"?

You may have learned to be a "good" boy or girl and repress your anger by acting "nice" even though you felt resentful and misunderstood. You may repress your anger now, as an adult, because being angry isn't compatible with your image of a good person, parent, spouse, or friend.

Denying anger for the sake of "forgiveness" is illustrated in the following scenarios:

A friend of mine has elderly parents who have their forty-five-year-old son living with them. They permit him to verbally abuse them regularly and to contribute almost nothing to the household. They believe they love him, and they want to help him. They want to be "good parents" and think that by not setting limits or making any demands on their son, they are being loving. They "forgive" him to keep the peace, while underneath there is a constant current of frustration and resentment.

Another friend experienced a personal crisis while out of town.

She called her husband from her hotel room for support. After only a few minutes, he abruptly cut the conversation short. She felt hurt and angry, but tried to make excuses and ignore his behavior by ignoring his unsympathetic response. She was determined to be "understanding and forgiving." The next morning she awakened still feeling angry—and with a pounding headache.

Genuine forgiveness cannot be offered if anger and resentment are denied or ignored.

Forgiveness is *not* assuming an attitude of superiority or self-righteousness. If you forgive someone because you pity them or consider them foolish or stupid, you have confused forgiveness with arrogance and being judgmental. For instance, a client's father, not conscious of his hostile attitude, offered "forgiveness" to his daughter by saying, "Never mind, I forgive you. I didn't think you could pull it off anyway."

Forgiveness does *not* mean you will or must change your behavior. If I forgive an old friend from whom I have been estranged, I don't have to start calling again—unless I really want to. You may forgive your husband for being careless with money, but that doesn't mean you have to give him your paycheck and the household finances to manage. You may forgive your mother for being too critical, yet you may still make the choice not to confide in her. You can forgive an incompetent employee and fire him if he's not doing his job.

Forgiveness does *not* require that you verbally communicate directly to the person you have forgiven. You don't have to go to them and declare, "I forgive you," although this may sometimes be an important part of the process of forgiving. Often the other person will sense your change of heart. At times it may need to remain a private choice. Perhaps the people you are most angry at are those you can't contact. Perhaps they have died or they are unwilling to speak with you. If direct verbal communication or an overt action were necessary for healing, then living forever with personal pain might be our fate. Luckily this is not so. Although we may choose to behave differently, forgiveness requires only a shift in perception, another way of looking at the people and circumstances that we feel have caused us upset and pain.

ANGER AND RESENTMENT

The most obvious reason for forgiving is to relieve ourselves of the debilitating effects of chronic anger and resentment. These are the most apparent emotions that make forgiveness a challenge as well as a welcome possibility for anyone wanting greater peace.

As we all know, anger and resentment are powerful emotions that consume our energy in numerous ways.

~~~~~~

P A U S E   A N D   R E F L E C T

Pause for a few minutes and think back on a time when you felt angry. How were you feeling? Or, if you are currently feeling angry, pause and become aware of how you're feeling now. . . . Now take a deep breath and go deeper into your feelings. What is going on underneath your anger? Were you or are you feeling scared? Sad? Insecure? Helpless? Powerless? Hurt? Abandoned? Were you or are you feeling the disappointment of unmet expectations and unfulfilled dreams? Look even deeper. Underneath the fears, frustrations, and/or sadness, were you or are you asking someone to really listen and pay attention to you? Were you or are you, consciously or unconsciously, calling out for respect, acknowledgment, caring, or love?

~~~~~~

As you peel away the layers, you will probably find that anger is actually a superficial feeling. Not superficial in the sense that it is trivial and inauthentic, but superficial in that there are many more feelings and dynamics underneath it. If we get lost in our anger, we become deaf to our deeper feelings. We learn to hear only those that have learned to speak the loudest.

Anger is a strong temporary emotional reaction to feeling threatened in some way. When anger arises, it may be expressed openly and directly, or it may go underground, quietly and persistently expressing itself as chronic resentment. Resentment is the feeling of chronic grievance or ill will that persists even long after the situation that provoked the anger is over. Resentment has been compared to holding onto a burning ember with the intention of throwing it at another, all the while burning yourself. In fact, the word *resentment* comes from the French *ressentir*—to feel strongly and to feel again. When we feel resentful, we feel strongly the pain of the past again and again. Not only does this take an obvious and dramatic toll on our emotional well-being, it can powerfully and negatively impact our physical well-being as well.

A physician who attended a workshop I facilitated on the use of visualization in healing complained of chronic back pain from which he could find no relief. Five hours into the workshop I led a visualization in forgiving. During the visualization he forgave his ex-wife. Much to his astonishment and relief, as he let go of the anger the pain in his back released as well.

THE BENEFITS OF HOLDING ON

For many of us, there are major stakes in letting go of anger and resentment because we feel that we get something from holding on to it. These benefits, referred to as "secondary gains," are frequently unconscious and very powerful until we become consciously aware of them and find healthier ways to respond.

Reflect on whether you use anger or resentment in any of the following ways:

Do you stay angry because it gives you a feeling of being more powerful and in control? Some people feel that getting angry and holding on to resentment demonstrates power, strength, commitment, and personal pride. But in fact, anger and resentment usually mask feelings of helplessness, disappointment, insecurity, grief, or fear, and are often used as substitutes for feelings of genuine personal power.

If, as a child, you were mistreated and had to deny and repress anger to survive, part of your healing includes giving yourself permission to claim these feelings now. Claiming anger may empower you to stand up for yourself and for the wounded inner child who couldn't stand up for himself or herself before. If you were denied your true feelings before, feeling angry now may give you the courage and power to stand up for yourself as you learn that you do indeed have a right to feel angry and assert yourself. If you were physically or sexually abused as a child, feeling anger may be a crucial part of the process of reclaiming and inhabiting your body as your own, and establishing and asserting personal rights and clear boundaries. Yet if you get stuck in needing anger in order to set boundaries, then the anger that is necessary at first to empower and heal you eventually disempowers you and inhibits healing.

Do you use anger as the impetus and fuel for getting things done? Some people believe that "if people weren't angry, they wouldn't work for social and political change." And indeed anger *can* be a positive motivator for change. Yet anger does not have to be the only motivation, the primary motivation, or, for that matter, any of the motivation for change. When we are in touch with our own true nature, with empathy and a sense of justice, we are often moved to take action with passion and conviction, and without anger. When anger is the primary motivation for change, it often creates resistance to the very change we are trying to elicit. It elicits fear in those we are trying to influence and, as a result, it often generates opposition rather than resolution.

One very sensitive and caring client had worked long and hard for organizations seeking to protect the environment. She felt passionate about this cause, yet her untransformed personal anger often got in the way of her effectiveness. She attended a public hearing with the intention of speaking out against a proposed industrial park that would increase pollution and destroy indigenous wildlife. Although she had hoped that her passionate outcry would engender much-needed support and inspire others to align with her cause, her anger pervaded her speech and the audience felt blamed and accused. Instead of rallying the support that she so very much wanted, she alienated many of those present and defeated her own purpose.

Do you use anger to control others? Have you ever noticed that when someone is angry, people around him or her become guilty and frightened and, as a result, sometimes allow themselves to be manipulated? If we use anger as a way to manipulate and control others, they, in turn, feel angry and resentful. We may get to control others by our anger, but as with all the secondary gains, we pay a high price in the process.

Another client, now thirty-five years old, had decided to move in with her boyfriend when she was twenty-three. Her father had never approved of his daughter's choice in men, and was particularly critical of this man who was of a different religious background from his own. When his daughter informed her father of her decision, the father flew into a rage and threatened to disown her if she followed through on her plans. She did move in with her boyfriend and there was no communication with her father for the next five years. Her father paid a high price for holding on to his anger.

Do you use anger to avoid communication? If you are afraid of taking the risk of sharing your thoughts and feelings, or of the possible consequences of telling the truth, then anger can be used as an effective avoidance mechanism. Anger may feel safer than intimacy and genuine communication.

Sherry is a friend whose parents had divorced when she was young. It was a difficult time for everyone in her family, and her mother became depressed and withdrawn. When Sherry got married she was determined to make it last. When her husband started staying late at work due to the pressures of his job, Sherry became terrified that he was cheating and would leave. She was afraid to share her anxiety and confront him with her suspicion. Instead she lashed out at him for small things and for working so much. Her husband felt attacked and criticized and started to find more reasons to work late. Sherry used anger to avoid addressing her real fears.

Do you use anger to help you feel safe? Does it seem to serve as a protection? When anger is projected toward others, they will often stay away. If they can't get too close, you don't have to feel so vulnerable. Using anger for self-protection may have been very creative and necessary when you were younger. Now as an adult you can learn to set boundaries and respond differently toward others who might try to disempower or dominate you.

Do you use anger as a way of asserting that you are "right"? You may be thinking as you reflect on this question, "You'd better

believe it! I am right and she is wrong!'' Forgiving does not imply that you are now acknowledging that the other person is right
or that you are now wrong. Rather it teaches that "there is another
way of looking at the world." It may be useful to ask yourself,
"Do I want to be right, or do I want to be happy?" Sometimes we
don't get to be both.

Do you hold on to anger to make others feel guilty? If you are
angry, you may want to punish the person toward whom you feel
angry. Reinforcing their guilt feelings is one way to do this. The
major problem with this strategy is that as we do this, we simultaneously—although not consciously—reinforce our own guilt,
which inevitably leads to personal unhappiness and low self-
esteem.

Do you use anger to avoid the feelings that are under the anger?
Sometimes it's much easier to feel angry than it is to feel the fear
and sadness underlying the anger. In fact, one reason it is sometimes so difficult to forgive is that in order to forgive we have to
bring to light and accept the truth of how we really feel. If we
have learned to live with denial and repression, this can be a painful
unveiling. Try to gently remind yourself, however, that on the
other side of the pain is relief and greater peace of mind.

Do you use anger to hold on to a relationship? As long as you
are holding on to the anger, you are in a relationship with the
person you are angry with. Many times a man or woman will get
divorced in order to get away from his or her spouse. Yet as long
as you hold on to resentment, you remain bound to the person
whom you resent. It may feel safer to hold on to the resentment
than to let go, because letting go may seem unbearably lonely or
new and scary. Many young adults move away from home to
escape from anger and resentment they feel toward their parents.
The move may be a wise and appropriate choice, yet if the anger
isn't resolved, they will always carry the unfinished business from
this relationship with them. When you harbor resentment, it is as
though you have a chain around your wrist and this chain is bound
to the wrist of the person you resent.

Does your anger keep you in the role of victim? If you spend
much of your life feeling like a victim, there may be a lot of
resistance to forgiving because when you forgive, you give up a

big part of that identity. If you forgive, it does not mean that you deny that you were a victim, but having been a victim doesn't necessarily dominate your present identity and emotional life. One workshop participant wrote, "If I give up all my favorite resentments, what will I have to talk about? Am I sure I can exist without the victim role in my life?" You may have been a victim, yet you have the possibility of living your life free from a victim mentality.

Do you remain resentful so that you don't have to take responsibility for your role in what's happening in your life now, or for how you feel? This may be one of the most powerful secondary gains of holding on to resentment, for as long as we hold on to resentment, we can blame someone else for our unhappiness. It's somebody else's fault. This doesn't mean that others don't contribute to our happiness or unhappiness, but ultimately we are responsible for how we feel. If we indulge in recurrent resentments, never attempting to see a larger picture, we avoid acknowledging the potential power we have in changing our relationship to the situation. As long as we see the problem as exclusively outside ourselves—i.e., that we have no role in how we feel—we keep ourselves helpless.

Chronic anger diverts us from the understanding that regardless of our current relationship with the people who originally provoked our anger, if we continue to carry it around with us, we are now responsible for holding on to it or for making a conscious decision toward letting it go.

Secondary gains, especially if you're not aware of them, can sabotage a conscious desire to forgive.

PAUSE   AND   REFLECT

Ask yourself, "What do I get out of holding on to anger and resentment?" Then complete the following:

What I get out of holding on to resentment is_____.

What I get out of holding on to resentment is_____.

What else I get out of holding on to resentment is_____.

And what else I get out of holding on to resentment is＿＿＿＿.

Be gentle with yourself as you notice these benefits. Try not to judge yourself. Rest assured that there are more positive, fulfilling ways to get what you genuinely want.

THE CASE FOR GENTLENESS

The act of forgiving requires us to reflect on basic perceptions that we may have taken for granted or never questioned. If you are like most people, you will have a tendency (sometimes a very strong tendency) to judge yourself for any number of things: "How could I think this way?" "I should be ready to forgive." "I'm angry and don't want to forgive!"

You may find yourself passing judgment on how quickly or how consistently you are able to integrate the practice of forgiveness into your life. You may feel that you just can't forgive.

As you work with forgiveness and do the exercises in this book, it is extremely important to notice your thoughts and reactions *without* judging them. If you experience fear, self-judgment, and doubts, be gentle with yourself. These are a natural part of the healing process. In fact, being gentle with yourself is, in itself, a great act of self-forgiveness. Regardless of what thoughts or feelings arise, affirm your commitment to being gentle with yourself.

You may not be sure what it means to "be gentle with yourself." Even if you think you don't know what it means, remind yourself to do it anyway. Hang a simple reminder—BE GENTLE WITH YOUR-SELF—around your house, on your refrigerator door, in your car, or anywhere that you will see it often. When you see the reminder, reflect on it for a moment. You may be afraid to be gentle with yourself, thinking it will just reinforce a "bad habit" or thought. Being gentle with yourself doesn't mean that you don't put forth effort and intention or that you condone thoughts and behaviors that you feel are inappropriate. It does mean that you can learn from them without beating yourself up. Being hard on yourself feeds a defeating cycle that disempowers you, encouraging guilt and a lack of self-respect. *Believe it or not, you have always done the best you could in any moment in time based on the degree of love or fear you were experiencing.*

REMEMBER TO BREATHE

As you participate in this book, or at any other time, pay attention to your breathing. Try to remember to breathe fully. When you don't breathe fully, you impede the natural flow of feeling and letting go. Breathing consciously and fully helps you feel and helps you remain grounded in your body. It is particularly important to remember to breathe fully when you feel especially challenged by certain concepts or specific applications of forgiveness.

CHAPTER TWO

FORGIVENESS:
THE KEY TO PEACE
OF MIND

There are many ways to define forgiveness, because forgiveness is many things. It is a decision, an attitude, a process, and a way of life. It is something we offer others and something we accept for ourselves.

Forgiveness is a decision to see beyond the limits of another's personality. It is the decision to see beyond fears, idiosyncrasies, neuroses, and mistakes—to see a pure essence, unconditioned by personal history, that has limitless potential and is always worthy of respect and love. Forgiveness is a choice to "see the light instead of the lampshade," wrote Dr. Gerald Jampolsky, author of many books on forgiveness. Actually, when forgiving, you may indeed see the lampshade (fear-based or conditioned identities), but you see it in the context of the light that illuminates the inner core of each of us.

Forgiveness requires recognizing that if a person is acting like a "jerk," or insensitively, then implicit in their behavior and attitudes are constriction and fear. Even though not obvious to the

unforgiving eye, underlying their behavior and attitudes is a call
for respect, acknowledgment, and love. It takes considerable insight to see this dynamic at first, because we are conditioned to
see the other person as wrong or stupid instead of constricted and
afraid.

One of my clients, Sally, lived this way in relation to her father.
While she was growing up, her father was critical and demanding.
Angry with him for not giving her the love she wanted, she held
her father responsible for all her problems. Believing he would
never change, she resigned herself to being angry with him, and
remained distant. In learning about forgiveness, Sally realized that
her father's critical behavior was the result of his own insecurities
and the fact that his parents had always been emotionally un-
available to him. Instead of continuing the pattern of feeling hurt
by every criticism and getting angry at him for his abrasive ways,
she began to feel compassion for him. She sensed his pain and,
with greater and greater consistency, could see beyond his behavior
and offer him kindness and acceptance. Gradually he softened
toward her. For the first time in her life Sally felt a loving connection with her father. A lifelong burden had been lifted.

Forgiveness is an attitude that implies that you are willing to
accept responsibility for your perceptions, realizing that *your perceptions are a choice and not an objective fact.*

Forgiveness is an attitude that favors looking at a person that
you may have reflexively judged and noticing that there is actually
more to him or her than just the "awful" or insensitive person
that you see. If someone reprimands you or acts disrespectfully,
your conditioned reaction might be to feel hurt, threatened, and
angry: "How could she say that to me?" or "How dare he yell at
me that way?" These are natural reactions. There are, as Sally
demonstrated, alternative responses that can give you the clarity
and insight necessary to prevent another's ignorant or fear-based
reactions from necessarily leaving you feeling angry and defensive.

A consequence of realizing that your perceptions are a choice
is that as you change your perceptions, your emotional reactions
change as well. In place of the angry man you saw attacking you
five minutes ago, you may now see a frustrated and scared little

boy. It is most often the wounded or frightened child in another who is responsible for their lack of caring or mature judgment. This wounded inner child lives within us as adults if our basic need for love, understanding, and comfort was denied as a child. The wounded child remains a driving force in the adult psyche until it is recognized and healed. Forgiving enables you to see the wounded child, the past conditioning, and the call for help and request for love and respect that is underneath insensitive behavior.

Forgiveness is a process that requires shifting your perceptions again and again. It is rarely a one-time event. Our habitual vision is clouded with the judgments and perceptions of the past projected on to the present. Here we are easily deceived by outer appearances. When we choose to shift our perspective to a deeper, more encompassing vision, we are able to acknowledge and affirm the greater truth of who we and others are. As a result of this shift, greater compassion naturally arises for ourselves and others. Each time we make this shift, we weaken the ego's monopoly on our perceptions and are enabled, as the derivation of the word *forgive* implies, to let go, to release, and to cease harboring the past. Forgiveness is often experienced as a feeling of joyfulness, peacefulness, love and open-heartedness, ease, expansiveness, confidence, freedom, lightness, a sense of rightness.

Forgiveness is a way of life that gradually transforms us from being helpless victims of our circumstances to being powerful and loving co-creators of our reality. As a way of life, forgiveness involves a commitment to experiencing each moment uncluttered by past perceptions—seeing each moment freshly, clearly, and without fear. It is the fading away of the perceptions that cloud our ability to love. When most people think about forgiving, they think about it as something to be done from situation to situation, angry incident to angry incident. Although forgiving is ultimately crucial for these times if we want to be free, healed, and able to move on, it is, in its broadest sense, a pervasive way of relating to life that is clear, compassionate, and understanding. Forgiveness teaches us that we can resolutely disagree with someone without withdrawing our love. It takes us beyond the fears and survival mechanisms of our conditioning to a certain boldness of vision that allows for a new realm of choice and freedom where we can put our struggles to rest. It guides us to where peace is not a stranger. It empowers us to know our true strength.

Throughout your day consider: ─────

Today I will see all anger (insensitivity, irritability, hostility, "stupid" behavior, etc.) as a call for acknowledgment, respect, help, and love.

The idea of seeing all anger as a call for acknowledgment, respect, help, and love can be a radical departure from the way we have learned to perceive and respond to anger.

TERRY'S STORY
A wonderful illustration of one person's choice to see anger as a plea for love and respect is this true story by Terry Dobson called *A Kind Word Turneth Away Wrath.*

A turning point in my life came one day on a train in the suburbs of Tokyo. It was the middle of a languid spring afternoon, and the car was comparatively empty—a few housewives out shopping with their kids in tow, some old folks, a couple of bartenders on their day off poring over the racing form. The rickety old car clacked monotonously over the rails as I gazed absently out at the drab houses and dusty hedgerows.

At one sleepy little station, the doors opened and the drowsy afternoon was shattered by a man yelling at the top of his lungs. A string of loud, shocking violent oaths filled the air. Just as the doors closed, the man, still yelling, stumbled into our car. He was a big man, a drunk and exceedingly dirty Japanese laborer. His eyes were a bloodshot, neon red, and his face was apoplectic with hatred and rage. Screaming unintelligibly, he swung at the first person he saw—a woman holding a baby. The blow glanced off her shoulder, but sent her spinning across the car into the laps of an elderly couple.

It was a miracle that the baby was unharmed. The couple jumped up and scampered towards the other end of the car. The laborer aimed a kick at the retreating back of the aged grandmother. "YOU OLD WHORE," he bellowed, "I'LL KICK YOUR ASS!" He missed, and the old lady scuttled safely beyond his reach. Beside himself with rage, the drunk grabbed the metal pole in the center of the car and tried to wrench it out of its stanchion. I could see one of his hands was cut and bleeding. The train rattled on, the passengers frozen with fear. I stood up.

I was still young, back then, and in pretty good shape. I stood six feet, weighed 225, and had been putting in a solid eight hours of Aikido training every day for the past three years. I was totally absorbed in Aikido. I couldn't practice enough. I particularly enjoyed the harder workouts. I thought I was tough. Trouble was, my skill was yet untried in actual combat. We were strictly enjoined from using Aikido techniques in public, unless absolute necessity demanded the protection of other people. My teacher, the founder of Aikido, taught us every morning that Aikido was non-violent. "Aikido," he would say over and over, "is the art of reconciliation. To use it to enhance one's ego, to dominate other people, is to betray totally the purpose for which it is practiced. Our mission is to resolve conflict, not to generate it." I listened to his words, of course, and even went so far as to cross the street a few times to avoid groups of lounging street punks who might have provided a jolly brawl in which I might test my proficiency. In my daydreams, however, I longed for a legitimate situation where I could defend the innocent by wasting the guilty. Such a scene had now arisen. I was overjoyed. My prayers had been answered. I thought to myself, "This slob, this animal, is drunk and mean and violent. He's a threat to the public order, and he'll hurt somebody if I don't take him out. The need is real. My ethical light is green."

Seeing me stand up, the drunk shot me a look of bleary inspection. "AHA!" he roared, "A HAIRY FOREIGN TWERP NEEDS A LESSON IN JAPANESE MANNERS!" I held on to the commuter strap overhead, feigning nonchalance, seemingly off-balance.

I gave him a slow, insolent look of contemptuous dismissal. It burned into his sodden brain like an ember in wet sand. I'd take this turkey apart. He was big and mean, but he was drunk. I was big, but I was trained and cold sober. "YOU WANT A LESSON, ASS?" he bellowed. Saying nothing, I looked coolly back at him. He gathered himself for his big rush at me. He'd never know what hit him.

A split-second before he moved, somebody else shouted, "HEY!" It was loud, ear-splitting almost, but I remember it had a strangely joyous, lilting quality to it—as though you and a friend had been searching diligently for something, and he had suddenly stumbled upon it.

I wheeled to my left, the drunk spun to his right. We both stared down at this little old man. He must have been well into his seventies, this tiny gentleman, immaculate in his kimono and hakama. He took no notice of me, but beamed delightedly at the laborer, as though he had a most important, most welcome secret to share.

"C'mere," the old man said in an easy vernacular, beckoning to the drunk. "C'mere and talk with me." He waved his hand lightly, and the big man followed as if on a string. The drunk was confused, but still belligerent. He planted his feet in front of the little old man, and towered threateningly over him. "WHAT THE FUCK DO YOU WANT, YOU OLD FART?" he roared above the clacking wheels. The drunk now had his back to me. I watched his elbows, half-cocked as though ready to punch. If they moved so much as a millimeter, I'd drop him in his tracks.

The old man continued to beam at the laborer. There was not a trace of fear or resentment about him. "What you been drinkin'?" he asked lightly, his eyes sparkling with interest.

"I BEEN DRINKIN' SAKE, GOD DAMN YOUR SCUMMY OLD EYES," the laborer declared loudly, "AND WHAT BUSINESS IS IT OF YOURS?"

"Oh, that's wonderful," the old man said with delight, "absolutely wonderful! You see, I just love sake. Every night me and my wife (she's seventy-six, you know) we warm up a little bottle of sake, and we take it out into the garden and we sit on the old bench that my grandfather's student made for him. We watch the sun go down, and we look to see how our tree is doing. My great-grandfather planted that tree, you know, and we worry about whether it will recover from those ice-storms we had last winter. Persimmons do not do well after ice-storms, although I must say ours had done

rather better than I expected, especially when you consider
the poor quality of soil. But, anyway, we take our little jug
of sake and go out and enjoy the evening by our tree. Even
when it rains!" He beamed up at the laborer, his eyes twin-
kling, happy to share the wonderful information.

As he struggled to follow the intricacies of the old man's
conversation, the drunk's face began to soften. His fists slowly
unclenched. "Yeah," he said when the old man finished, "I
love sake too . . ." His voice trailed off.

"Yes," said the old man, smiling, "and I'm sure you have
a wonderful wife."

"No," replied the laborer, shaking his head sadly, "I don't
got no wife." He hung his head, and swayed silently with
the motion of the train. And then, with surprising gentleness,
the big man began to sob. "I don't got no wife," he moaned
rhythmically, "I don't got no home, I don't got no clothes,
I don't got no tools, I don't got no money, and now I don't
got no place to sleep. I'm so ashamed of myself." Tears rolled
down the big man's cheeks, a spasm of pure despair rippled
through his body. Up above the baggage rack, a four-color
ad trumpeted the virtues of suburban luxury living. The irony
was almost too much to bear. And all of a sudden I felt
ashamed. I felt more dirty in my clean clothes and my make-
this-world-safe-for-democracy righteousness than that laborer would ever be.

"My, my," the old man clucked sympathetically, although
his general delight appeared undiminished, "that is a very
difficult predicament, indeed. Why don't you sit down here
and tell me about it?"

Just then, the train arrived at my stop. The platform was
packed, and the crowd surged into the car as soon as the
doors opened. Maneuvering my way out, I turned my head
for one last look. The laborer sprawled like a sack on the
seat, his head in the old man's lap. The gentleman was looking down at him kindly, a beatific mixture of delight and
compassion beaming from his eyes, one hand softly stroking
the filthy, matted head.

As the train pulled away from the station, I sat on a bench
and tried to re-live the experience. I saw that what I had
been prepared to accomplish with bone and muscle had been
accomplished with a smile and a few kind words. I recognized

that I had seen Aikido used in action, and that the essence
of it was reconciliation, as the founder had said. I felt dumb
and brutal and gross. I knew I would have to practice with
an entirely different spirit. And I knew it would be a long
time before I could speak with knowledge about Aikido or
the resolution of conflict.

Terry's story brings home so poignantly the basic truth that people
don't victimize, aggress upon others, or try to control others unless
they feel out of control, helpless, and powerless themselves. Realizing the psychological dynamics underlying aggressive behavior
doesn't mean that you or I should respond the way the elder
gentleman in Dobson's story chose to. You can hear a call for help
under another's raving and ranting and still choose to speak up,
leave, make certain demands that must be met in order for you
to remain in the relationship, etc.

If I had been on the train in Dobson's story and was able to
recognize the laborer's pain and plea for help, I probably still would
not have asked him to sit next to me or tried to carry on a conversation with him. I would have, in all likelihood, looked for the
closest way out. Forgiveness is not about what we *do*, it is about
the way we *perceive* people and circumstances. It is another way
of looking at what is being, or has been, done. Regardless of what
I choose to do, seeing his behavior as an expression of fear and a
call for love and respect would have allowed me to be less likely
to contribute to escalating fear and, as a result, more likely to
respond in a truly helpful way.

A PSYCHOLOGICAL FRAMEWORK
FOR UNDERSTANDING
FORGIVENESS

The underlying and often unconscious beliefs that we hold about
ourselves and human nature influence and ultimately determine
our ability and willingness to risk, to trust, to love, and to forgive.
Because this is so, I have found that before encouraging workshop

participants to put forgiveness into practice, it is invaluable to offer a perspective on human nature that makes it possible to understand why forgiveness is a wise and expedient choice.

The following model is based on transpersonal psychology, the study of human nature and development that includes the spiritual dimension of human experience. It is rooted in the assumption that human beings possess potentialities that surpass the limits of the normally developed ego. Although strongly influenced by the Psychosynthesis model developed by the Italian psychiatrist Roberto Assagioli, the model presented here integrates a number of influences and schools of thought.

This perspective of human nature is based on an assumption that within everyone is a center, core, or essence, the nature of which is:

1. Awareness—the ability to see clearly, without defensiveness and without distortion
2. Free will—the ability to choose how we respond to situations

This core nature and fundamental capacity for clarity, conscious choice, and action is referred to as the Self, a term that is used differently from what we usually call the self.

~~~~~~

P A U S E   A N D   R E F L E C T

Imagine you have an important appointment and you are stuck in the middle of a traffic jam. You start to worry, you feel a headache coming on, your shoulders are getting tense, and you envision the worst consequences of being late. Now imagine a moment while anxiously sitting there when you realize that your worry and anxiety isn't moving the car in front of you or the car behind you any faster. You take a deep breath and breathe out a sigh. You tell yourself to relax. You feel some relief. You decide that when you get to your meeting you will simply communicate what happened. You put on your favorite music station. You remind yourself again that you do have a choice as to how you respond to this situation, and you reaffirm to yourself that you might as well relax. You take another deep breath. You sit back, breathe deeply, and enjoy the time you have alone.

~~~~~~

You have just made the shift from feeling like the helpless limited little *self* to being identified with the core or essential *Self*, the source of your personal power.

The ability to step back and be aware of yourself getting caught up in anxiety, and the ability to choose to respond in a clear, wise, and deliberate way, are natural functions of the Self.

SUBPERSONALITIES AND THE SELF

Diagram A on the following page shows the Self at the core of your being, and a variety of smaller selves around it. (The words *small selves, partial selves, subpersonality,* and *ego* are used interchangeably.) These myriad aspects of the personality or ego are referred to as subpersonalities. They are organized patterns of identification consisting of emotions, roles, and beliefs. To the degree that we identify with any particular subpersonality, we see the world through the colored glasses (the beliefs and perspectives) of that particular identification. Part of the process of growing up, of healthy development, includes developing and identifying with the many subpersonalities—with the emotions we feel, the roles we adopt, and the beliefs we hold.

A subsequent stage of healthy adult development demands self-awareness, the ability to stand apart from and identify our governing subpersonality (or subpersonalities) at any time. Such an awareness allows us to recognize that there is more to us than the pattern we are experiencing at any particular moment. Recognizing this is the first step in shifting from experiencing the world through the eyes of a little self to the more expansive perspective of the essential Self. Ultimately the whole of who we are is far greater than the sum of our subpersonalities.

Subpersonalities are an essential part of a whole and healthy

A. SUBPERSONALITIES AND THE SELF

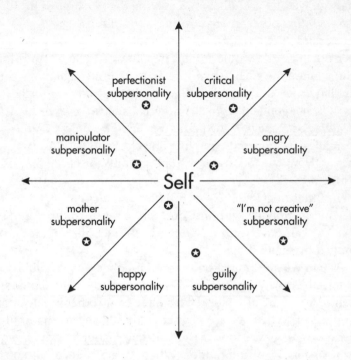

human being. Yet overidentification with any of them can debilitate us or stunt our growth. When subpersonalities based on fear or the early survival tactics of childhood show up recurrently, they will inevitably inhibit well-being. For example, imagine a three-year-old who can only get her need for attention met when she is manipulative: she is likely to (unconsciously) decide that manipulating people is the best way to get what is needed. This is a very creative and reasonable decision for a three-year-old. It may still be creative at age five or ten. But if this person is now twenty or thirty, forty or fifty, and is still manipulating people as a way to get what she wants or needs, it is obviously no longer creative. Now it is a historical and outdated way of relating that is sure to inhibit, among other things, spontaneity, happiness, and self-esteem. Although the role of manipulator was first adopted to secure acknowledgment and love from others, now it is most likely to be met with judgment and anger from others. Like many of the patterned roles that become a way of life, the role of manipulator has outlived its usefulness, preventing the person lost in this role from finding other, more positive ways of relating.

Besides "the manipulator," examples of other patterns or sub-personalities that would inhibit happiness and Self-expression include emotions such as chronic anger, chronic agitation, chronic anxiety; roles such as victim, controller, martyr; and beliefs such as "I'm not good enough," "I'm responsible for everything," "Life is always a struggle." As adults we often become identified with a small part of ourself, and, like an actor who gets lost in the part he's playing, we forget that we are the director of the play as well as the actor.

In order to grow into our full human potential, we need to go beyond identifying with just our partial selves to our core Self so that we can have our emotions, roles, and beliefs without being limited by them.

When we are limited by them, not only are we inhibited from being objectively aware and free to respond to the situations at hand, but we are also blocked from the many other innate qualities of the Self. When we are aligned with our Self we naturally experience greater wisdom, trust in ourselves, courage, joy, creativity, compassion, love, and humor. When we are aligned with our Self we discover greater effectiveness, and access the confidence and power to act on our deepest instincts of what is right.

Being aligned with our true Self quite consistently is an experience that few of us in "civilized" society have had. Very few people, especially in modern Western culture, have been consciously aware of the existence of the Self. Our traditional psychological theories have reinforced a limited view of the adult psyche, one that is dominated by the ego (personality) and unaware of the Self. And yet the Self is always where we are.

Notice in Diagram A that the Self has no boundaries, but that the subpersonalities have definite boundaries. When we are primarily identified with a certain subpersonality, all our perceptions are defined by it. Remember the traffic jam. At first you may have felt fear and worry. If you are primarily identified with worry, you will experience the world through a filter of anxiety and distress. If you are primarily identified with anger, you will experience the

B. INTERACTIVE SUBPERSONALITIES

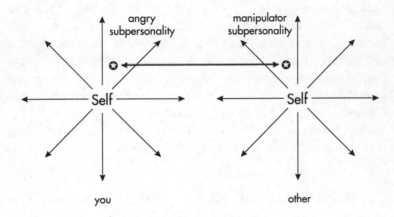

world accordingly, tending to blame and judge others. You will feel anxious and hostile. And as with worry, you will probably be fixed on one way of interpreting situations at hand.

Often our most trying interactions happen when our subpersonalities engage another's subpersonalities.

Take a look at the dynamics in a relationship where you feel anger or resentment. It's unlikely that you are angry at someone who is responsive and loving. Most likely your anger is directed toward someone who is fearful and constricted around one of their subpersonalities, i.e., someone who is manipulative, controlling, unresponsive, critical, or angry. Their anger, manipulation, unresponsiveness, or criticizing, which is caused by their own reflexive stance of self-protection and fear, is threatening to you. You react with anger and judgment of your own. Then what you have is the fear-based subpersonality in you reacting to the fear-based subpersonality of the other person.

Diagram B illustrates this dynamic. For example, the angry sub-

personality of one person may react to the manipulator subpersonality of the other. Or the victim subpersonality of one may react
to the controlling subpersonality of another. Many marriages play
themselves out like this for years—one subpersonality relating to
another.

Regardless of the name you give them, whether it be "the controller," "the critic," "the miser," etc., what fuels subpersonalities
such as these is fear—fear of loss, fear of humiliation, fear of
helplessness, fear of abandonment. And underneath the fear is a
call or request or plea to be safe, respected, heard, loved, and
acknowledged—even though this may be difficult to discern when
you are caught up in a tangle of conflicting emotions.

How do you find your way out of the tangle and into a new
way of relating? The practice of forgiveness is the key.

GETTING CLEAR: FORGIVENESS
VS. AVOIDANCE

Sometimes choices are made in the name of forgiveness while what
is occurring isn't forgiveness at all. It is important not to confuse
being forgiving with denying your own feelings, needs, and desires.
Forgiving doesn't mean being passive and staying in a job or relationship that clearly doesn't work for you or is abusive. It is
important that you are clear about your boundaries. What is acceptable for you? If you are willing to allow unacceptable behavior
again and again in the name of "forgiveness," you are more than
likely using "forgiveness" as an excuse not to take responsibility
for taking care of yourself or as a way to avoid making changes.
In a job situation, for example, forgiveness doesn't excuse you
from figuring out what you want to do, confronting the issues, or
looking for another job if you are unhappy where you are. Often
the boundaries between forgiveness and avoidance are subjective,
and the truth of which it is for you is to be found by being completely honest with yourself. Look to what is true in your gut-level
feelings and listen to your heart.

A PRACTICAL APPLICATION

For the sake of illustration, let's look at some scenarios within a work situation of how the dynamics of anger, resentment, or forgiveness could play themselves out.

Imagine that you work in a job where your boss is incompetent and arrogant. You are angry with him and his performance. You've said a few things to him, but he doesn't seem to listen. You basically enjoy your work but depend on your boss for expediency and support in certain projects. You can usually get your work done without his support, but it takes more effort and causes much more aggravation.

With greater frequency, you find yourself lying awake at night steaming from the dissatisfaction that you feel. Getting up Monday through Friday is becoming more of a chore.

You have complained about him to your co-workers, and although they perceive him similarly they aren't willing to take any firm action. You've mentioned your dissatisfaction to a few people in appropriate positions, but they have essentially ignored your concerns. You are beginning to realize that you work for a dysfunctional organization. Most people in the system live in denial of the real issues, and up to this point, your efforts to effect change have been futile.

When dealing with your boss you appear reasonable, but now there is never a time when you think of him or interact with him when you don't feel angry. Although he senses your anger, it has not effected positive change on his behalf. In fact, he is responding to your anger by becoming more defended, and as he does, you are becoming even more distressed and scornful.

What do you do if you work in an organization where there is no support from the hierarchy for getting appropriate feedback and supervision for your boss so that he is made accountable for competence in his position? How can you work with a situation like this so that you don't emotionally stay the victim of another's incompetence and passivity?

One scenario is that you stay in your job with no change of perspective and remain very angry. This is not what you call a good time.

Another scenario is that you stay in your job and decide to forgive your boss, or more accurately, you decide to practice forgiveness. Forgiveness, especially in a situation like this, is not something you do and then it's over and done with. Here it would surely be an ongoing process. To forgive your boss in this situation is an example in which forgiveness is truly a bold choice, because it would necessitate a willingness to intercept a way of relating to him that is now reflexive and has had a very powerful emotional charge. It would take will, nerve, and daring to choose an alternative response.

What would it look like to forgive in a situation like this?

Forgiving would entail allowing yourself to see that there may be more to this person than meets the eye. Forgiveness means seeing him as a human being, with both magnanimous possibilities and very human feelings and insecurities to deal with. Forgiving would entail the willingness to acknowledge and relate to the Self in your boss, to the wise, reasonable nature in him, *even though your ego might assure you that that is ridiculous, that he does not have a Self—and that his light is out.* It requires affirming his wholeness regardless of what fragment you see.

Forgiving him doesn't mean that you will avoid communicating directly about how you feel and what you think about what is happening; it doesn't imply that you will hesitate to call him on the issues. But it does mean that you are willing to see beyond his persona and relate to him about these issues from your Self to his.

There are many ways that your boss may respond to your forgiveness. One possibility is that he may sense that something has changed. Since you are not lost in anger and judgments, and are more openhearted in your interactions with him, he may feel less threatened—and loosen the hold on his position. As a result you may find yourself having an easier, more workable, and productive relationship with him. This is probably the most cheerful scenario.

Another scenario is that you practice forgiveness, but your boss is so shut down in habitual fear-based subpersonalities that he doesn't seem to respond at all. With greater and greater consistency, day after day, you try to see the bigger picture and relate to his Self. You address the issues you need his support with while being as reasonable, honest, and clear as possible—but he, for the most part, isn't any more responsive. (In fact, if he is that constricted and frightened, he may not even notice your change.) Because every moment of choosing to relate to the Self of your boss is a moment when you are strengthening your identification with your own Self, even if the circumstances remain very difficult, you will naturally experience greater power and perspective. Even if he doesn't change, by choosing to forgive, you are responding to the situation creatively and actually using your once-perceived "enemy" to nurture yourself and grow.

What are your options now?

On an inner level, there is only one option if you want to be as peaceful as possible and not live as the angry victim of your boss—this, of course, is to continue forgiving. However, forgiving him does not imply that you should or will stay in the job. One option would be to stay in your job, with new awareness and insight, heightened objectivity, and detachment, doing your job as effectively as you can. If this is your choice, it would be very helpful to have some daily rituals such as meditation, affirmations, exercise, relaxation, prayer, or journal writing to nurture and support you in being and staying as centered as possible. As you work at staying centered, you may even find yourself experiencing compassion for the sure misery that your boss experiences (whether he acknowledges it or not).

Another scenario is that you are forgiving, you see the situation differently and are not getting so emotionally distraught, yet the situation doesn't feel workable. Although you are forgiving, you decide to leave your job. Frequently when people make the choice to leave as a result of difficulty on the job, there is a great deal of anger that one carries for months or years. By forgiving, you discover that it doesn't have to be this way. You may still experience anger, frustration, and sadness about leaving, yet by forgiving you are able to move on to acceptance and letting-go with much greater ease.

MEGAN'S STORY

I was ready to quit my job. It had gotten to the point where I would dread waking up in the morning already filled with

anxiety about the day to come. The truth was, I loved my
position in sales. I liked the product line and most of my co-
workers. It was my boss, the manager of my department,
who drove me crazy. Hardly a day went by without her
finding something wrong with my work, and although I was
the highest-earning salesperson in the division, still my boss,
Joanna, always found something wrong with my work. I'd
be sitting at my desk processing paperwork when my line
would buzz. I'd fill with fear and anger when I heard Joanna's
cold voice ask to see me in her office.

As I walked down the hall I'd notice my jaw clenching
and my hands curled in fists. Once inside her office, facing
her angry face, I had to respond to a ritual checkoff list of
"Did you do ____? Did you take care of ____? She would go
on until I was ready to throttle her. She would often find
some small omission to criticize me for.

By then I was so angry that I would go back to my desk
and spend some time stabbing holes in my desk blotter with
my pen while fantasizing scenarios of revenge.

When I went for my annual physical, my doctor warned
me that my blood pressure and cholesterol were inching
steadily upward. He inquired about my stress level at work
and made a point of telling me that I'd better do something
about it. The next week a friend invited me to a lecture on
"forgiveness." I didn't even think of Joanna when I went to
the lecture—she was beyond forgiving as far as I was concerned. But I thought perhaps it was time to think about
forgiving an old boyfriend—and besides, it was a night out
with my friend.

The concepts that were presented were completely new
to me, and to my surprise, I was inspired to actually start
applying them to Joanna. The next day I promised myself
that no matter what Joanna said or did, I would see it as a
sign of her fear or insecurity—and once I thought about it,
I knew this was accurate. When her call came, I took three
or four deep breaths and walked as calmly as I could into
her office. The routine went as usual, only this time I remembered to breathe and tried to practice forgiveness. For
the first time ever, I looked closely at her face and saw deep
lines of what looked like pain and fear. This time I elaborated
on my answers, trying to reassure her that I was taking care

of business and would make sure everything was covered. Unexpectedly, Joanna's face softened a bit. The questioning was shorter than usual and she said good-bye with an uncharacteristic warmth.

Later that day I found out that her teenage son was having some rare health problem (this came only a few months after her divorce). My perceptions of Joanna shifted from seeing her as a blaming, critical mother figure to seeing her as an overburdened, stressed-out, frightened woman. As I cultivated this new understanding, I began to see that beneath all that fear, blame, and judgment was just another struggling human being trying to get love, acknowledgment, and attention in the best way she knew. Her job had become for her the last bastion of control, so she desperately fought to ensure the success of her department. Now, instead of wanting to kill Joanna, I began wanting to help her. The more I did that, the less frightened she became. Amazingly, she began to confide in me and become a friend. Although she sometimes still reverts back to her old behavior when she's under a lot of pressure, I don't take it personally anymore. I look forward to my job and seem to be more productive since I don't spend so much energy being angry or recovering from my meetings.

CHAPTER THREE

LEARNING TO FORGIVE
ON NEUTRAL
TERRITORY

Practicing forgiveness is something you can do right away even if there are certain people you don't feel ready to forgive. To begin practicing forgiveness, I recommend starting on neutral territory—in other words, with people whom you don't really know. Although you may feel an urgency to forgive particular people with whom you have a difficult relationship, starting with people with whom you don't have such a relationship will allow you to ease into the process by starting with some of the basics.

Sometimes people ask, "Do you have to forgive yourself before you can forgive others?" or, "Do you have to forgive others before you can forgive yourself?" I think it's a little bit like "What came first, the chicken or the egg?" In Al-Anon it is suggested that the only person you need to forgive is yourself; everyone else will naturally be forgiven as a consequence of self-forgiveness. Although the experience of forgiving yourself will ultimately lead to forgiving others, the most difficult person for most of us to forgive is ourselves. Since it is easier to forgive others (at least some others), we'll begin there.

As mentioned before, forgiving is more than just something to do when you are guilty, angry, or resentful, although it is clearly most useful in these instances. In the most expanded way of working with forgiveness, we can practice with anyone—and everyone becomes our teacher.

Forgiveness is a practical matter at first, as choosing to see situations in ways that may be unfamiliar requires a conscious decision, desire, and commitment. It also requires a lot of repetition to master, to become integrated, and to feel natural.

Starting on neutral territory is like practicing and learning something with which you are unfamiliar and unskilled before you are required to use it in more demanding ways. Like any new skill, it may seem somewhat awkward at first. If you are a novice at skiing, you can't just put your skis on, stand up, and head down a mountain. Starting with the basics is least threatening and most useful: first getting used to just having skis on (getting acquainted with new concepts), then learning how to maneuver (checking out what it is like to use some of these new perceptions), then skiing down some gentler slopes (practicing forgiveness with people with whom you have no personal history of anger and pain—this, again, is what is meant by "neutral territory"), and then going for the slopes that require more skill (forgiving those whom you are angry and resentful toward, where greater clarity, compassion, willingness, and intention are required). Starting by forgiving on "neutral territory" can be like a warm-up for forgiving in relationships where something was done to you.

When we meet someone, the ego's impulse is to judge and make the distinctions that determine whether we are dealing with a potential enemy or friend. Within moments the ego often firmly establishes whether we should like the person or not. These judgments act to keep our hearts closed and separate us from others: "I can't stand people who sound like that," or "I think women who wear nail polish are foolish," or "I don't like foreigners." We set ourselves apart by an assumption of superiority. Or, we set ourselves apart by establishing our inferiority: "I'm not as bright," or "I'm less attractive," or "I feel insignificant next to John." When we are chronically confined by the boundaries of the ego, this separation manifests itself as a pervasive sense of unworthiness or an inflated sense of arrogance and superiority. We either belittle and judge ourselves and make ourselves "wrong" or we project the separation from ourSelf, making others wrong and creating scapegoats to carry the burden of our insecurities and fears. By forgiving on neutral territory we can start to heal the habitual judgments, fear, and separation that often pervade much of our lives.

By starting to practice forgiveness on neutral territory, we begin to acknowledge and shine a light on the essential Self of others that is fundamentally good and innocent. By doing this we also begin to affirm and relate from our own essential Self. Forgiving in this way doesn't imply that we or others are not guilty of particular acts, but it does mean that the act that was committed does not vaguely sum up our entire character or the entire truth of who we or others are.

PUTTING THEORY INTO PRACTICE

When we greet someone, we most often demonstrate our recognition with the greeting of "hello." This is usually an acknowledgment of our awareness that another person (personality and body) is there. In a segment of the African culture people are greeted with the word "Sawubona." This greeting literally means "I see you." Not "you" primarily as a body but "you" as a pure Self. It is a recognition of the core nature of another that is always worthy of our respect, acknowledgment, and love. Imagine going through your life acknowledging and being acknowledged in this way. Imagine how your life might be different now, had you been recognized for this shining Self while growing up.

Exercise: Seeing the Light
For at least a few minutes, three times a day, for the next month, take the time to practice forgiveness with people you haven't met before or don't know well. Allow yourself to see beyond their outer appearances and see, instead, the Self—the light. Inwardly acknowledge that each

person you see has a peaceful, loving, and wise nature. You can do this as you walk down the street, ride an elevator, stand in a line—virtually anywhere when there are others around (or even in your imagination when there aren't others nearby). No words or outer gestures are needed. Just a quiet inner recognition is sufficient. In essence, you are silently saying, "I see You."

Dr. Gerald Jampolsky describes a form of this practice as "Person-to-Person." When you practice Person-to-Person, you scan people for signs of peace, gentleness, and love. "In other words," he explains, "we seek their innocence, not their guilt. We look at them with our heart, not our preconceived notions." This kind of seeing requires inner vision—the willingness to acknowledge and trust in what may be hidden from view. It is a willingness to trust what the other person may not even know or trust in themselves. Goethe wrote, "If you treat a person as he appears to be, you make him worse than he is. But if you treat a person as if he already were what he potentially could be, you make him what he should be." (Or, in the language of forgiveness, what he "is".)

Practicing Person-to-Person can be like a lifeline to sanity when living in big cities, especially in a city like New York. The daily insults and assaults, and dealing with people on the streets and in the subways who look somewhat "weird," could easily annoy us or entrap us in fear even long after any potential danger is over. The practice of forgiveness on neutral territory gives us an incredible opportunity to observe our reactions—in particular, the fear and judgment of "different-ness." Author and teacher Hugh Prather says that "forgiveness is not some futile act in rosy self-deception, but rather the calm recognition that below our egos, we are all exactly the same."

When I first started working with forgiveness, I would practice on neutral territory as I walked through my neighborhood in Boston. I would look at people and acknowledge their Self. When I interacted with people, I would create and recognize that in front of me was a person of peace. When I recognized this in others, I felt peaceful myself. I remember one neighborhood person whom I frequently saw. He was affectionately known as Mr. Glad Bags. Mr. Glad Bags was a tall, heavyset man who wore green garbage bags on his feet, a green garbage bag for a jacket, and a garbage bag for a hat. Needless to say, the lampshade on this person was most striking. He carried a broom and, of his own accord, would sweep the streets. It was a wonderful challenge to keep seeing the light in Mr. Glad Bags. It offered me the gift of remembering who we were. Had I not consciously practiced forgiveness with him, I might have constricted and been threatened by his appearance. Instead, I felt safe, as indeed I was.

As you practice forgiveness, because you are coming from the Self, you learn to trust your gut reactions and instincts more and more. You will be more likely to know whether there is an actual threat to your physical well-being or not, rather than living as if someone were always out to get you.

SANDRA'S JOURNAL

During the first week of an eight-session forgiveness course that I facilitated, participants were encouraged to practice forgiveness on neutral territory with strangers. Following are descriptions of one person's experience.

I got home in a glorious mood—feeling like a beacon and loving it. Just shining, shining, shining. Strangers were reaching out to me, saying hello unprompted, thanking me with great sincerity for letting them pass, etc. I went out for a walk with my dog and shortly came upon two men arguing loudly. For an instant I felt the fear in my belly that always appears in the face of conflict, and then I began to chuckle, and thought, "There are two subpersonalities going at it." Certainly there was distancing there, but for the first time I felt safe in earshot of anger. It no longer had the power to roar out of control and devour me.

As I walk down the street trying to be aware of the fundamental goodness within others, I am frightened by a world full of light. It's an almost-overwhelming concept/reality. Once recognized, it changes everything. While the possibility is so exciting, it entails loss. The loss of my blinders, the loss of freedom from responsibility, and most importantly, the loss of my own little world of misery, uniquely mine.

There is such perfect wholeness revealed in this "exercise" of looking into another's heart. The very second I open my heart, it receives love. As soon as I send out understanding, I am understood. I wonder how I could have lived for thirty-one years in ignorance of such an essential concept. I have noticed so many blind people this week. Strangely enough, I am referring to those with physically impaired vision. It feels as if I have been tripping over white canes for days now. I am stunned by how little I am accustomed to look, much less see.

Even small acts of forgiveness always have significant ramifications at a personal level. Even small acts of forgiveness contribute to one's sense of trust in oneself and the potential of others; they contribute to a human spirit that is fundamentally hopeful and optimistic rather than pessimistic or defeated; they contribute to knowing oneself and others as potentially powerful people who can choose to lovingly create, versus seeing humans as basically selfish, destructive, and sinners.

Throughout the week reflect:

There is another way of looking at the world.

CHAPTER FOUR

WORKING WITH ANGER:
LETTING PAIN BE PAIN

Before moving on to using forgiveness in more intimate relationships, it is important to address the personal pain—the
sadness, anger, resentment, and guilt—that may have brought you
to this inquiry into forgiveness in the first place.

Forgiveness is essential for healing and experiencing our wholeness. Yet, in order to experience our wholeness, no part of us can
be repressed, denied, or overlooked. Just as our wholeness includes
great wisdom and an extraordinary capacity for loving and caring,
it also includes anger, resentment, hostility, shame and guilt, and,
for many people, rage. These emotions often stay hidden, and
whether quietly muffled or raging below the surface, until fully
healed, they take their toll on our ability to be happy and have
healthy and satisfying relationships.

This is particularly true for those who have grown up in a
dysfunctional home where primary caretakers were significantly
emotionally impaired. Experts estimate that as many as 90 percent
of adults in this country grew up in dysfunctional homes. The

damaging consequences of such an environment are becoming
better understood, and support groups such as Adult Children of
Alcoholics have developed to help people deal with their common
issues.

Anyone who was reared in a home where they experienced
physical or emotional abuse, rejection, or abandonment must forgive in order to heal *fully*. But before they forgive, they must own
the pain that was experienced.

Owning the pain is recognizing, acknowledging, and admitting
what is true. Once it is owned, the pain of the past can then be
turned into the richness of life itself. Eva Pierrakos's poem in her
book *The Pathwork of Self-Transformation* describes the great value
of this process:

> *Through the gateway of feeling your weakness lies your
> strength.*
> *Through the gateway of feeling your pain lies your pleasure
> and joy.*
> *Through the gateway of feeling your fear lies your security
> and safety.*
> *Through the gateway of feeling your loneliness lies your ca-
> pacity to have fulfillment, love and companionship.*
> *Through the gateway of feeling your hopelessness lies true
> and justified hope.*
> *Through the gateway of accepting the lacks in your childhood
> lies your fulfillment now.*

Our pain needs a safe, appropriate place to be vented and allowed, without judgment, to be. Claudia Black, author of *It Will
Never Happen To Me*, a popular and respected book on adult children of alcoholics, says that "the recovery process includes responding to one's emotional pain." She refers to "a compulsion
to be happy"—a compulsion based on the denial of pain that adult
children of alcoholics (and others raised in a dysfunctional family)
often suffer from. We cannot fully heal if we deny what Carl Jung
called the "dark" or "shadow" side of our personal history and
psyche. One cannot skip this essential step of owning the
"shadow"—the anger, rage, sadness, etc.—if forgiveness is to be

totally integrated and real. It can't be neatly placed on top of fear and sadness pulsating below.

Numbing or denying our pain and anger with drugs, alcohol, shopping, work, or a veneer of sweetness and acceptance is no release from pain and anger. As theologian Matthew Fox points out, "Then we become pain's victims instead of the healers we might become." He explains that "liberation begins at the point where pain is acknowledged and allowed to be pain." We have to enter into it, and befriend it in order to let it go.

LETTING PAIN BE PAIN

Even though by practicing forgiveness you may be able to dissipate and transform anger that arises in current circumstances, or perhaps not even get angry in the first place, it is still important not to deny the existence and impact of anger that you may have felt (consciously or unconsciously) for many years. Understanding and even having compassion for another's abusive behavior now (i.e., understanding that someone abused you because of their own repressed anger and rage from having been abused themselves) does not automatically liberate you from the trauma, helplessness, and fear that you experienced in the past. Unless you have since found a safe and supportive context in which your feelings could be honored (acknowledged and allowed without judgment or punishment), these emotions from childhood, adolescence, young adulthood, and perhaps adulthood are likely to have remained repressed, suppressed, and denied to this day. If there is no safe place to be emotionally vulnerable and express pain and fear when traumatic experiences occur, then the trauma can get stored in the musculature of the body and held in the psyche for years.

Sometimes these chronic feelings somatize and find a home in the body. They may appear as chronic headaches, stomach upsets, backaches, etc. When persistent, these repressed or suppressed feelings may dominate the personality, become explosive, and/or shut you down. They may result in an inner battle between helplessness and anger, creating a state where anxiety reigns. When anger isn't released, it often seeps out at the edges of the personality as fear, sarcasm, withdrawal, hostility, self-deprecation; or it exposes itself clearly in anger, rage, depression, passive-aggressive behaviors, self-abuse, abuse toward others, an inability to be effective in the world, and the inability to have emotionally intimate relationships.

When we try to forgive while denying anger and guilt, if indeed it is within, the "forgiving grown-up" can become a subpersonality rather than a true expression of the Self. Or, we may forgive from time to time, but then the forgiveness is easily displaced with recurring anger and guilt. After attempting to forgive we might wonder why we still feel angry or empty inside. If we are repressing anger and guilt, the forgiveness we extend can't be rooted in our being, because the repressed feelings become a barrier to our core experience. The body and psyche that hold too many restricting and repressed emotions have little room to embody love and joy with much consistency and depth. We may experience the joy and relief that forgiveness offers from time to time, but it will remain on the surface. It's like trying to plant a magnificent flower garden with a very shallow root system. A brief drought or a passing wind can sweep it all away. But if we give our pain acceptance and, in a safe context, feel what may have been too unsafe and scary to feel in the past, then the pain can be released and transformed. The process of honoring our feelings is like tilling hardened or shallow topsoil so that it becomes rich and deep. Only then will our forgiveness and understanding have room to take root deep within us.

SURVIVAL MECHANISMS

If you try to embrace forgiveness, denying repressed fear, guilt, and anger, you continue the legacy of rejecting your feelings. Before, it was others who didn't respect and honor your feelings. Now, if you continue to ignore the feelings that are there, you are doing the very same thing to yourself.

If you grew up in a dysfunctional home, it was not safe to be emotionally vulnerable. If your tears were routinely met with "Keep crying and I'll really give you something to cry about," or if your feelings were met with ridicule or anger, you undoubtedly learned that your feelings were unacceptable and, in your wisdom, you adopted survival mechanisms to cope. These coping strategies may have been essential to deal with your fears and reduce the potential for more abuse and more rejection.

Some of the more common survival mechanisms that keep our "negative" feelings below the level of our everyday consciousness were first recognized and defined by Freud.

Denial is a refusal to accept things as they are. For instance, instead of recognizing when you're angry, you insist that you're not. You simply deny what is true. "I don't feel that way."

Repression is a total, unconscious, reflexive blocking of an unacceptable feeling or desire from your awareness. Here your conscious mind has no awareness that anything is being repressed. You don't deliberately choose to repress; it is often activated reflexively in order to cope with incidents and feelings that are overwhelming, incomprehensible, or terrifying. For instance, rage about sexual abuse might get completely repressed because it has been too terrifying and unsafe to allow these memories or emotions to surface. This rage might manifest as anxiety attacks or physical symptoms, or get projected as hatred toward a particular people or group.

Suppression is the conscious exclusion of painful or unacceptable feelings, desires, or urges. When you suppress an emotion, you consciously and deliberately keep it from surfacing. For instance: You were at a family outing, and your aunt, as usual, was sarcastic and demeaning toward you. You were infuriated, but you knew if you gave her a piece of your mind you would be harshly punished. So you actively opposed your desire to tell her off and appeared cool and unbothered. You adapted.

Like any of these mechanisms, suppression can be healthy or unhealthy; and as we grow and see things differently, many of these may outlive their usefulness.

Projection is the process of disowning your feelings and desires and unconsciously attributing them to others. When an uneasy feeling comes up, instead of saying, "I feel angry," the feeling is denied and is then displaced onto another and manifests as "He's angry at me." If confronted with your feelings, you deny their existence. Or, rather than acknowledging feeling guilty, you externalize the guilt and place the blame on others.

Rationalization is the invention of stories, excuses, and alibis that serve as a rationale for unacceptable behaviors and motivations. "I'm not angry at her for hitting me because I know she had an abusive childhood." Or, "I'm not angry at him because I know he tried." These statements may be true, or they may be rationalizations. A rationalization can be an intellectual understanding used to deny uncomfortable feelings, and it can also be a way to avoid looking at the truth.

RELEASING PAIN AND ANGER

There are many ways of releasing feelings, and different theories about the best way to do this. Some psychotherapists believe that actively releasing feelings is necessary for healing; others do not.

Sometimes people who need to actively vent the energy that has been held back by giving their anger expression will feel self-conscious and foolish banging on a pillow or yelling. It's important to remember that the person who needs that release is often not you, the adult—although you may need it, too—but the child within you. It is the four-year-old within who was emotionally abandoned or the ten-year-old who was put down who needs to express his or her sadness and anger and be accepted and validated. In order to do this, we must be able to hold the paradox of being the adult as well as the hurt and angry child. If there are unhealed emotions, the two parts sometimes co-exist. Rather than seeing your anger, rage, sadness, etc., as bad or unacceptable, it is just accepted as a feeling and as energy. It is simply the truth of your experience.

Releasing or venting painful memories and feelings does not necessarily mean directly confronting those who have hurt you or treated you unfairly. As mentioned before, directing the full force of your anger directly toward another is, in fact, often not useful; it is apt to reinforce and perpetuate underlying fear and separation for both of you.

TECHNIQUES FOR RELEASE

Opinions vary as to the most effective methods and techniques of
working with these feelings in order to heal. None of these is suited
for everyone. The various approaches include working with rational thoughts, the unconscious mind, emotive release, and directly with the body.

Body-oriented therapies are rooted in the premise that the mind
and the body are a unity. Since the work of Wilhelm Reich dem-
onstrating that memory is a psychosomatic experience (stored in
both the mind and the body), there has been growing interest and
application of techniques that trigger awareness and physical and
emotional release and integration through working directly with
the body. Some of these techniques include Rolfing, massage, bioenergetics, Feldenkrais, the Alexander technique, Lomi Body
work, and Soma.

There are other powerful techniques that do not intentionally
encourage overt emotional release but nonetheless provide a context in which feelings can arise and be worked with in transformative ways. These approaches include meditation, visualization,
journal writing, dream work, and expressive arts such as painting,
singing, and movement.

The techniques that have most influenced me both personally
and professionally have been meditation, Guided Imagery and
Music (developed by Dr. Helen Bonny), and intensive breath work.
The best-known approaches to the powerful technique of intensive
breath work are Grof Holotropic Breathing (developed by Dr. Stan-
islov Grof) and Rebirthing, also referred to as Conscious Connected
Breathing. The evocative techniques of Guided Imagery and Music
and intensive breath work require experienced guides in their initial use.

There are a number of well-known techniques for releasing
anger that do not necessarily need an experienced guide or teacher
like many of the techniques referred to above. Some cathartic
techniques to help release anger and let off steam are writing out
angry feelings in a letter that you can later tear up, punching a
mattress or pillow, screaming and letting out feelings in a room

where you won't feel inhibited or in a car with the windows closed, and any variations on these.

If you have often witnessed anger in others that was misplaced, destructive, or out of control, know that your anger need not be like that. It can be channeled in ways that are safe, appropriate, and liberating as in the cathartic exercises mentioned above.

The process of experiencing and releasing your anger and pain can be extremely liberating, yet it can also be a trap. Matthew Fox notes "how important it is that we not glorify pain or cling to our pain or wallow in our pain. That is not letting pain be pain—that way lies letting pain be our boss . . . What we must do ultimately is to let go of our pain." It is important to pay attention and to stay conscious while working with emotions so as not to get perpetually stuck in anger and let "pain become your boss." We work with pain in order to heal. If indulged in, pain and anger can become another addiction.

SEEKING SUPPORT

If you grew up in an environment where your feelings were not respected and you feel there is still "unfinished business," or if you feel a desire or need to be supported in working with some of your current feelings, it may be very useful to seek the support of a counselor or therapist. When choosing a therapist, I recommend that you interview a variety of therapists to find the person best suited for you. Look for (1) someone who is comfortable working directly with feelings and can allow for their expression, (2) someone who is nonjudgmental and noncontrolling, (3) someone who is warm and acknowledging, and (4) someone who truly understands the value of forgiveness for healing—but does not exert pressure to forgive before one is ready.

WHEN YOU'RE NOT READY TO FORGIVE

There may be certain people you feel you don't want to forgive or who you don't feel ready or capable of forgiving at this time. Respect where you are. Your process of forgiving is uniquely yours, and this resistance may be a healthy response for where you are in your growth. Be gentle with yourself.

Even when you aren't ready to forgive certain individuals, you can be practicing forgiveness on neutral territory. This is always helpful in reminding you of what is possible, and in reminding you of who you truly are.

WHEN YOU WANT TO FORGIVE, BUT DON'T FEEL ABLE TO

You may notice as you consciously begin to practice forgiveness that at times, despite new insight and a genuine desire to forgive, your emotional responses remain unchanged—you may still feel aversion, hostility, and anger, and not find forgiveness in your heart. Sometimes it takes a while for new understanding to be integrated into our emotional experience. At times like this, patience and self-forgiveness are important. Also, when you want to forgive but continue to feel angry, it is useful to go within and look back over your life to see whether your "unforgiving" feelings are a sign of old pain and hurt that has not been acknowledged or healed. Present circumstances may trigger unresolved feelings from the past that are directly or tangentially related to what is going on now.

A clear-cut example of this dynamic happened with my friend Pam.

Hal, my friend Pam's boyfriend, had an affair with another woman while living with her. When Pam found out about the affair, she knew it was time for her to end the relationship. With a lot of pain but with little ambivalence she demanded that he leave the home where they had been living together for two years. Hal was genuinely pained and remorseful, and wanted to remain friends even if their romantic partnership was over. As Pam reflected on the relationship, she became aware of how Hal's behavior was part of a pattern he had repeated with other women he had been involved with before her. He had been so deeply wounded as a child and so unsure of his mother's love that he would latch onto one woman after another, not daring to let go of any of the women until they got clear about their boundaries and demanded he leave.

Despite Pam's awareness of the pain and emptiness that motivated Hal's behavior, she felt betrayed, as indeed she was. She was furious with Hal. For many months she gave herself permission to feel her anger and pain. After about a year she got some distance and worked through some of the anger. She then started actively working with the principles of forgiveness. She could see who Hal really was—this was the person she had fallen in love with in the first place. She felt compassion for the pain and woundedness that drove him into the stream of unworkable relationships that he painfully re-created again and again. Yet even though she understood what drove him to ultimately self-destructive behaviors, and even though she could see that under his hurtful and neurotic behaviors there was a genuinely good person, anger and rage would surface again and again.

When she sat with her feelings and tried to explore what was going on, in addition to feeling angry at Hal, images of her father would appear. Pam began to realize that she felt tremendous anger toward her father for having had a string of affairs while married to her mother. She had never been aware of how much anger she held toward her father since she always kept a tight cap on it, lest her father abandon her, too. Until she acknowledged and worked through some of the feelings that had been repressed for years in relation to her father, she realized they would always get triggered when attempting to work through her feelings in relation to Hal. Pam decided, with the prompting of her new therapist, that it was time to start dealing with the past.

CHAPTER FIVE

FINDING AND TELLING
THE TRUTH

As you've already learned, in many circumstances words never need to be exchanged for forgiveness to be authentic and complete. Yet in any ongoing relationship where mutual cooperation is called for (whether this is with a co-worker or a boss, a roommate or a spouse) the ability to communicate clearly and honestly is essential for nurturing an atmosphere of forgiveness. Sometimes it is necessary to complete a matter. Sometimes it is necessary to keep intimacy intact. In a close ongoing relationship, if there are unresolved issues and there is no real communication, there will inevitably be anger, resentment, frustration, and a lot of second-guessing about what the other person is thinking and feeling.

In order to verbally communicate in a way that nurtures forgiveness it is necessary to (1) be aware of what the real issues are for you, (2) be in touch with the truth of how you feel, (3) decide what thoughts and feelings would be useful to share, (4) articulate these thoughts and feelings in a clear, nonblaming way, and (5) share your truths while keeping your heart open.

My friend Jake was frequently furious with his wife for not taking more responsibility around the house. When he looked closely at what was really going on for him and what he was feeling under the obvious anger, he discovered a profound sense of disappointment and sadness that his marriage was not the supportive partnership he once thought it would be. As a result of this new awareness, the next time he got angry at his wife, rather than being hostile he shared his heartfelt disappointment and sadness with her. Instead of his wife's usual counteraccusations for feeling judged and misunderstood, she listened, felt his disappointment, and responded with a sincere willingness to work as more of a team.

If Jake hadn't acknowledged the pain and disappointment under his anger and taken the risk to communicate these feelings to his wife in a nonaccusatory way, he and his wife would probably still be living in their own emotionally isolated worlds. True communication (communion) always inspires connection rather than separation.

Exercise: Discovering the Truth

The following phrases are designed to help you get clear about what you are feeling and what the real issues are in a relationship where you are angry or upset. Even if you don't or can't actually speak with the person you choose, completing the following will help you understand your circumstances and yourself better—and self-understanding always leads to greater freedom.

As you complete the following sentences, allow yourself to be open to whatever thoughts or feelings that arise. It can be very useful to actually write your responses and reflect on them after you have completed the writing.

Before you do the exercise, close your eyes and take a few letting-go breaths. Then think of a situation in your life where you often feel angry or upset. (You can use this exercise in relation to anyone.) Keeping this person and situation in mind, complete the following:

The issue is _____.
The issue is _____.
The real issue is _____.

The real issue is _____.
The real issue is _____.
The issue is really _____.

(Continue using these phrases, filling in the blanks, until you have exhausted your responses.)

In relation to this person or situation, what I'm feeling is _____.
What I'm feeling is _____.
What I'm really feeling is _____.
What I'm also feeling is _____.
I also feel _____.
And under that feeling is _____.
And under that feeling is _____.
And under that feeling is _____.

Breathe. Look inward and complete the following:

What I'm afraid of is _____.
What I fear is _____.
What I'm afraid of is _____.
What scares me is _____.
What really scares me is _____.
What I'm really afraid of is _____.

Be gentle and compassionate with yourself.

In order to step out of ineffective patterns of relating (one of which may be a pattern of not telling), it is also important to reflect on what is acceptable and unacceptable for you in the context of the relationship. Now that you know what you are feeling, think about what is acceptable for you in this relationship. What is acceptable to you is a *highly* personal decision. You may determine that it is unacceptable for your boss to berate you verbally or for your spouse to have affairs. If these are truly unacceptable, and your attempts at negotiating change are thwarted, you may decide to end a relationship that has provided a certain security until now. After this kind of introspection, you may also decide that certain behaviors that you held as unacceptable are really not all that important—or that they are important to you, but not important enough to consider ending or changing the form of the relationship. You may find yourself less judgmental and more accepting of another's habits and idiosyncracies.

Continuing to reflect on the relationship or situation you have been working on, complete the following sentences:

What is unacceptable to me is _____.
What is unacceptable to me is _____.
What I can't handle is _____.
What I can't handle is _____.
I can't handle it because _____.
I can't handle it because _____.
What I need to do (if anything) to make it acceptable is _____.
What I need to do to make it acceptable is _____.
What needs to change to make this acceptable is _____.

Note: Even if you are dealing with the same relationship, your responses to these sentence completions may change from time to time. Be gentle with yourself and allow for change and flexibility when it is the truth of your experience.

When there is a lot of dissatisfaction in intimate relationships, it is also useful to make distinctions between your needs and your wants. For instance, in an intimate relationship you may have a *need* for honesty. You may have a *need* for attention and affection. These are the threads that form a bond of intimacy between two people. On the other hand, you may *want* your partner to clean the kitchen regularly or dress well when you go out on the weekends. Although these may be important to you, they're not likely to be the basis for your relationship.

The distinction between needs and wants is also highly personal. As you reflect on your needs and wants, certain ones will naturally be more important to you than others.

Bringing to mind a person toward whom you feel angry (you can bring to mind the person you thought about in the previous sentence completions), complete the following:

In this relationship (situation) what I need is _____.
What I need is _____.
What I need is _____.
What I need is _____.
What I want is _____.
What I want is _____.
What I want is _____.
What I want is _____.

- At this point in your relationship, which issues have become a chronic source of irritation and frustration?
- Are these issues in relation to your wants or needs?
- If they are about wants, are they masking deeper needs?
- Which wants, if any, are you willing to let go of so that you can share more ease and love?

If others don't give you what you feel you need, don't assume they know what you need. Tell them. If your needs and wants are significantly different from the needs and wants of the person you brought to mind, and you don't talk about these differences with honesty and compassion, working at coming to some understanding, there is apt to be a lot of resentment. Try to prioritize and negotiate your needs and wants to greater mutual satisfaction.

P A U S E   A N D   R E F L E C T

Once again, call to mind the situation that you reflected on during the sentence completions. Reflect on the following questions:

- Am I growing as a result of this situation?
- Am I able to maintain a sense of self-worth or do I feel dragged down by this situation?
- Do I have enough support from others to feel strong and loved?
- Do I have a limit in terms of time or behavior as to what I am willing to accept?

If you are in a difficult, challenging situation and you don't feel like you are growing and you feel like the situation is "dragging you down," seek out a supportive person or group to help you gain perspective and strength.

~~~~~~

GETTING YOURSELF HEARD

When we're angry, there is often a tendency to withdraw or express anger by verbally blaming, accusing, and berating another. Despite the fact that this withdrawal or verbal attack creates more distance, our innermost desire is to connect, to get another to hear us and empathize with our experience. Getting the people we are angry at to actually hear what we have to say is not something we can take for granted by virtue of the fact that our voice is audible to them. How many times have you heard someone say, "I'm listening, I'm listening," when you've sensed they don't hear a word that you're saying? Getting people to really listen often takes some skill.

There are times when verbally discharging your anger and letting your frustration and hurt just hang out is a very human response. Verbal outbursts, if they are not destructive, do bring attention to the issues. These angry releases may feel wanted and needed to help you let go and shake up the situation so it can hopefully settle in a more workable place. However, if this is the predominant way you deal with your anger, there are other ways of verbally expressing yourself that will more effectively accomplish getting yourself heard.

To create the greatest likelihood of being heard, first you have to get someone's attention. It helps to have an appropriate time and place. Trying to talk to your mate while they are running out the door to an appointment pretty much guarantees that you won't get heard. Second, try to set the person you're speaking to at ease. If they feel like you're getting ready for battle, they are not likely to be in their most receptive state. Third, tell your truths as clearly as possible, without blaming. Try to be very aware of the intention of your communication and the spirit in which you do your truth-telling. These will largely determine whether the cycle of anger and pain is continued or interrupted.

I suggest working with the following communication skills: The first is learning to translate your anger into clear, nonblaming statements. The second is learning the skill of active listening.

By taking responsibility for your feelings (rather than projecting them onto others), and honestly communicating the effect that another's behavior has on you, you create the optimal emotional climate to be heard.

One of the most important and basic ways to implement this way of relating is to use *I* statements rather than *you* statements. A *you* statement is often interpreted as an attack, while an *I* statement is often experienced as an invitation to listen. A *you* statement might sound like *"You* make me angry" . . . *"You're* a real jerk" . . . *"You* are acting like an immature twelve-year-old" . . . "Why don't *you* act like an adult?" These statements tell another how inept and inadequate they are, and they frequently invoke mutual blaming and name-calling. When you're angry, many of these statements end up being exaggerated and absolute. *"You always* do that" . . . *"You're never* there for me." While these statements may in fact be accurate, they are rarely, if ever, useful in moving toward a positive resolution. The *you* statements sound like, and are interpreted as, a final negative judgment or statement of fact. They will almost inevitably evoke the effect of emotionally distancing the person you are addressing, and any immediate expectations for real communication are likely to be frustrated.

In contrast to these *you* statements, *I* statements are personal assertions of how *you* feel and how *you* are impacted by what is happening. These assertions communicate how you feel without blaming or necessarily reinforcing guilt. The process of making *I* statements helps you to extricate yourself from being lost in just anger while allowing a bigger picture to emerge. If you are angry at your mate for working long hours, changing from a *you* to an *I* statement might sound like changing *"You're* never there for me, *you're* incredibly selfish" to *"I* feel scared and alone when you work so many hours. *I* miss your companionship and *I'm* afraid you don't care anymore." Or *"You* make me so angry" might sound like "When you ____, *I* get angry because *I* feel unack-

nowledged and abandoned.'' Other *I* statements might sound like
"*I* really worry when you come home late and don't call" . . . "*I*
feel tired and overwhelmed when most of the responsibility falls
on me" . . . "*I'm* worried about the children and *I* feel sad and
hurt by the distance between us.''

Unlike the *you* statements, the *I* statements are much less threatening and invite the person you are speaking with to assume more
responsibility for their behavior. They offer a message that you
trust him or her to respond to the situation by having more respect
for your needs. An *I* statement simply states the truth of your
experience, and as a result it isn't likely to evoke the resistance
and defensiveness one might experience if they feel blamed or
controlled.

Sending honest *I* statements sometimes calls for a lot of courage
because, rather than pointing your finger at another, you are expressing your true feelings. Thus, you risk having your authentic
feelings known and rejected. You are letting the other person know
that you are a person who is capable of being angry, hurt, frightened, sad, disappointed, discouraged, etc. The payoff for this honesty and openness is that it fosters mutual truth and intimacy.

Despite more honest, skillful communication, you won't necessarily evoke the response that you want. Others may not be
ready or want to take responsibility for their attitudes and behaviors. Even if this is the case, you help to disentangle yourself from
a neurotic dynamic and you empower yourself to proceed with
responding to the situation at hand from a healthier vantage point.

Exercise: Communicating Self-to-Self
*Take a few deep relaxing breaths. Bring the person to mind whom you
thought about in the sentence completions in the previous pages. Recall
what the real issues are for you. Recall what you are feeling in relation
to this person . . . Recall what you feel you need in this relationship
for it to be workable for you . . . Breathe in and feel the wholeness
within your own being . . . Now imagine yourself in a safe place and
imagine being with this person, telling him or her the truth of your
perceptions and feelings. Let go of any blame and judgments and own
your feelings and perceptions as your own. Let them know, as simply
and clearly as possible, the truth of your experience. Tell him (her),
When you _____ (or when _____ happens), I feel _____.*

Let him (her) know what you perceive to be the real issues. Speak from your Self to their Self. Tell them your truth while keeping your heart open. Imagine that they really listen and hear you. . . . When you are ready, bring your attention back to the present moment.

If it feels appropriate and safe, allow yourself to actually communicate with this person in this way.

HEARING ANOTHER'S TRUTH

In addition to learning how to communicate in a way that you are likely to be heard, skillful communication also requires that you are able to listen as well. Especially in ongoing troubled relationships, one can become so accustomed to judging, threatening, preaching, and shutting down that the ability to truly listen and hear what another has to say can become significantly impaired. We may often look like we are listening, while a stream of judgments undermines the integrity of our apparent receptiveness.

Active listening, putting aside one's own agenda to really hear what another has to say, is a skill that for most of us needs to be nurtured. Active listening is a quality of attention that is experienced as caring and loving. As such, it promotes safety, respect, trust, understanding, and intimacy. It encourages people to be honest and get things out into the open.

To genuinely listen to another, you must take the time to listen and want to hear what they have to say. You must want to come to a peaceful and workable resolution. In order to really listen you have to be willing to temporarily suspend your own judgments so that you can fully attend to the experience of another. While listening, you must be genuinely willing to try to see the world as they see it, even if their view is completely different from your own.

In addition to hearing words that are obviously perceptible, there is a level of hearing that analyst Otto Rank referred to as ''listening with the third ear.'' This listening has to do with hearing the words and feelings that may not even be spoken. It is hearing between the lines. When people are frightened and angry, they may be unaware of the greater spectrum of their feelings and be unwilling or unable to articulate the truth. Being open and listening with your heart and full attention enables you to hear the nonverbal messages in the communication. It calls for a receptiveness and willingness to hear the truth behind another's words.

If you have a tendency to be controlling or defensive, this can be very threatening, for you may have to expose yourself to views that are different from the ones you may hold to so dearly as "right." Just as sharing the truth of your feelings with another takes courage, so does genuine listening. Just by listening, you risk having your attitudes changed and you risk hearing truths you may not want to hear.

When you listen empathically, you get to better understand that person. Empathy and insight into another's genuine feelings and motivations can open your heart and mind and change your thoughts and emotional responses toward them.

A friend and co-worker of mine became irritable and uncommunicative while working one day. I asked her if there was something disturbing her. She responded by saying that everything was fine. Her body language and tone of voice clearly indicated that this was a far cry from the truth. I sat quietly alone in a relaxed state and imagined conversing with her. I listened for the truth behind the words she had actually spoken to me. I heard her saying that she was afraid that she was not good enough at her work. She was afraid that people didn't appreciate her. I heard her insecurities and trusted my intuition that this was indeed what was behind her irritability. The next day I sincerely expressed my appreciation for her and her work. It opened up a needed discussion and reassured her. Her mood was radically different after that encounter.

If we listen deeply, we can usually hear the primal universal human calling to be respected and loved.

SELF-TO-SELF COMMUNICATION

In addition to taking responsibility for your experience and talking to another in a clear, nonattacking, nonblaming way, in forgiveness it is essential to remember to share from your Self to another's Self—keeping your heart open, remembering there is a place in them that is wise and caring. This will help you stay centered, and supports an atmosphere of safety so that both of you can let down your defenses and be more open to hearing each other.

In order to share from your Self to another's Self, you have to have *the willingness to see another newly.*

P A U S E   A N D   R E F L E C T

Consider a person you are feeling angry toward: Is the way you perceive this person limited to how he or she has been in the past? Do you already have your mind made up that this person is a certain way and is hopeless and will never change? (i.e., "Anthony will always be a jerk." "My husband is always stubborn.")

It may be perfectly understandable why you would think this way, but forgiving requires that you release or at least suspend negative and limiting perceptions as being the complete and final truth. Seeing beyond another's historic limits is a sure way to move beyond one's own.

FORGIVING YOUR FAMILY

II

CHAPTER SIX

FORGIVING YOUR
PARENTS

Now that you have had an opportunity to practice forgiveness on neutral territory, it is time to bring it home. Forgiving our parents, siblings, children, spouse, or "significant other" is usually our greatest challenge, and because this is so, it offers the most profound opportunity for healing—short only of fully forgiving ourselves.

Coming to peace in our relationships with our parents and other family members is crucial to our own inner peace. No matter how much we might cut ourselves off from them, we remain connected. As Paul Pearsall, Ph.D., writes in his book *The Power of the Family: Strength, Comfort and Healing,* "We can not disown what we have not purchased. . . . Such love [the love within the family] is not purchased, earned, or chosen, it is assigned through your humanness, through your evolution, to and within your own family. . . . The energy that is the universe bonds you all together forever, and a failure at reconciliatory loving only causes needless and endless pain in your soul while you lead a life in the illusion of separation."

BIRTHING INTO ADULTHOOD

There is no relationship potentially as important as our relationship with our parents. It is most frequently upon this relationship that the emotional foundation of our life is formed.

After nine months in a safe, nurturing womb, we make our way into the outer world. The natural birthing process ushers us to the point when the umbilical cord is cut and our physical autonomy is established.

We arrive impressionable, open, picking up our cues from our parents, the temporary directors of our life. Then, and in the years that follow, we learn our initial lessons about love and fear, safety or insecurity, generosity or fear and greed, self-respect or shame and low self-esteem, the need to be in control vs. safety in vulnerability.

When we come to adulthood we have the opportunity to actualize another kind of autonomy, one that is central to continued emotional growth and essential to spiritual maturity. If we don't have a healed relationship with our parents, this new autonomy requires that we go through another birthing process. Rather than cutting a physical umbilical cord, we now must cut an emotional umbilical cord to our parents, one that has grown out of a past of unmet needs and unfulfilled expectations. Often this cord is composed of anger, judgments, blame, shame, and guilt. If it remains connected, it will keep a part of us small, close our heart, and, like all resentment, hold us an emotional hostage to the past. Cutting the cord requires that we no longer expect or depend on our parents to nurture, love, and support us if they aren't capable of doing so at this time. Forgiveness serves as the merciful scalpel with which the umbilical cord is cut and we are all set free.

BRINGING IT HOME

If you are among the lucky few who grew up with two loving, supportive parents who were able to respond in a responsible, warm, and heartfelt way to your need for love and guidance, you aren't likely to feel the need to forgive in order to heal feelings of anger and resentment. However, you can still use forgiveness to help transform even the small irritations and minor conflicts that arise in most any relationship.

However, you may be one of the majority of adults who did not have two parents who were reliably able to recognize and meet your basic needs for bonding in love and affection, for physical and emotional safety and respect, and for innocence and play. If your parents did not meet these basic needs and you have not yet healed yourself and your relationship with them, your "inner child" is likely to become activated when you interact with or even think about them. (This "inner child" may also be activated in many other relationships if its needs are significant and unmet.) The activation of your inner child is not a conscious response— it's more like a reaction you don't get to vote on. It may get triggered by an innocent remark from a parent, the sound of their voices, or just by their presence. Sometimes you may even surprise yourself when you are with one of your parents and not feel like the mature adult your friends and colleagues know you to be. You see one of your parents, and the seven-year-old within may get triggered. Your parents' judgments feel devastating. Their demands and need for control are infuriating. Their denial leaves you feeling rageful. Their anger is met with yours. You find yourself still demanding a love they aren't capable of giving.

Letting go of the hope that your parents will ever meet your needs is often the antecedent to a profound sense of loss and a deep sadness which requires acceptance and grieving to heal.

Carol was the firstborn in a family of four children and two alcoholic parents. Her father often abused her mother, whom Carol felt the need to protect and rescue while growing up. When Carol entered therapy at the age of forty-one, she was enraged at her mother for never having been there and she was demanding that her mother now be there for her in a way that she had never been there before. Her anger was replacing a deep fear of loss and abandonment. For the first time in her life she felt angry and was expressing it to her mother. But it was not until she felt the full impact of the truth that her mother could not provide her with what she so deeply needed that she could let go into her intense

sadness and woundedness, release the deeper pain, and begin to
heal. Carol recognized that the child within her wouldn't get the
love and support that she needed and deserved from the person
whom it felt most instinctive to seek it from.

Like Carol, when healing your pain and wounded inner child, you
may need to look to effective, empathetic therapists and coun-
selors, to loving, supportive friends, therapeutic groups, and other
family members, to God or to what the Twelve Step Anonymous
programs call "a higher power" and to yourSelf. As the child
within you feels loved, accepted, and secure enough to feel and
grow, you naturally birth into a more secure experience of adulthood.

LETTING GO OF EXPECTATIONS

There can be a lot at stake in forgiving in a relationship that is so
primary and important. There is a lot to let go of and a lot to gain.
One thing that you need to let go of is an idealized image of how
your parents should be even though as a child you truly needed
them to be different than the way they were.

Forgiving your parents requires letting go of the expectations
that demand what they cannot give. You may want your parents
to be different, you may actively support them in changing, but
in order to forgive and have peace of mind, you have to let go of
any attachment to your parents' being a certain way. If you continue to demand—even at a subtle level—from your parents what
they may not be capable of giving you at this time, you will keep
anger, resentment, and guilt alive for all involved.

~~~~~~

P A U S E   A N D   R E F L E C T

Think of something you want from your mother—i.e., love,
acceptance, affection, approval. In your imagination, see yourself
with your mother. Remember to breathe. Now tell her what you

want from her. Say, "Mother (or whatever you call her), what I want from you is _____ and _____." List as many things as you need to until you feel complete. Take a deep breath. Feel the wholeness within your own being. Then say to her, "Mother, I no longer hold you responsible for giving me _____ (whatever you listed before)."

Now imagine you are with your father and repeat this exercise.

~~~~~~

The job of nurturing yourself must shift from your parents to yourself. It is up to you to proceed with your life, making the choices that nurture and support you. What you had needed, wanted, and expected them to give you, you will need to seek from others and yourSelf. Coming to terms with this reality may activate a lot of anger for you. You may find your inner child screaming, "It's not fair. They were supposed to take care of me. It was their job to give me these things." Although this may be a very deep and authentic response, there comes a time when letting your parents off the hook is a necessary step toward self-empowerment.

LETTING GO OF THE STRUGGLE

In order to forgive, you have to be willing to let go of the struggle implicit in resentment. This may feel very threatening at first. The struggle may make you feel strong or alive, and in letting go of the struggle with your parents you may find yourself threatened by feelings of defeat or hopelessness. Yet sometimes in order to heal, one needs to allow oneself to temporarily feel these feelings, trusting that on the other side of these feelings is an inner strength deeply rooted in the Self. Surprisingly, struggle or tension may have become a trusty companion, ever present and familiar. Letting go of struggle would fundamentally change the relationship with yourself as well as with your parents. You may have struggled as a way to feel separate from them, and yet the struggle has kept you bound not only to them but to yourself as a child.

Think about a tense and stressful relationship with one of your parents. (If this isn't the case, think of someone else with whom you have had a long and difficult relationship.)
· What would it mean to let go of the struggle in the relationship?
· How would your relationship be different?
· What would be left in the relationship?
· What would post-struggle interaction with your parent look like?
· How would you feel?
· How would your life be different?

Bruce is a thirty-two-year-old cook. His father is a workaholic insurance agent. Bruce's father often worked late, and when he was home he either sat in front of the TV or worked in his home office. When Bruce was young his father was a master at giving him orders, but any attempt for meaningful interaction by Bruce was aggressively treated as a nuisance and distraction from "more important things to do." His father would, with a scornful look, tell him "not to bother him now." As an adult, Bruce was furious with his father for continuing this pattern and for having emotionally abandoned him as a child.

After working with the principles of forgiveness for a few months, Bruce responded to the preceding questions in the following way.

What would it mean to let go of the struggle with your father?

It would mean I'd have to stop hating him for the way he's been. I've hated him for a long time. I'd have to give up the only relationship I've ever had with him. I'd have to look to see why he has always been such a miserable person, something I've never really done before.

How would your relationship be different?

I don't know if he would react other than the way he's always reacted, but I'd try to talk with him—something I gave up trying to do over twenty years ago. I'd stop hating him; actually, I know I'm already doing that. I haven't asked my father for anything since I was a kid. I'd ask him to do something with me, go to a ball game or something—he likes baseball—and I wouldn't easily take no for an answer. I'd hope that I could break the ice, but if I couldn't maybe I'd stop asking again. When I see him I'd try to relate to him with some genuine kindness—that would be very different!

What would be left in the relationship?

I'm not sure. If he responded positively to me, there would be some excitement and hope on my part that we could finally share something. If he couldn't respond to me, there would be more sadness and disappointment. I know I'd have to accept the sadness—actually I'm feeling that more and more—and I'm realizing that if I don't want to set myself up for a lot more anger, I have to let him be the way he is, if he just won't or can't come around.

What would post-struggle interaction with your father look like?

At the very least, I'd feel different inside. It might not look too different on the outside, but I'd be more aware and less reactive in a blaming way.

How would you feel?

I would feel much freer. I also think I might still feel angry at times. I know there's a lot of sadness under the anger now, so I'd try to acknowledge and feel that. I'd feel more peaceful—that's new.

How would your life be different?

I'd be more accepting and stop putting so much energy into denying my feelings or getting lost in negative thoughts. I think I'd feel stronger and better about myself.

David is a forty-two-year-old dentist. He is dating a woman of another religion. His parents are angry and intolerant about his choice to continue dating her. Every time he sees them, they are verbally abusive or totally withdrawn. His parents have always been extremely controlling, but up until now his personal, academic, and professional choices have been acceptable to them. He came to me for counseling, wanting to deal with this issue.

After working together for a few months, I asked David to respond to the following questions:

What would it mean to let go of the struggle with your parents?

First I'd have to do what felt right to me, accept my choice, stop struggling with myself, and stop trying to please them.

How would your relationship be different?

I wouldn't argue with them anymore. We've been through that enough times to know that it doesn't make a difference. At this point either they would accept my right to choose my own relationships or they wouldn't. If they don't start to respect me and my choices (and it doesn't appear that they have any inclination to do so), I will stop visiting them.

What would be left in the relationship?

For them, anger, judgments, and fear. For me, sadness and a growing acceptance that I can't be myself and have a workable relationship with them at this point in time.

What would post-struggle interaction with your parents look like?

I wouldn't have any contact with them for a while.

How would your life be different?

I'd stop trying to run my life for my parents. I have a deepening awareness of how addicted to control and how miserable they really are inside. It's sad—sad for them and sad for me. I'm realizing that I don't have to stay angry at them.

Although I do get angry at times, I have more understanding and compassion, and a more forgiving attitude. I wish it were different. I really would like to have a good relationship with them, or at least a cordial one, but I'm not willing to sell out on myself in order to please them. I have to be more my own person now.

David's particular experience of forgiveness illustrates some important points. David had cultivated a forgiving attitude toward his parents *and* he chose to cut off any active communication for a while. In this instance forgiveness didn't improve the working relationship on a day-to-day basis. He decided that having an active relationship with his parents didn't serve them or him for now. As long as they were consistently demeaning and negative toward him and opposed to any resolution other than their own, he decided separation (not phoning or visiting them for a while) would be best. Forgiveness did, however, empower him to be free of his parents' manipulations and to do what was in his own best interest. It allowed him the objectivity to avoid making his parents' prejudice and need for control a source of guilt and remorse. It allowed him to avoid getting pulled into the great melodrama that his parents were staging (and pulling his siblings into as well). Forgiveness gave him the inner strength to get some emotional and physical distance. Paradoxically, this distance allowed him to transform his anger into deepening compassion.

BUT I HAVE A RIGHT TO BE ANGRY!

As you consider the possibility of forgiving your parents, you may think, "But I have a right to be angry after what my father did." "I have a right to be angry after the way my mother treated me." And indeed, you absolutely *do* have a right to be angry! And again, it is important to feel the anger if it is how you feel.

Yet anger, like all emotions, usually follows a natural course if it is safely allowed to be, without your holding onto it or pushing it away prematurely. Over time it is likely to arise, intensify, peak, and fade away of its own accord. However, if you are attached to your anger or afraid to let it go, in order to heal, you will need to take a more active role in dealing with it. Making a conscious choice to practice forgiveness will enable you to heal the anger and ultimately feel more powerful, peaceful, and secure.

Many people fear forgiving their parents because they believe that by forgiving they will once again make themselves vulnerable, open to being taken advantage of and hurt.

If your parents have been abusive and you have historically responded to their behavior with anger of your own, your anger may have been the wall that served as your protection. And up until now it may have served you well. Yet by persistently using anger to establish boundaries and serve as a source of strength and protection, you deny yourself the opportunity of knowing what genuine strength is. Maintaining anger as a source of strength is a form of self-deception. As a stance, it always reestablishes your sense of powerlessness and fear because you unconsciously relinquish the power you have to the person with whom you are angry. Moreover, it ensures perpetuating a struggle where no one ever wins.

Like David, you can forgive and still set clear nonnegotiable boundaries. You may decide, for instance, that despite your forgiving attitude toward your parents, you are no longer willing to be around them when they are drinking or being hostile and demeaning. You can forgive and choose to leave a family gathering, end a phone conversation, stop visiting, etc. Or, you can choose to stay. However you choose to act, you can choose to not take the anger and fear-based behavior of your parents so personally. You can choose to not get hooked into the drama, seeing it for the fearful and learned behavior that it is.

Forgiving moves you from feeling defensive to feeling powerful—not because you are now a more superior person, but because forgiveness is an expression of the Self and the Self is, by nature, powerful. *A Course in Miracles* reminds us, "In my defenselessness lies my safety." When we no longer need to defend ourselves because we are aligned with the Self, the true meaning of safety and strength reveals itself.

THEY SHOULD KNOW BETTER!

Sometimes there may be resentment toward your parents because you think that somehow they should "know better," and yet, at a conscious level, they may not. Perhaps they've never dealt with their own insecurities and are still identified with their own scared and hurt "inner child."

Exercise: A Native in Their Land

Take a few deep relaxing breaths. Now see your mother as a young child. Imagine her in her childhood. Imagine what shaped her personality. Was she emotionally nurtured and supported by her parents? Were her feelings honored and validated, or dismissed, or treated with contempt? What fears and successes shaped her sense of security and self-love? Did her parents serve as models as to what a loving parent could be?

Now imagine your father as a little boy. Repeat this exercise keeping your father in mind. Allow yourself to become a native in his land.

Now consider:

Are you willing to entertain the possibility that for the level of self-love and self-respect your mother and father experience, for the level of fear, shame, guilt, and confusion they may live with, for the degree of emotional and spiritual maturity they have integrated, they have done and are doing the very best that they can?

The last question implies not only considering what influenced your parents' development, but also questioning beliefs that you may have unconsciously carried from childhood into adulthood—namely, that your parents still necessarily know more, and are wiser or more powerful than you. Without questioning these beliefs as an adult, you may live in denial of your own wisdom and power. In a certain respect it means giving up being "the child" even though you may not have received the parenting you felt you needed in order to grow up.

Again (and again), understanding that your parents may have done the best they could doesn't mean that you condone their behavior or that you should hesitate to firmly assert yourself and directly address the issues or feelings that remain unresolved—if you feel it would be useful to do so. Be vigilant, however, to make sure that by addressing the issues you are not expecting that your parents will necessarily change. Expectations will once again set you up for a sustained struggle if you don't get the response you want. Do it for yourself. Even if your communication falls on deaf or resistant ears, you will know that you have tried to open communication and heal the relationship. In order to let go of the struggle, your decision to address the issues requires a conscious decision to do so as effectively as you can (sharing the truth of your experience from your Self to their Selves while suspending judgment and blame). Be willing to let go of the outcome of your interaction—if their reaction evokes more anger and pain, get the support you need or take it upon yourself to deal with the feelings that are evoked. Just your sincere effort to communicate and initiate positive change can result in a feeling of greater freedom and completion for you. At least you will know that you have tried your best.

BETH'S STORY

Beth had never gotten along with her father. Forgiving him changed their relationship.

> I spoke with my father last night and really did have an easy, effortless experience. When he initiated a topic of conversation, familiar in its intent to evoke sympathy for him and disgust for the rest of the world, I had a moment of panic. My reactive button got pushed and I felt the unconscious surge of powerlessness, resentment, anger, etc. Just for a second, until I remembered who we are—who he is, who I am—and then I was able to respond to him as I never have before. Normally I would have made faces, rolled my eyes, and silently pummeled the sofa while uh-huh-ing in sweetly bored tones. I would have been saving away the more obnoxious remarks to sneer over later with my sisters. Last night, however, I answered him. I responded with the understanding that I needn't be cruel, nor of the same mind. I found myself capable of being gentle to him and firm in my right to my opinions, both born of this realization that we are not responsible for one another. To my surprise and de-

light, he listened a little, and moreover, he did not become defensive or angry. It was by far the best conversation I've ever had with him.

Once you are ready, you make the choice to step out of old neurotic patterns of relating, not because you have to, but because you know other choices work against you.

As more and more people develop awareness and insight into how their thoughts, attitudes, and childhood experiences impact their present experiences, it's not unusual for them to move beyond many of their peers and elders in emotional and spiritual understanding and maturity. If you develop greater insight into a situation than the person with whom you are in a relationship, then the greater responsibility for not getting lost in neurotic patterns becomes yours. You could see this as a burden ("Why do I always have to be the one to change?") and resent it, or you could see it for what it is—an incredible opportunity to grow and love.

HAVING RESTS ON GIVING, NOT GETTING

Oftentimes people mistake loving someone with doing things for them, as though love can be quantified. More accurately, love is where you come from in your relationships with people. Joe thinks buying his daughter a new car is an indication of his love for her. Barbara thinks visiting her father every Sunday is an indication of her love for him. While these may be tokens or symbols of love, they should not be confused with the unconditional recognition and acknowledgment that is at the core of a loving relationship.

When love is an action, you offer the beloved what they need, not what you want to give them as a token of your love. The purest expression of love requires that you are in touch enough with yourself to feel a true connection and empathy with another.

Because so many of us lack self-esteem, it is often hard to give of ourselves. Often we hold back from giving of ourselves because we feel inadequate, because we don't feel there's enough of ourselves to give. Paradoxically, the more we give of our true selves, the better we feel about ourselves.

It follows that what we often ask from others (i.e., true recognition, acknowledgment, respect), we have difficulty giving.

P   A   U   S   E   A   N   D   R   E   F   L   E   C   T

Do you want your parents' (or anyone else's) unconditional love? Have you been willing to love them unconditionally?

Do you want their approval? Have you been willing to accept them as they are?

A Course in Miracles says that "whatever we give to others is given to ourself." By extending love, we naturally experience the peace and love we are extending. In truth, having rests on giving, not on getting.

ELLEN'S LETTER
Ellen believed for many years that a loving, forgiving relationship with her father was not possible.

Dear Daddy:

As we both know, this isn't the first earnest letter I've written to you. In the past my messages have frightened and angered you, and I hope that won't be the case this time. If, on the other hand, you are hurt by what I have to say, I am truly sorry for the pain, but recognize it as yours and not mine.

I love you more than words will convey. You are my father, the man I grew up loving. I doubt that anything in the world can compare to that. Consequently, you have been the man with the greatest power to hurt me, and I have been hurt.

I want you to know that I no longer hold you responsible for that pain. I can now see how we made it together but it was I who have carried it all these years. I chose to make it part of my life, just as I choose today to put it down and walk on unburdened. I'm afraid that we both expected unrealistically of one another. Neither of us had any experience with this father-daughter business. You wanted a perfect daughter and I a perfect father; we couldn't see that it was already so. Over the years I demanded things of you which I could only receive from myself, and I know that you have done likewise. I ask your forgiveness for it as I forgive you.

I have done you an injustice in not seeing you as you are. Perhaps more importantly, I have deprived myself of years of knowing you. I am ready to see you anew today, and I am also prepared to come out from behind my little girl and stand in the open for you to see and know if you want to.

This was to be a letter of forgiveness, so I feel for the sake of completion the necessity of telling you that I do forgive you without reservation. It feels like a rather pro forma statement to me, though. Once I decided to step outside of the circle of expectation and disappointment, which has always comprised our relationship, once I chose to be who I am rather than a failed example of who I thought you wanted me to be, there was no need to forgive. The past simply melted away, exposed at last for the doomed pattern of reactions it was. Forgiveness was merely looking at you with clear eyes, *knowing* that you love me and that I love you and seeing that we are both whole already.

I also need to ask your forgiveness. There are myriad individual things I have done, said, not done, left unsaid, which I'm sure have hurt you. Many things with intent. And undoubtedly often without awareness. I am truly sorry for anything I've done which has caused you pain or fear, but most of all, I am sorry for the suffering I have caused you by looking away. I know that this may sound like just more ranting from your insanely introspective first child, but for me this is a reality, Daddy, and I do ask your forgiveness.

Finally, let me say that I love you, I have my eyes open and focused and am beginning to see you. Despite the not infrequent cruelty and pain we have visited upon one another during the last thirty-one years, my heart is opening. For the first time I can say that I am glad and honored that you are my father; that I would rather be no one's daughter more than yours. With growing love.

As we forgive, we become more aware and insightful. As our compassion for and understanding of others and ourselves grows, we begin to experience a greater reality of love in our life. As my friend and colleague Naomi Raiselle so beautifully describes it, "Love is no more and no less than the simple, honest and natural expression of our own wholeness, our full self-acceptance. But until we can truly accept, without judgment, all of who we are— our seeming shortcomings as well as our innate glory—love waits patiently behind the fragile illusions of romance, or else it is mistaken as a medium of barter and exchange, or it feels like an object of addiction and is experienced as a constant need."

It is through forgiving that we learn to grow in love. As we learn to accept, without judgment, the seeming shortcomings (the fears, the calls for help, the idiosyncrasies) as well as the innate glory (the wise, loving, capable Self of others), we come to know ourSelf, for forgiveness is the key to knowing our true identity. It is an understanding of reality that gives us the courage to engage more effectively with our personal trials, in whatever form they come.

FORGIVING YOURSELF AS A CHILD

As with any relationship where there is resentment, you may feel that the person in the relationship whom you really need to forgive is yourself. If you were abused you may feel guilty or angry at yourself. Perhaps you feel you could have stood up for yourself, fought back, or run away from the abusive situation. No matter what you did as a child, no matter how "bad" you were told you were, you did not deserve pain, rage, or humiliation. Above all, it is critical for you to know and accept that none of the abuse was your fault. If you want to heal, it is critical to remember that you did the best you could have done considering the scope of your awareness and the depth of fear you were experiencing. You can make other choices now.

Many parents blame their unhappiness on their children. For instance, my friend grew up hearing, "If it weren't for you, your

father and I would be so happy." Her healing began with forgiving
herself, recognizing that she was not responsible for her mother's
unhappiness. Her healing continued by feeling angry at her mother
and later forgiving her mother for having burdened her with that
guilt for so many years.

You may now be angry at yourself as an adult child for not
having forgiven your parents sooner. Hindsight is not useful if you
use it to condemn yourself. You may feel, "I've wasted so much
precious time." This may be particularly true if your mother or
father has died. The truth is that during the time you feel you
"wasted," you were moving toward that time when forgiveness
would be possible. No one can forgive before they are ready.

CAN YOU HEAL YOUR RELATIONSHIP WITH YOUR PARENTS AFTER THEY HAVE DIED?

If you had a painful relationship with your parents and they died
before you had a chance to heal that relationship, you may feel
remorse that you've lost your chance to come to peace with them.
Considering the options that were obvious to you, forgiving may
not have been possible earlier. Remember to be gentle with yourself.

If you had a painful relationship with deceased parents, their
death may have felt like a welcome relief. You may have thought,
"The relationship is finally over and I won't have to deal with
them anymore." Yet even if they have died, if you have "unfinished business" with them, it takes its toll on your well-being until
it is resolved.

If your parents have died, regardless of how you felt about their
death or how you related with them while they were alive, it is
possible to heal the relationship now.

Certainly it is still possible for you to forgive them. Your willingness to forgive them only takes you.

It has been my experience that a profound sense of mutual
healing is also possible. Toward the end of forgiveness workshops

I facilitate a visualization called "Love and Forgiveness." Before the visualization begins, participants choose someone toward whom they feel some anger or resentment *and* toward whom they are open to the possibility of forgiving and sharing a healed relationship. In the visualization, participants are encouraged to invite the person they have chosen to an imaginary safe place. When I lead this visualization in a large group, almost without fail, a deceased person (frequently a parent) will come into a few of the participants' awareness. (Sometimes the participant has chosen someone other than a parent and, to their surprise, a deceased parent appears.) In the course of the meeting and exchange with this person, forgiveness is often expressed both ways. Through hearing the deceased person talk in this process, insight is gained into their side of the experience. The opportunity to empathize with the other's experiences and points of view allows the opportunity to both understand and deal with the hurt. As a result, an authentic and profound emotional healing often occurs.

Whether your parents are deceased or alive, if you are willing to open to the possibility of healing your relationship with them, try the Love and Forgiveness visualization that follows.

Visualization: Love and Forgiveness

Find a comfortable position, close your eyes, and take some long, deep breaths. As you breathe out, feel the tension releasing from your body and mind. Repeat this several times.

Now imagine that you are in a safe and comfortable place. You may have been there before, or you may create such a place in your mind. Notice how this place looks . . . how peaceful it feels. Feel yourself being comfortable here . . . calm and relaxed. Breathe in and feel a calm strength within you. Now think of someone for whom you feel some resentment . . . perhaps someone from the past or someone you see every day. Picture this person in your mind. Breathe in and feel your own inner strength. As you breathe out, let go of any fear or worry. Now invite the person you just pictured in your mind into this safe place. Breathe in and feel the wholeness within your own being . . . and allow yourself to look at this person . . . and now begin to relate to them, communicating the thoughts and feelings that until now have been left unsaid.

With a willingness and courage allow yourself to share the truth of your experience. . . .

Now allow yourself to hear as this person shares with you. Listen fully for the words and feelings that may not even be spoken. With openness and patience listen to them. Fully hear what they have to say . . . listen for the truth behind their words. Let go of any blame and judgments . . . let go of the pride that holds on to resentment. Breathe in and feel the wholeness within your own being. Allow yourself to look into their eyes. Let go of your fear and see beyond their fear. Let go of the burden of resentment and allow yourself to forgive. Let go of judgments and see with new clarity. Look beyond this person's mistakes and errors and allow yourself to see their wholeness. . . .

Now again look into their eyes and allow the seeming issues that stood between you to grow dim and disappear. Breathe in and feel your own inner strength. If there is anything else you wish to tell this person, take a few moments to share it now. . . .

Now allow yourself to let go of the past and see this person as if for the first time, in this moment, each of you knowing who the other person really is. Now with a sense of freedom that goes beyond even understanding, say good-bye and watch as this person leaves. Now allow yourself to extend this forgiveness to yourself . . . letting go of any guilt or self-blame . . . let go of self-judgment . . . make room for yourself in your own heart . . . open your heart to yourself, knowing that you always deserve your love. Feel a growing freedom and joy as your heart opens fully to your power to love, to be fully alive. . . .

Get ready to open your eyes . . . feel yourself becoming alert . . . and when you are ready, open your eyes and go on with your day.

Love and Forgiveness can be used to help heal your relationship with anyone.

I encourage you to return to this visualization often as you practice forgiveness with others.

. . .

The more you choose a loving awareness, the more consistent, integrated, and natural an expression forgiveness becomes, and forgiving always leaves you feeling more peaceful and whole.

Remember, however, that forgiveness doesn't necessarily last in time (especially at first when there has been a lot of judgment and anger in the past). You may feel like you have finally forgiven someone and then minutes later a remark or memory evokes anger again. Often, the stronger you become, the more you are able to allow the deeper and more hidden anger to come forth. Remember that forgiveness isn't an achievement as much as it is an ongoing process. *Be gentle with yourself.* The issues that are unresolved with your parents, or in other areas of your life, keep arising *for the purpose of healing*.

As it says in *A Course in Miracles,* "Choose once again. Together you remain prisoners of fear, or leave your house of darkness and walk into the light that forgiveness brings."

ERICA'S STORY

Erica, a successful urban architect, shares a painful history and her unique process for forgiving her father.

All kids crawl in bed with their parents, I suppose. It seems such a safe place to be—an escape from thunderstorms, nightmares, loneliness. It must be one of the great joys of being a parent to awake to the sight and touch of a child.

I was probably three or so the first time my father got in bed with me. I can't remember the first time it felt bad, or I felt bad, or it seemed not right or not safe. There was always a scenario. Daddy's here to give you a backrub. Daddy's here to play with you 'cause Mommy's cranky in the morning. Daddy's here.

He used to curl up behind me and fondle what would have been breasts had I been older. Unless I've totally repressed it, I don't think there was other activity. But what it lacked in activity, it certainly made up for in longevity. For the record, the last time my father tried to get in my bed I was thirty years old.

His visits were always in the morning. School mornings and weekend mornings. To this day, I am an incredibly light sleeper in the mornings. I have what I call retroactive wakefulness. If I hear a sound, it is as if my mind plays back the few moments leading up to that so that I can sort it out for its meaning. I am wide awake in a flash.

My father created all the laws in the family, though the family was not at all closely knit. He was the boss. You could ignore him sometimes, but you could never defy him. In thinking back to those morning visits now, I realize I had no sense at all that I could have said, "Stop," or that I had any power. Probably the sense of being disempowered was stronger in its impact than the incest. Men can still disempower me with a loud word.

The strongest memory of a single incident that I recall took place when I was about ten years old. I think it was a Saturday morning. Daddy came into my bed quite early. I clenched my arms to my sides to prevent allowing him access to my chest, and I pretended to be asleep. I don't know how much time elapsed before I got up and left my room. I think I went first into the guest room. He followed me there. I then got up and went into my mother's room (actually, strictly speaking, my parents' room, but my father slept in the guest room). He followed me there. They had a king-size bed, and he curled up right behind me with my mother in the other half of the bed. So, I crawled out of that bed and went back to the hallway. I had run out of beds. I went into my bathroom, locked the door (against Daddy's law), and got into the tub with whatever towels were there and tried to sleep.

I got in trouble for locking the door.

The day I first got my period (I was thirteen), I remember thinking that now my father wouldn't be able to get in my bed anymore. I wasn't a little girl now. But the very next morning he was there again with me.

I was very fortunate to be able to go to a boarding school when I was fourteen, so for nine months of the year I was safe. Odd, I still feel safer when I am alone.

People with whom I have shared this story always ask what my mother was doing all this time. I have spent a lot of time thinking about that. I think my mother felt equally disempowered by my father, and I think that she also didn't feel she could tell him to stop. But remember, it was the 1950s and 1960s, and *Time* and *Newsweek* hadn't yet discovered incest as a breaking trend. I think also that it was pretty clear in my family that my father didn't divorce my mother for two reasons: me and his swimming pool. Maybe subconsciously she thought if she pried him away from me she would lose him—or at least the family unit—altogether. I was a pawn. He could only swim five months a year.

The last time my father got in my bed I was living in New
Haven. He was visiting for the weekend, and on Saturday
morning he came into my room with the promises of a backrub. Armed with a couple of years of therapy and a sense of
independence, I said no. He said, "But sweetie, you always
loved for me to give you backrubs!" "No, Dad, I just don't
want my father in my bed." "Jesus, what do you think I'm
going to do, make a pass at you or something?"

Denial runs in the family. I was twenty years old before I
mentioned this to anyone. I was seeing a therapist and about
two months into therapy, after a lengthy disclaimer about
how I didn't want him getting all Freudian on me because I
knew this was my father's problem and not mine, I told him
about it. He got the short form. I didn't go into detail because
I didn't want him making a big deal out of it.

He listened quietly, and when I had finished he waited.
Then he said, "Do you know what you did before you told
me that story? You buttoned your suit jacket up to your neck."

I had to acknowledge there was more to this than met my
eye. So, after all these years of denying that it was of signif-
icance, all of a sudden, I was kind of vomiting the information. It was like coming out of the closet—I started telling
people about it. To be more specific, I started telling people
about my father, because I don't think at that point I yet saw
myself as part of the scene. I shudder to think about who I
must have told in those days. Thank God it was the hippie
era then, and maybe they were stoned and forgot.

One thing that surprised me was that people who heard
the story tended to start hating my father. That seemed a
rather extreme reaction to me, because after all, my father
had other parts to him besides this, but I think I stopped
telling people eventually because I didn't want to have to
keep defending him.

That first round of therapy when I was in my twenties was
helpful because it got me to deal with the information and
to acknowledge that that situation may just have had some
effect on me. The fact is, I am extremely skittish to this day
when men touch my breasts. I tend to disassociate myself
from them somewhat—I use them more as punchlines than
anything else. It's as if men have fingers of emery-board
material. I wonder how much the Daddy-in-my-bed scenario

is responsible for my being forty-one and alone. Happy, but alone.

Seeing other people in therapy in my early twenties I saw a lot of them being constantly angry, and it always seemed to me that this was a part of a process, but that therapy wasn't over until you worked through the anger. I think there are some people who have a lot of anger in them. Some aren't so interested in working it through. And then there are some who strive for calmer waters and greater harmony. I fall into the latter category.

I had never thought of forgiveness as an action. It always seemed to me it was an evolution, that over time your anger would wane. I didn't think that forgiveness was something you could create; I thought you just had to wait for it to happen. Given these assumptions, it's hard to explain why I went to an evening lecture called "Love and Forgiveness."

The "Love and Forgiveness" meditation that I did around my father asked you to envision yourself in a safe place. I picked Brace's Cove, a rocky beach about a mile from my house where I used to walk early in the mornings when I was feeling great. It is not a swimming beach—it's full of debris and driftwood. One year a whale washed up there.

The meditation said I should invite my father into this safe place. What I saw was my seventy-year-old father, who has a bad back, bad feet, bad knees, one eye, and walks (badly) with a cane, making his way across this craggy beach to join me. I was overwhelmed with the awareness that this man loved me more than anything in his world, and that he would do anything in his power to help me. What became clear was that the key words were "in his power." His incestuous and overpowering treatment of me wasn't really in his power.

I saw it another way, too. Having that excruciatingly clear awareness of how much he loved me, I thought how strong those "bad" feelings must have been to overpower his incredible love for me. In all other aspects of my childhood, I was always completely confident of his love for me. He would do anything for me; make any sacrifice; protect me from anything—anything except, of course, from himself. He couldn't protect me from himself, and from whatever dark drives exist in him.

The meditation is helpful, too, because it gives both you

and the other person a chance to say what you need to say to each other. In my case, what I needed to say was precisely what my father needed to hear. I needed to say that while I don't understand what drove him, I forgive him. I know that somehow this was all unrelated to his loving me. It didn't mean that he loved me less. The most painful moment of the meditation was when I said good-bye to my father and had to watch him walk away, stumbling a bit across the sand in a place that was completely unfamiliar and uncomfortable for him, but doing it without hesitation because he loves me so.

Throughout your day consider:

I am responsible for what I see in myself and others.

CHAPTER SEVEN

FORGIVING YOUR SPOUSE

A primary committed relationship is like a stone mill: It will either grind you down or polish you up—which it does is ultimately up to you. It's helpful to reflect on this in the light of the wisdom of Confucius: "The gem cannot be polished without friction, nor man perfected without trials."

No adult relationship is likely to cause more friction, or offer as many trials, as the committed intimate relationship of marriage. (The term *marriage* is used to refer to any committed, intimate relationship.) Unlike many relationships, in marriage you come face to face every day with each other's needs, desires, and expectations.

Without forgiveness in marriage there can be a great deal of emotional pain—because without it there is always the tendency for each partner to get lost in their small selves, separate from their greater Self, and consequently, separate from each other.

Nothing inspires mutual love and understanding more than a forgiving attitude. And regardless of whether you stay together forever or physically part and go your own ways, by forgiving, you bring alive the primary goal of forgiveness in a relationship— to establish a personal commitment to truth and to genuine respect and peace.

MODELS OF RELATIONSHIPS: IMAGES OF LOVE

Models of happy, healthy, fulfilling intimate relationships are relatively rare. As recently as our grandparents' and parents' generation, marriage was not necessarily a relationship that one entered into with a high degree of choice and awareness. Many people got married because that's what was expected at a certain age—get married, have children, and adapt to fulfill perceived roles and functions. For many it was enough to keep a marriage intact. Each partner's personal development and fulfillment, and the deepening of the partnership in emotional intimacy and love, may have been considered somewhat irrelevant to the marriage's function and success.

Besides the models of marriage that many of us personally grew up with, our cultural image of love is a sorry one. Developmentally this image is stuck in adolescence. Soap operas, true-romance magazines, tabloids, gothic romances, and Hollywood movies rarely portray "true love" as anything more than acquiring the perfect partner and satisfying sexual desire.

Forgiving offers us the opportunity to grow up and go beyond the confining romantic archetypes that are doomed to leave us feeling lonely and betrayed. Forgiving offers us ways of relating and being that remove the obstacles to the presence of love, caring, friendship, and commitment. Forgiving kindles a willingness to engage and work with what arises in a relationship, because it enables us to relate to a person and not to a romantic ideal. Forgiving is the stuff that great relationships are made of.

One client described her marriage and its healing through forgiveness in this way: "I spent the first ten years of my marriage trying to make Steven over into my image of a husband. I was angry at him for having failed by not fulfilling my ideals. And I've spent the last year of my marriage discovering who he really is and falling in love with him again."

Culturally, marriage and the love that consecrates it have been viewed in only a small fragment of their potential meaning and possibility. As Robert Johnson in his book *We: Understanding the Psychology of Romantic Love* says, "We are the only society that makes romance the basis of our marriages and love relationships and the cultural ideal of 'true love.' " The romantic image of love is masqueraded as the fulfillment of all that is possible. We come to expect the other to always be the strong, handsome prince or the beautiful, perfect princess. If we are duped by this fantasy, we expect romantic passion to be sustained, and we lose compassion when it isn't. This static image allows us to glimpse a certain transient potential in relationships, but it will inevitably leave us feeling angry, resentful, and betrayed when the illusion that this can be maintained is inevitably shattered. Lost in pain, we are then distanced from a deeper passion for true intimacy and a more mature, less neurotic love. Johnson states, "Usually we blame other people for failing us; it doesn't occur to us that perhaps it is we who need to change our own unconscious attitudes—the expectations and demands we impose on our relationships and on other people."

HEALING THE PAST: SETTING THE STAGE FOR A LOVING RELATIONSHIP IN THE PRESENT

Until we heal our relationships with our parents and siblings, we're likely to reenact at least some of the problems of our "family of origin" in our primary relationships. It is commonly known to marital theorists and therapists that adults tend to repeat the themes of early childhood or of previous generations in the context of their intimate relationships. For instance, a woman who had a physically abusive father may find herself married to a spouse who is abusive; a man who had a domineering mother may find himself married to a woman who is bossy. Adults who were abused as children are more likely to abuse their own children than those who were not. Becoming aware of family dynamics and compassionately facing your wounds is important to assuring that you don't reenact these patterns in your adult life. Until we heal these relationships, we aren't likely to have fresh relationships with others.

If you are resentful, angry, or otherwise unresolved with your family of origin, make it a priority to heal these relationships. If your work of forgiving your parents and siblings is complete, or something you are currently engaged in, it will positively and profoundly affect your relationship with your partner (and everyone else).

Every marriage contains two inner children as well as two adults, and it is the job of the partners to love these frightened children in each other so that they may heal and grow. It is sometimes the unmet needs of the inner child that are unconsciously demanding to be met in a relationship: "Take care of me! Be there to gratify my needs upon demand (even if you have to put aside your own needs to do it). Be the mommy or daddy I never had." In addition to each partner being there for the inner child in the other, each partner needs to take responsibility for healing the inner child within themself. This self-responsibility and self-healing is necessary if the relationship is to thrive and grow.

Each person brings to the relationship the love and the obstacles to love that have been learned. The ways of love are learned and chosen. Some adults have felt so alienated from love, so wounded by what passed for parental "love," that feeling worthy of genuine love and being able to extend love must be learned and nurtured as an adult. If you heal old wounds and learn to love and accept yourself, you naturally bring the light of love to your relationship.

ANGER AND RESENTMENT IN MARRIAGE

Marriages are often easy arenas in which we can see the negative effects of anger and resentment as well as the transformative effects of forgiveness. When two people fall in love, they often see the pure Self of the other and experience their own Self mirrored in their partner's eyes. As time goes by, the partial selves begin to emerge in the dynamic of the relationship, and disillusionment, resentment, and confusion often set in. Each partner thinks the other has changed, that they have somehow been misled and deceived by those first loving impressions. In truth, everyone brings all the aspects of their being to an intimate relationship—the noble nature and high radiance of the Self, as well as the darker, more fearful aspects of some of the partial selves.

In marriage, as in many relationships, anger and resentment may exist as a result of an isolated incident—your partner embarrassed you in front of friends or was unfaithful to you. Or, it may be a reaction to daily behaviors and attitudes that you perceive as undesirable or distressing—your partner has ignored you, been unkind to you, been uncommunicative, or unwilling to take responsibility around the house. He or she has been too demanding sexually or too unresponsive. You may disagree about money or child-rearing, or your partner may be addicted to alcohol, drugs, sex, or work. And yet there is a bond and you are together.

Some unnameable force seems to draw two people together; there is a pull that interweaves lives, offering a possibility for growth that parallels few others. It is said that if you want to walk the path of fire, get into a relationship. Friction is sure to generate heat. And heat can be the catalyst to your healing and to Self-discovery and fulfillment.

How do you use the friction to grow in a relationship where resentments are running high?

You have to have a willingness to forgive.

THE WILLINGNESS TO FORGIVE

If you are holding on to anger and resentment toward your partner, pause and reflect on any secondary gains you may be getting.

~~~~~~

P A U S E   A N D   R E F L E C T

Notice your responses to the following questions with a gentle, nonjudging awareness:

· Is holding on to resentment a way to prove that you are "right"?
· Is staying angry a way to reinforce that your partner isn't worth loving?
· Is holding on to anger a way to control the situation?
· Is it a way to maintain some illusion of control?
· Is being angry a way for you to avoid intimacy?
· Is it a way to avoid deeper feelings of sadness, despair, hurt, abandonment, and rejection?
· Is it a way to be heard?
· Is it a way to hold on or let go?
· Is it a way to punish and get back?
· Is it a way to maintain the position that the problem is your partner's?
· Is it a way to maintain life as it is and avoid a degree of clarity that may risk change that you are afraid of?

~~~~~~

Maybe you're just feeling tired of forgiving. You don't want to do it one more time! Be gentle with yourself. You have a right to be tired. Be kind to yourself. Get support. Let it be okay if that is what you feel right now. Yet, know that staying angry will be more exhausting in the long run. Even if forgiveness has been the furthest thing from your mind, be willing to open the door to forgiveness just a crack. And know that in each moment you have the opportunity to choose forgiveness again.

In Chapter One we looked at how forgiving (or not forgiving) might manifest in a job. Let's look at some possibilities of how the dynamics of anger, resentment, or forgiveness might play themselves out within a marriage:

If there is anger and resentment you could:
1. hold on to the anger indefinitely and be miserable;
2. forgive—in which case you will be more peaceful, clearer

about what the real issues are, and empowered to stimulate positive change;

2a. your mate might respond, let go of their fear and defenses
(assuming they are fearful and defensive), and a new level
of mutual relating based on clarity, respect, and responsibility could now ensue. Here intimacy would have the
opportunity to be reestablished or established for the first
time;

2b. forgive—and your mate might be too defended and fearful
to outwardly respond at this point in time—here you could
stay involved in the relationship having greater peace and
perspective, *or* you could choose to forgive *and* decide that
you're not going to remain committed to maintaining this
partnership as a primary relationship.

As mentioned before, forgiving does not imply that you overlook
behaviors or dynamics in the relationship that are truly unacceptable to you. Forgiving involves forthrightly addressing these
issues and, if they are a pattern, setting clear boundaries and consequences for unacceptable behavior in the future. Getting clear
on what is acceptable and unacceptable for you is a testimony to
the love and respect you have for both of you. To allow truly
unacceptable patterns to persist maintains resentment, guilt, and
dysfunctional behavior and disempowers both you and your partner.

If you are experiencing friction in your primary relationship, take
some time to look deeply into what the real issues are, what you
are feeling under the anger, what is acceptable and unacceptable
for you. Return to pages 59–62 and pause and reflect on the
sentence completions in relation to yourself and your partner.

Be gentle with yourself as you do this. It takes boldness to
acknowledge your deepest feelings and truths. Appreciate yourself
for having the courage.

Now take some time to participate in the *Love and Forgiveness*
visualization on page 88 once again. This time bring your partner
to mind. Getting in touch with and sharing the truth of your

experience, and letting go of judgments and listening to your mate's honest experience, even if only in your imagination, can significantly open your mind and heart.

If you have been feeling angry and resentful toward your partner for a long time, it may be particularly difficult to break the pattern. Perhaps whenever you think of your partner, what comes up are the judgments you have about him or her and the feelings of separation that have grown between you. If this is the case, it's extremely useful to take some time every day to reflect on the reality of his or her Self—his or her "light."

~~~~~~

P A U S E   A N D   R E F L E C T

Close your eyes. Take a few deep, relaxing breaths and get in touch with a place of peacefulness within you. Picture your partner in your mind's eye and allow yourself to suspend all judgments about him or her for now. See the reality of your partner that is beyond his or her personality, physical appearance, subpersonalities, and fears. See his or her light, wholeness, and essential innocence. Open your heart . . . don't hold back.

~~~~~~

Even if you are not angry at your partner, it is most helpful and healing to do this exercise on a regular basis as an expression of your commitment to inner peace and to creating a loving relationship. Relating in this way always nurtures warmth, safety, and connectedness at the deepest level.

The most effective communication is a result of your willingness to remember this reality of your partner's greater Self. If you feel incomplete and have a need to communicate to resolve a particular issue, communicate from your Self to your partner's Self. Share the whole truth of your experience. Share your perceptions. Own them as your own. Share your feelings, *all the while keeping your heart open.* If you are frightened, then tell the compassionate Self of your partner that this is so. If you are frustrated, take responsibility for what you want, what you fear, what you need—and from yourSelf, share it with your partner. If you feel passionate about something, say so, but share this with his or her Self. Keep the lines of communication open.

FORGIVENESS AND INFIDELITY

Often one of the most disruptive and upsetting experiences that people encounter in a monogomous relationship is sexual infidelity. (Sexual infidelity as it is used here refers to sexual relationships outside the marriage that are kept secret and hidden from the partner.) This breach of trust destroys the intimacy within the couple because when there is dishonesty and secrecy, intimacy cannot exist. The discovery of the secrets and lies usually leaves a crisis in its wake, and many betrayed persons continue to feel resentful for a lifetime.

The fallout upon confronting the truth about what has occurred can send you opening the door to the divorce lawyers or opening the door with your mate to a more intimate and honest relationship than you had before. I strongly recommend getting the support of a couples' counselor to help you deal with the issues if you find yourself in such a situation. If you have a mutual commitment to restoring the relationship, it can be done—*and* it takes work.

Reestablishing a bond of trust calls for honesty. It takes looking honestly at the relationship, and at each person's feelings and truths. It calls for a willingness on the part of the person who has had the affair to admit responsibility for their behavior and to get clear about their commitment. And as Frank Pittman, M.D., author of *Private Lies: Infidelity and the Betrayal of Intimacy*, wrote, "The issue is not one of emotion, but one of choice—whether the commitment of marriage has or has not been abandoned." Reestablishing a bond of trust necessitates exploring one's motivations, and trying to understand them. The person who has had the affair needs to be willing to be present and hear the rage, anger, hurt, and fears of their partner if the relationship is to really heal.

In an article addressed to men about admitting and dealing with infidelity to their mate, Pittman writes, "She will need to express her anger and hurt. . . . Her anger is a necessary part of the repair process. Accept her anger. You earned it. Underneath that anger is great hurt, fear of losing you, fears of her own inadequacies, concerns about how she could have been so blind not to have known about the affair earlier. She's scared. . . . She's afraid to rely on you again. She's torn between wanting to be comforted by you and wanting to become her own separate person and never see you again. She needs to run through all these feelings, and it takes a while. Don't try to cut it short."

With honesty, genuine willingness to recommit to the relationship, and a willingness to work through the issues, the relationship can move over time to a stronger, more intimate relationship than ever before.

JOYCE'S STORY

For a while I had sensed something going on between my husband, Ted, and Ann, a woman he worked with. One evening Ann called our house saying she was going to take her life in some dramatic fashion. My initial response was that of trying to comfort Ted. I found myself saying, "Don't worry. It will be all right. Call her husband. This is his responsibility, his business."

I asked Ted if he was having an affair with Ann and he denied it. He said, "No, I am not involved with her." As he was denying his involvement, I had this click in my head and I remembered a story about my mother and father and my father's involvement with another woman and my mother comforting him through some crisis with the woman he was having the affair with. I thought to myself, "Wow, are you doing the same thing your mother did? How naive can you be?"

When I finally realized that Ted had been having an affair with Ann, I felt as though I was kicked in the stomach. I wanted to keel over and hold myself. I felt a sense of wonder. Not a sense of wonder in a positive sense, but rather, "My God, who is this man? I don't believe it. How could he? How could he be involved with that woman?"

My first thought after the initial wave of feelings was, "This has nothing to do with me." This seems demented. I had just

finished analysis and I felt loving and kind toward Ted. I felt
as though it was a new beginning. It was going to be our
twenty-fifth wedding anniversary. I was excited about life.
In a few minutes the joy was replaced with a feeling of profound betrayal.

He wouldn't talk about it at first. I became rageful. I remember sitting in my office feeling so stricken, thinking, how
can I work? What could I possibly bring to my work? I told
close friends of ours in the strictest of confidence and the
males' reactions were laughter. I'm sure it was nervous
laughter, but at the time it was humiliating. I felt injured,
tender, vulnerable. I felt devastated. Truly devastated.

My daughters didn't know what was going on and I
wanted to scream it from the housetops, from the roofs.

I asked myself, why am I staying? But I had this attitude
that you work things out. And I had made this enormous
investment for twenty-five years.

Ted ended his affair and on the surface things went along,
but the closeness wasn't the same. It took years to heal. I
carried anger for a long time, as much as seven years. Everything felt like a pretense when we were with other people.
I felt like I didn't care—which was a cover-up for a whole
lot of caring.

Two years after that incident with Ann I began seeing a
therapist. A year later Ted and I got into a couples' group
and into individual couples' therapy. I was rageful. Rage that
I had felt toward my father was added to my rage. I think I
was carrying fifteen or sixteen years of old feelings from my
parents' relationship. I began to see that there was much
more to this than appeared on the surface. That all kinds of
things had played into this. I had carried into this marriage
an idea of marriage that was based on what I had known,
what my parents' marriage was. I had deferred to Ted a lot.
I think I was afraid of my own power. Somehow a powerful
woman was aggressive and nonfeminine, and I feared that.
In subjugating, I realized I wasn't true to myself. There was
anger with myself for having lost myself and gone along in
this way. I hadn't made a lot of my needs known. I wasn't
me. I wasn't paying attention to me. I started to allow myself
to get in touch with what was important to me and become
my own person.

For years Ted just sat in therapy and didn't say much of anything. In the couples' group he just went through the motions. I would become angry and agitated because this was the same thing he did in life. I felt, "This is ridiculous. This marriage is empty." Finally I was ready to leave. Retrospectively, I think I had to be ready to leave. Rather than being held by one or the other, we both had to really want to stay in the relationship for anything to happen. Things began to really change at that point.

In therapy we did an opening-the-heart exercise facing each other looking into each other's eyes. We sat there looking at each other. I was opening my heart trying to feel what I really felt for this man. One of the things that kept coming up time and time again about Ted was that I always felt there was an essence to him. What I call an essence. There was something underneath that kept me there. I felt that if he could take the rind off, that essence was there. I realized that what had sent him underground was all these things that had been imposed on him in his growing up. All the don'ts. The joyless kind of family he came from. There was within him this tremendous capacity for life, for joy. He had a wonderful dry sense of humor. What had sent me underground was the need to be "a good girl." In this exercise something clicked. Something happened and things were different from then on. This sounds crazy, but it's true. I was able to feel love coming from my heart and something coming from him. The signals were coming through loud that this person really loved me. Maybe this was true before and I didn't feel it. Something healed and we were both more accessible to each other. Ted is still in therapy. For years he went to therapy to save the relationship. Now he goes for himself. We've shared an enormous amount of pain, but what we now share was worth working through the pain for.

The affair is a dead issue now. It's in the past. Yet even though it isn't alive in our relationship, how it all happened is almost like a mystery in some ways. But it's okay to leave it a mystery because there's been a maturing. There's a tendency for me to want to tie everything up neatly in a package now. I can live with the ends not woven neatly and still be able to open my heart.

·   ·   ·

In most relationships, an affair is not the problem but the manifested symbol of many problems that already exist within the relationship. For Ted and Joyce the discovery of the affair served to bring to the surface non–life-affirming patterns in themselves and in their relationship. As they were willing to have the courage and perseverance to face their own pain and the conspiracy of denial in their marriage, they learned to be true to themselves and to be there for one another. Now in their sixties, Joyce and Ted are great friends to one another. They have an alive, intimate, and loving relationship.

Unlike Joyce, you may never have the opportunity to work through your feelings in the context of your relationship. Even if your partner is physically present, perhaps she or he is not able to be there for you, hearing or witnessing that hurt and anger aroused by the infidelity. If your partner is unwilling to work through the issues that led up to the infidelity, this may feel like another abandonment—and perhaps one too many for you to stay in the relationship. The anger may be what you need at that point in time to give you the impetus to make changes. Honor your feelings. You have a right to feel the way you do. But as time passes, consider that without forgiveness you will always be bound to the relationship. Without forgiveness you will remain in pain and anger and feel your heart deadened to love. And it is only through forgiveness that you will reclaim your capacity for aliveness and love again.

IF THE MARRIAGE ENDS

Frequently when marriages fall apart, one partner loses faith in the other and in what he or she can become. It may seem easier not to forgive, to see the other as an idiot or wretch. It might then be easier to harden your heart, to distance yourself, and move on. There will be a broader range of experiences if you forgive. As you peel away the different layers of feelings, you will probably uncover love and the desire to be loved. In some relationships you may open yourself to forgiving after you have already decided to separate and go your own way. At these times it may feel particularly painful to open to the truth of this love. When your heart is open, you may feel more sadness, disappointment, or loss. And yet, if you keep your heart open through forgiveness, even in the face of painful circumstances like divorce, you will nurture your healing and experience a deepening peace, clarity, equanimity, and greater confidence in yourSelf and in your future.

Whether you choose to stay together or go your separate ways, healing yourself and the relationship through forgiveness is crucial to resolving your feelings and getting on with your life.

PATRICIA'S STORY

About seven years ago, my husband, Jeff, fell in love with another woman and moved out, leaving me with two young children. I was more frightened and angry than I had ever been in my entire life. For six months after his leaving, I was consumed by murderous feelings toward Jeff and his girl-friend, Karen. My whole life was about being a victim of divorce. Whenever Jeff came over to see the kids, as soon as I heard the doorbell ring, I'd be flooded with conflicting feelings. I hated him, yet I wanted him back.

Finally, in desperation, I decided to try using some lessons from *A Course in Miracles*, a book which teaches about forgiveness, to defuse my feelings. In particular, I was intrigued by a lesson which tells us to try to see people as if we've never seen them before—to greet all of the people we know with fresh eyes, leaving behind the baggage of the past.

I devised a plan. At night I would practice seeing Jeff in a new way in my imagination. The next day, when the doorbell rang, I would come down the stairs, look at the door, and say to myself, "I am determined to see things differently." Then I would open the door and try to be present in the moment. When he said "Hello," I would try to just say "Hello" rather than saying something nasty like, "How can you possibly say 'Hello' after what you've done to me?"

It took a long time, but it worked. I got to the point where I could actually see him as a new person. On the days when I could open the door and see him without remembering all of the bad things, I found myself actually feeling compassionate toward him. It seemed sad to me that he had to come to the front door and ring the doorbell in order to see his own kids. He didn't live with them. He didn't even have a key to the house. And, every time he wanted to see his kids, he had to face me, a person who would likely scream at him. This felt like an awful burden for him.

As I continued with the practice of forgiveness, I started to be able to see that he was simply a person going through life just like anyone else. His main goal in life was not to wreck me. It's just that he wasn't happy in his marriage, and he wanted to be with someone else. As I began to see this more clearly, I began to be able to see my own part in the breakdown of the marriage. Jeff would often say to me, "I always loved you, but you were never very interested in me." I had always vehemently denied that, but when I began to see him just as a person living his life, I was able to also see that I hadn't ever really been that much in love with him, and I didn't really think we were very well suited for each other. I even felt that way when we were first married, but I hadn't been willing to acknowledge it.

The thing that made letting go of anger and forgiving Jeff most difficult was having to accept what was happening in my life. I don't think some divorced couples ever do—so they stay in the same place as if everything just happened yesterday. Though it took me a long time, I feel liberated by being able to forgive.

FRIENDSHIP IN MARRIAGE

If a marriage is to really flourish, each person must have a desire to build a mutually supportive friendship. A friendship in its fullest expression is based on generosity: you are generous in your listening, generous with your affection, generous with all that you have and are. In a friendship, each person cares for the other's wants and needs as well as their own, celebrates each other's successes, and offers support and reassurance when things don't go so well.

- Are you willing to encourage your partner's growth even if it brings up some anxiety for you?
- Are you willing to make an effort to be patient and accept the differences between you?
- Are you willing to offer honest, nonjudgmental feedback?
- Are you willing to honor your partner's needs, even if they are different from your own needs?

Notice your responses with a gentle, nonjudging awareness.

If you sincerely work toward forgiveness, your ability to become a friend will grow, and friendship will become the reliable foundation of your relationship. There may be times in your marriage when you are willing to remain a friend to your partner even if you're not actively getting much response from them, because in your heart you are committed to them. *In order to nurture and sustain the peace that forgiving offers, ultimately you need to allow your effort and intent, rather than another's reaction to your effort, be your reward.*

Without forgiveness there is no friendship; and without friendship there is no real partnership. It's not until you step back and see yourself and your partner more compassionately that you will have the clarity and strength to act in ways that are ultimately most satisfying, honest and loving for both of you.

Even if you and your partner are extremely committed to forgiveness, anger is apt to arise from time to time. It is necessary and healthy for any relationship to have the room for anger to arise. Each person needs the freedom to express himself or herself without the threat of rejection or emotional abandonment. In a relationship that nurtures growth and mutual respect, neither person has to suppress and deny feelings in order to be loved and accepted. Each person needs the freedom to express upset and fear as well as joy. Our willingness to allow for another's fear without necessarily reacting with fear of our own, and our willingness to see and accept the whole truth of a situation without projection, is the peace that forgiveness offers. If a loved one is distressed, afraid, and hurting, there is concern and compassion. There is room for their pain and fear while knowing and affirming their strength as well.

The purpose of forgiveness in marriage isn't to necessarily encourage you to stay together. It is to help you discover the glory of your Self in a context where it might be easy to lose your Self in a disarray of judgments and conflict. It is to teach you the reality that giving and receiving are one. It is to allow you to experience the joy of friendship and the fulfillment of genuine relating. It is to give you peace, and having peace you are in a position to share it and teach your fellow traveler that peace is possible. It is to teach your partner, whether he or she knows it or not, that he or she is worth loving. It is to give you the means for living a life responsibly and fully.

Throughout your day consider:

I am determined to see things differently.

CHAPTER EIGHT

FORGIVING THE
CHILDREN

If you have never raised children or spent much time around them, it may seem unlikely that they would even require forgiving. One might look at young children and observe that so much of their behavior is purely innocent and uninhibited and, therefore, blameless.

If you are a parent, however, you know the emotional intensity and enormous challenges and frustrations inherent in raising a child. Young children are naturally self-centered; they are often messy, noisy, and demanding. They aren't likely to be concerned with your needs, nor should they be, yet your patience may wear thin, particularly when you're feeling tired, worn out, or distracted by other concerns.

Even if you are a very forgiving and conscientious parent, you will get angry at your child from time to time. This is especially true with children who are particularly dependent, clingy, and needy or independent and rebellious. Getting angry at your child can be useful at times; it serves to discharge your anxiety and can teach your child about the consequences of his or her behavior. If your six-year-old wanders to the other end of the beach after you've made an agreement and warned her to stay close-by, your anger may clearly and appropriately express the potential danger of disobeying rules. Getting angry in situations like this certainly isn't necessarily negative.

However, if you repeatedly get angry over minor issues or you find yourself constantly criticizing and yelling at your child, you need to reexamine the source of your feelings. Staying angry and blaming your child for your anger gives the child the message that not only is her behavior unacceptable but that she is a bad person. As Matthew McKay, Peter D. Rogers, and Judith McKay point out in their book *When Anger Hurts: Quieting the Storm Within*, "Children have only one motivation for behavior: to satisfy basic needs. Their primary goals are to be fed, to belong, to be safe, to be significant . . . blaming doesn't help children to behave more appropriately. It simply labels them as 'bad' for trying, as best they know how, to take care of themselves."

Clear boundaries and discipline are a necessary part of learning for children. Some external discipline is a prerequisite for internalized discipline. Setting clear, understandable boundaries for children can be done in loving, positive ways. The behavior of a parent not only sets the limits for the specific situation, but creates a role model for the child, who may observe that conflict and stress can be handled in an honest, fair, nonpunitive manner. On this level, forgiveness is the willingness to see a child's dissonant acting-out and/or withdrawal as an expression of fear, and thus a call for love and acknowledgment. The message is clear: it is not the child who is bad but the behavior that is unacceptable or inappropriate.

Forgiving reminds you to keep your heart open while setting limits and taking specific action. When forgiving, discipline is imparted by remembering and relating to the Self in the child and communicating with the part of it that is wise and that knows and understands that there are certain consequences for particular unsafe or inappropriate behavior (even though they may appear light-years from this level of awareness and understanding in that moment).

On the other side of anger is the experience of guilt. Even if you don't feel angry much, guilt often seems to come with the territory of parenting: "I should have been more patient," "I should have shared more quality time," "I could have done that differently. I feel guilty for . . ." The stresses of single parenting and of the household where both parents work frequently add to the ammunition for guilt and self-judgment. Be gentle with yourself. Remind yourself that if you have done things that you judge yourself for, you can choose differently the next time. Your willingness to be gentle and offer yourself forgiveness will absolutely help you to be more of the parent you want to be.

There may be many times when parenting feels joyful and effortless. Yet there may be times when the most loving behavior may feel very difficult, demanding tremendous clarity and inner strength. If you are experiencing fear and difficulty in certain aspects of parenting and feel that you could use some additional support, it may be very useful to seek counseling. Approaches like Parent Effectiveness Training (P.E.T.) can be very useful. Many communities have support groups for parents. Numerous books and workshops are available to help teach effective communication and to support healthy, loving relationships.

As our culture is becoming increasingly aware, more and more people who have had difficult childhoods are bringing a strong commitment to conscious parenting, and in the process participate in reparenting themselves. The process of forgiving your child simultaneously releases you from your guilt. As you see your child as guiltless, you heal the child within yourself.

As with other intimate relationships, unfinished business from your childhood is likely to arise in your relationship with your children. If you had a painful and difficult childhood—unless you have the conscious intent to be aware and loving in this role— you are inclined to carry on dynamics in the relationship with your children that you enacted with your parents when you were a child. Even if you are trying to be very conscious, you may find yourself repeating a behavior with your child that your parents inflicted on you. Be gentle with yourself and allow yourself to get support if you can't heal this pattern on your own.

Unfinished business from your adult relationships can also dramatically influence your ability to have a loving, open relationship with your child. You might need to forgive your child for looking like your ex-spouse or even for reminding you of yourself. Many parents get furious at their children for echoing back their very own words and behaviors.

FORGIVENESS AND SELF-ESTEEM: TEACHING OUR CHILDREN

Another level of forgiveness is expressed by the willingness to see and acknowledge the essential Self of the child even when circumstances are peaceful. Pablo Casals summed it up well:

When will they teach our children in school what they are? We should say to each of them: Do you know what you are? You are a marvel. You are unique. In all of the world there is no other child exactly like you. In the millions of years that have passed there has never been another child like you. And look at your body—What a wonder it is! your legs, your arms, your cunning fingers, the way you move! You may become a Shakespeare, a Michelangelo, a Beethoven. You have the capacity for anything. Yes, you are a marvel.

At home, at school, and in our culture at large, we need to teach our children who they are.

Everyone who affects and influences children—parents, daycare workers, teachers, coaches, administrators, doctors, nurses—must bring full awareness to this most imperative and far-reaching responsibility. We must question our perceptions and reeducate ourselves. The philosopher Tagore once said, "Each newborn child brings the message that God has not lost his trust in man." Yet by not teaching every child that he or she is a marvel, we betray this trust.

Forgiveness offers us the means for honoring this trust. It gives us the way to acknowledge the truth about the very nature of each and every child. Too often children have been thought of and treated as "inferior creatures" to be controlled. As a result, says Jungian analyst Marion Woodman, we have "a preconceived notion of what a child ought to be and try to force the child into that mold." This misperception instills in the child a deep-rooted sense of lack or inner deficiency. As a result our children are deprived of the essential relationship of respect and trust that is necessary for establishing positive self-regard and self-esteem.

I LOVE YOU WHEN . . .

Because the culture has been so ego-bound, external achievement has been sanctioned as the most significant factor in defining self-worth. As a result, when we experience emptiness, depression, or a spiritual void, we tend to look to outer circumstances for the cause and the solution. Many parents teach their children what they themselves believe to be true—that achievement in the world is the prerequisite and guarantee for success and happiness. Some have made it their responsibility and mission as parents to encourage external achievement as the highest priority for their children in child-rearing.

No one can deny that achievement can contribute to happiness. Academic, physical, and artistic achievement most certainly contribute to self-esteem and a fulfilling life. It's important for parents to encourage and inspire their children to achieve in these ways. But making a child's worth contingent upon external achievement has the opposite effect, inspiring feelings of inadequacy, fear, and guilt. When a relationship is based on control rather than respect, on judgment rather than love, on projection rather than honor, good intentions can become a great disservice to both the parent and the child—and the end result becomes a generation that is highly neurotic, addicted, unfulfilled, bewildered, and frightened.

Without unconditional love and respect, a child's sense of self-worth will always be fragile, no matter how outstanding his or her achievement. With such a shaky foundation, as an adult one may find oneself lost in self-doubt or caught in the frenzy of the illusory pursuit of perfection. In her book *The Drama of the Gifted Child*, Alice Miller clearly conveys how feeding the "performing self" of the child instead of the "essential self" tends to lead to depression or grandiosity as the child grows older. Every child needs to hear and feel "I love you no matter what."

The "I love you when . . ." message includes other conditions as well. They may be obvious or unspoken: I love you . . . when you behave the way I want you to . . . when you are quiet . . . when you perform . . . when you look the way I want you to look . . . as long as you don't question my authority . . . as long as you don't reveal family secrets to anyone . . . and countless variations on these themes.

Children who are not loved unconditionally may be labeled and seen through a filter of changeless judgment that he or she then internalizes. These labels may be communicated out of frustration, unwittingly, even in jest, but they significantly impact a child's sense of self-worth and identity. "Bobby or Suzy is . . . a brat . . . a pest . . . dumb . . . not too bright . . . unruly . . . a nuisance . . . obnoxious . . . perfect or 'such a good child' (in a way that doesn't allow for humanness) . . . a kid you can't expect much from." All these constitute a belief, a conclusion, a resignation and final judgment about the child's very nature, which the child is likely to take in as true. Even if these judgments aren't overtly expressed, they are communicated loudly and clearly.

P A U S E   A N D   R E F L E C T

Think of a child whom you are related to, or who you teach, coach, or care for in some way, etc. (If not current, think of someone from the past.) Identify any judgments you have about this child . . . Reflect on whether your judgment is held as a fixed fact about the child . . . Allow yourself to let go of your preconceptions and see and acknowledge the essential Self behind the child's transitory mood or personality trait(s).

Early in life, when the sense of self or ego is first being developed, the more judgments, the more conditional the love or the more controlling the relationship, the more guilty, ashamed, and disempowered the child (and later, the adult) becomes. The more unconditionally loving, respectful, accepting, and forgiving the significant adults are, the more self-trust, self-respect, spontaneity, self-expression—in short, *joie de vivre*—the child develops. By forgiving our children in this way, we give back to the generations to come the spiritual inheritance that has been too long denied.

Visualization: Forgiving a Child

I invite you now to participate in an inner journey of forgiving a child. As with previous visualizations, this may be most effective for you if read aloud by a friend or play back from a prerecorded audiocassette tape.

Make yourself comfortable and allow yourself to take some deep relaxing breaths. Feel all your muscles relaxing. Feel your entire body relax. Let any concerns slip away. Feel yourself becoming more relaxed and peaceful with each breath. . . .

Now bring a child to mind whom you would like to forgive. This can be a child you are angry with or a child you aren't angry with but with whom you wish to share and affirm even greater love. (Perhaps it is the child within you.) Allow yourself to see the light in this child. Imagine that she or he is very wise, radiant, and loving. Just reflect on the reality of this Self for a few moments . . .

Now imagine that you are actually with this child. You may be outdoors, or in a favorite indoor place. Imagine greeting this child with genuine warmth and caring. Imagine being delighted to see him or her. Allow yourself to experience the joy of forgiving this child in this new way.

Allow any fear, judgments, anger, or guilt from the past to slip away. See this child as a gift in your life. Imagine you were destined to meet for the purpose of sharing love . . . You understand now that through your realization of who she or he is, you can serve her or him, and in this understanding you are served as well. Seeing with inner vision, see the radiant light within the child. You see her or his sweetness and uniqueness. Imagine interacting grounded in this vision . . . You give and receive love. You let this child know how lovable, beautiful, and special she or he is.

Imagine putting into your heart a promise to remember this child (and every child) as a marvel, and as the light of the world . . . Imagine promising yourself to grow in inner peace so that you can experience peace more consistently and share it with this child and others . . . Now return once again to seeing the eternal light in this child. Bringing this vision with you, whenever you are ready open your eyes..

TEENAGE CHILDREN

Even if your children are older, it is never too late to offer them forgiveness. It may seem easier to forgive younger children, since their behavior is often due to developmental stages which change quickly. And after all, they *are* children. But when children grow into their teen and adult years, forgiveness may not be offered as charitably. Now you expect them to be more reasonable and mature.

Abby, the daughter of a neighbor, is now fourteen. She frequently defies both her parents. Although she is bright, she isn't doing well in school. She hangs around with kids who get into trouble. She is sexually active, and has come home from parties smelling of alcohol. Her parents have been absolutely clear with her about what constitutes acceptable and unacceptable behavior. They have grounded her on many occasions. They have used every way they know to get her to behave differently, and yet Abby persists in acting irresponsible and rebellious. Her parents often feel angry. They express their anger to Abby but also try to see beyond the current situation.

Abby's mother, who has attended workshops on forgiveness, says, "For me the idea of 'seeing the light instead of the lampshade' has been really helpful. I actually imagine Abby's body like a fog and I see a light within her. Sometimes I think of it as her soul. Her behavior isn't what I want it to be, but it isn't *her*. It helps me to separate her inherent goodness from her behavior. I have to keep remembering to do it, it doesn't just come automatically. And I have to keep doing it over and over and over, moment to

moment. I also have to keep forgiving myself for losing it sometimes, for being human, for not having been there in ways that in
hindsight I wish I had been. The willingness to forgive intervenes;
it stops the anger from escalating. Rather than the anger building
up into a mountain, it builds into a molehill."

Getting angry is natural from time to time and is never the issue
in and of itself unless it is abusive. Staying angry for long periods
of time and maintaining an undercurrent of hostility is an issue
because it will always generate greater problems. Chronic resentment fosters emotional distance that ultimately leaves both parent
and child feeling guilty and wrong. For the teenager, as with any
child, the resentment gets interpreted as "I'm not worth believing
in. I'm not lovable. I'm a bad person." "My parents don't care
about me."

Even though forgiving is the process of reawakening again and
again to the awareness of your child as lovable and good, it doesn't
preclude "tough love"—the difficult choices that one must sometimes make out of love for another. As a parent, this might mean
allowing your child to face the consequences of drug abuse or
drinking and driving, even if it means being arrested or being
expelled from school. It might mean being committed to taking
certain actions at home such as grounding your child, even though
you know this will be met with tremendous resistance. When a
child is acting in ways that are clearly self-destructive and seriously
disruptive, it is never forgiving to ignore what is going on. Forgiveness is never to be misunderstood as a mask for avoidance,
neglect, indulgence, or passive parenting.

In addition to setting firm guidelines, Abby's parents also in-
sisted on individual counseling for Abby and family counseling as
well. Family counseling can be extremely useful in helping to
unravel the real issues that are at the root of disruptive or inappropriate behavior. In many situations parents may be unknow-
ingly contributing to their child's problems. If parents are
overcontrolling, or provide little or no structure, or are themselves
experiencing a lot of hostility or tension, a child's behavior may
reflect these imbalances. Exploring the underlying issues can lead

to significant change. Family counseling can also reinforce the sense of "we're in this together" instead of placing all the blame on the child.

ADULT CHILDREN

Each stage of growing up has its own set of potential challenges. As children become adults, new issues may emerge.

Dan was raised in a strict Catholic household. He was sent to parochial schools and graduated from a Catholic college. His father worked hard and sacrificed to pay for his education, giving Dan the chance to "get ahead" that he never had. After graduating with a degree in political science and prelaw, Dan decided to become an artist. He took small jobs that allowed him to get by financially so that he could dedicate his time to sculpting. His father felt hurt, angry, and disappointed. He couldn't understand why Dan would "throw away" his education.

"Dropping out" of the mainstream, marrying into a different religion, marrying the "wrong" person, being gay, making a particular career decision, and moving away are all common causes of a parent's chronic resentment concerning his or her adult child. The reasons for such resentments are endless, but the underlying issue often boils down to the frustrations of the parents whose expectations are not being met. Convictions run deep as to what is right and wrong. When parents have fixed and inflexible judgments about the "right" lifestyle for his or her child, anger and resentment inevitably occur when their child wanders from the approved path. Parents who insist on the career path or mate for their child are often projecting their own fears and unlived ambitions. When parents reject their adult child's choices, the message is, "Trust me, not yourself. I know best." Your adult child may sometimes make choices that seem clearly wrong or unnecessarily difficult. As a parent, it may be quite painful to watch your child stumble and fall; it may be even harder to allow your child to "hit bottom" and let them resurface on their own when they are ready. But although you may know better, you can never truly predict the lessons they need in order to learn their unique life's lessons and to mature.

This does not mean that you should hide your feelings or observations, or hesitate to state a strong and impassioned case for what you feel would be best. But after sharing your perceptions and expressing your feelings, often the most loving and respectful choice is to let go. When your child is troubled or chooses a different path, you may need to acknowledge the anger, guilt, grief, and loss you feel before forgiving is possible. But allowing adult children to make their own decisions and "mistakes" can eventually inspire the kind of mutual love and respect that leads to a fulfilling adult relationship.

THE DISABLED CHILD

Every parent wants children who are healthy and well adjusted. Yet children who are physically disabled, learning disabled, emotionally handicapped, or chronically ill sometimes fail to meet the hopes and expectations of their parents. Instead of the anticipated joys of parenting, there may be displeasure, sadness, anger, disappointment, and pain.

Families and marriages often disintegrate under the enormous emotional, financial, and practical pressures of raising a handicapped child. Most parents faced with these challenges have felt angry at times—angry at God, their spouse, themselves, and perhaps even angry at the child. Feeling angry at the child may be embarrassing and hard to admit. Or, the anger may feel like a more tolerable or acceptable emotion than feelings of anguish, hopelessness, helplessness, sadness, and grief that may be within.

Author Hugh Prather and his wife, Gayle, ran support groups for parents whose children had died. They noticed that parents who held tightly to their anger (toward God, doctors, the system, etc.) could not grieve, and thus could not begin to heal. Their anger walled off their grief. Separate from their grief, their suffering was kept perpetually alive.

If social-service agencies, schools, and medical care are not responsive to your child's needs, getting angry can express your frustration and may even result in better and quicker attention. Many social movements, such as Mothers Against Drunk Driving, have been prompted by a parent's angry reaction to unjust or uncaring attitudes or policies. Turning anger into constructive action is healthy, but it is important to be aware that you transform the anger so you are free to move on with life.

Anger can also serve as a cover for guilt—guilt that you are somehow responsible for your child's condition, guilt that you could have done something differently, guilt that you could be doing more right now. Like all guilt, if it goes unexamined it can undermine your relationship with yourself and others, and your efforts to care for your child now. Compassion and self-forgiveness is crucial in helping you free yourself of the burden of guilt. If this is an issue for you, you may find Chapter Nine, "Self-Forgiveness: A Great Birth," particularly useful.

Forgiving your child requires that you remember and relate to that part of your child that is healthy. It doesn't mean denying the reality of his impairment, or the impact it has had on you and your family. But forgiving allows you to see and affirm a part of the child that may not always (or ever) be obvious. If you only see your child in terms of his illness and disability, you rob yourself and your child of joining in moments of joy and pleasure. You are more likely to identify yourself only as caretaker and become preoccupied with guilt, anger, pity, and pain.

IN THE CLASSROOM

Children, our most precious resource, are in their early developmental stages put in the trust of teachers and the educational system. Society has not, however, wholly prepared teachers for this vitally important role.

A child's self-esteem and self-concept is shaped in response to his repeated social contacts and experiences with other people. Because of the amount of time a child spends in school, and a teacher's authority, teachers become a major factor in the development of the child's self-esteem and self-concept. Despite this most significant fact, the design of nearly all educational systems has lent itself to particular blindness when it comes to responsibly influencing this aspect of a child's growth and development.

This fact isn't intended to point blame at the teaching profession. Rather it is to point to the potential and responsibility of all educators. It is to say that educators, in order to move toward their potential and fulfill their responsibility, must open to and choose new perceptions of themselves, their role, and the children they teach. Forgiveness again offers the means for doing this.

The function of the teacher or educator is to educate in the fullest sense of the word—"to lead out, to bring forth—to get from the inside to the outside." Yet, the primary concern in teaching has been to instruct (put in) rather than to facilitate education (lead out). From within come creativity, imagination, intuition, intelligence, the capacity to love and care, a natural curiosity, and great potential for achievement. Contrary to popular belief, these qualities are universal, not merely confined to the exceptional or privileged few.

Forgiveness offers a way for a teacher to relate to a student's essential Self, not to just the performing or conforming self. Forgiveness releases the teacher from comparisons and former judgments so that she or he can nurture self-esteem through unconditional positive regard. In this atmosphere the child can feel relaxed and safe; then there is room for the creative instinct to flourish, for optimal learning to occur, and for self-esteem to be nurtured. Learning and retaining information becomes easier. Students are more likely to seek new challenges, take intellectual risks, and express themselves creatively.

Of course, being skilled, knowing the subject matter and the most effective ways of teaching it, and maintaining appropriate order are an essential part of the whole; but without an atmosphere of faith in the student's potential and positive regard for who each child is now, the teaching and learning process become devitalized. Creativity is stifled, thwarting the connection to one's spirit and to the source of self-expression, happiness, and confidence.

Teachers have a vitally important role in each child's life. Every student needs unconditional love and respect. By recognizing and intentionally relating to the lovable, creative, smart, and sensitive Self in each student, teachers will, in a most fundamental way, nurture their student's intelligence, nurture them as whole people, and bring new vitality and enjoyment into the work and art of educating.

PYGMALION IN THE CLASSROOM

In 1968, Robert Rosenthal of Harvard University and Lenore Jacobson of the San Francisco public schools published the book and classic study entitled *Pygmalion in the Classroom*. In it they explored the hypothesis that one person's expectation for another's behavior often serves as a self-fulfilling prophecy. Such a hypothesis has been researched in many areas of the social sciences for years. Studies were conducted with animals, as well as with human subjects. In these studies the animals performed poorly or in a superior way commensurate with whether the experimenters believed their subjects were or were not genetically endowed. In reality there were no genetic differences between the animals that had been pointed out to be smart or dull. Rosenthal and Jacobson noted, "If animal subjects believed to be brighter by their trainers actually became brighter because of their trainer's beliefs, then it might also be true that school children believed by their teachers to be brighter would become brighter because of their teacher's beliefs."

A study was designed to test this hypothesis at the Oak School, a public elementary school in San Francisco. Children were randomly selected and identified as students who would show dramatic intellectual growth in the academic year ahead. The predictions were allegedly made on the basis of scores of tests of academic potential. Actually, these "potential spurters" had no more ability, according to the real achievement-test scores, than their classmates. The belief or expectation of the teachers that these students were brighter became a self-fulfilling prophecy. The belief by the teachers that these children were brighter got communicated, and the children responded to this belief and faith in their ability.

Perhaps what was most significant in this study was that the children who had been expected to bloom intellectually were rated as more intellectually curious, happier, and in less need of social approval. Similar replications of this study all showed significant effects of teacher expectations. Teachers who expected children to excel were likely to be friendlier, less critical, more accepting, and warmer toward them. Dramatic changes in the students' performance were influenced not by changes in teaching methods, but by teachers' perceptions alone.

Unfortunately, most teachers aren't held accountable for their attitudes toward their students. The value placed on subject matter almost always supersedes the value placed on communicating positive regard and faith in the child's potential. Too often the teacher's tasks are limited to the curriculum and maintaining control. Disregarding the vital task of enhancing self-esteem is a serious oversight, particularly because many individual and social problems, including academic failure, chronic anxiety, loneliness, and drug abuse, are rooted in poor self-esteem.

An antidrug campaign that is based on "Just say no" may have its usefulness, but it is ultimately a naive approach. People "say yes" to drugs (and to other addictions) not because they necessarily want to or are making a fully conscious choice. People say yes because, at some level, they hurt inside, feel badly about who they are, and are drawn to numb the pain. Actively nurturing self-esteem, from the first day of school on, is the most important preventive measure against drugs that can be taken in today's educational system.

Self-esteem is the most relevant determining factor of success in any endeavor in life. The greater an individual's self-esteem, the more likely they are to be at peace with themselves and others. The more likely they are to treat themselves and others with respect and kindness. The more they will live with love rather than fear.

In a speech given by Luis Alberto Machado, former cabinet-level Minister for the Development of Intelligence of Venezuela, he said, "Everything that we teach in the classroom has to have the goal of the happiness of human beings. Intelligence is an instrument in the service of love."

In the process of forgiving the student, self-esteem of both the student and the teacher is enhanced. Meaning and value are infused into the teaching process. A vital part of the teacher is resuscitated. The teacher's Self and the student's Self meet. The student feels acknowledged and important. A trusting relationship is created. Belief in his or her beauty and potential is communicated. Disciplinary action, when necessary, can be carried out with clarity and wisdom. Education is humanized and classrooms become accepting and loving environments where children are eager to come and participate.

Fifteen years ago, I was the director and head teacher of a school for children excluded from the Boston public schools because of truancy and severe behavioral problems. About ten years after leaving that job I had the following dream:

I was going to take a leave from my work as a stress-management consultant and workshop facilitator to once again become the teacher and director of a small school. There was going to be one other teacher. We were both extremely excited about the year of teaching before us. We scheduled the day so that every morning we would arrive at school with enough time to do any preparation that was needed, plus an hour to relax, meditate, and visualize together. In this visualization our intention was to reflect on the incredible light and limitless potential of each child. We would see how totally lovable and beautiful each and every child was. We would see ourselves welcoming the children with joy and bringing this awareness throughout the day. Although we would be intentional about creating engaging and valuable learning experiences in terms of lessons and projects, our first and foremost goal was to bring the spirit of love and forgiveness to each student and every interaction. The following visualization on forgiving your students is based on this dream. A particularly good time to do this is shortly before your class begins.

Visualization: Forgiving Your Students

Allow yourself to take some deep, relaxing breaths. Imagine breathing in a soothing, peaceful energy. Allow yourself to release tension as you breathe out. Allow any fears to slip away. Breathe in and feel the wholeness within your own being. Feel a peacefulness within and feel it radiating out, filling you and surrounding you with a peaceful radiance. Thank yourself for taking this time for you.

Now seeing with inner vision, imagine a student toward whom you feel some displeasure . . . Affirm to yourself, "I am willing and determined to see (their name) newly". . . Allow yourself to let go of judgments and limiting perceptions about this student . . . Acknowledge his or her essential Self. See this student's light and limitless potential . . . Imagine being very caring, loving, and accepting . . . See all their "negative" behavior as a request for help and a call for acknowledgment and love . . . Imagine seeing this child as creative, intellectually bright, and considerate (even if they have been blocked from this expression in the past) . . . See yourself really enjoying the opportunity of making a positive difference in their life . . . Inwardly acknowledge how important forgiveness is in this relationship for both of you. See yourself practicing forgiveness with this child as you go through your day.

Repeat this visualization or any aspect of it with each one of your students.

· · ·

Creating a context of warmth, acceptance, and respect for each child by the intentional practice of forgiveness is by far the most important responsibility each teacher has—even if the student is not causing any particular difficulty. There may be those students who elicit anger, irritation, and judgment over and over again. Remember that forgiveness isn't a one-time event. It is a process that involves repeatedly exercising our power to choose and our gift of vision.

WE ARE ALL TEACHERS

We are all teachers much of the time. When we interact with others, some interactions may be neutral, yet in most interactions we are teaching fear or teaching love. Becoming aware of what we are teaching gives us the opportunity to choose once again. It gives us the opportunity to teach only love.

ANNA'S STORY

Anna, a nurse in a psychosomatic unit of a major urban children's hospital, attended a few forgiveness presentations. She immediately resonated with the power of this way of seeing and relating to people and circumstances. She actively chose to practice forgiveness with the children that were assigned to her care. After experiencing the enormous power of forgiveness first-hand, she began to teach the concepts and practice of forgiveness to other staff members as well.

After participating in a forgiveness visualization, I had the dramatic realization that each time I identified someone in my clinical work with whom I was having great difficulties, or toward whom I had very tense, angry, or fearful feelings, I paid an exorbitant price if I chose not to forgive. I sacrificed a great deal by clinging to anger and resentment. Over time, I became irritable, judgmental, and less focused in my work. I was less open and honest, less centered and empathetic, and more rigid. At first I felt uneasy and anxious, then bitter and miserable. Only through forgiveness could I travel full circle to regain what I had lost. I needed to forgive.

Gary, a nine-year-old boy on the unit, was incredibly impulsive, destructive, and aggressive. Initially, in order to understand his outbursts and develop empathy for him, I tried to view his behavior as either an expression of love or an expression of fear. Even though intellectually I was trying to think this way, I still held intense anger toward him. At work, I found myself avoiding him, and he sensed my physical and emotional distance. So I expressed my thoughts and feelings to him within the forgiveness visualization. In the visualization, I was furious with him. I was disturbed and indignant that he was hurting other people, destroying his belongings and those of others. After I vented my hostility in the imagery, it was my turn to listen to him. He told me all about his fear. He said his behavior was the only means he knew at that moment to express the panic, mistrust, and terror he felt toward other people and toward himself. He said,

"I fear abandonment.

"I fear I'll be taken from my mother and put in a residential school.

"I fear kids hate me.

"I fear I'll never have a friend.

"I fear staff just hate me.

"I fear no one can keep me safe.

"I fear no one wants to take care of me for the rest of my life.

"I fear I'm stupid and dumb.

"I fear people think I'm crazy. I've heard them say I am.

"I fear no one wants to know how bad I hurt.

"And if they do want to know, I fear they won't be able to handle how bad I hurt . . ."

He spoke volumes about his fear. Immediately, a striking discovery was before me. As I developed compassion for him, I could go on to forgive him. My tolerance and understanding of him and his suffering aided me in being truly and completely present with him through his most demanding and tumultuous times.

Concurrently, another striking discovery unfolded. I appreciated how I was sitting with my own anxieties longer. A parallel process was in motion. As I sat with my own discomfort, I cultivated compassion for myself. The longer I could endure my own feelings, the longer I could simultaneously acknowledge Gary's pain and embrace him rather than become immobilized by anger's powerful grip.

Each time I forgive someone in my clinical setting—a child, a parent, a peer—a door opens. Behind this door stands another person, usually outside the clinical arena, a person who has had a deeper, more profound, and oftentimes painful and intense impact on my life.

As soon as I recognize this person, as soon as I face them, confront them, listen to them, and finally forgive them in the imagery, only then can I begin to peel away the crankiness, the judgments, the impatience, the projections, the tensions, the bitterness, the anger, the fear, and come straight to my heart. Now I expose my misunderstandings, my hurt, my unmet needs, my misery, and my sadness. I need to shed tears and forgive myself. As soon as I forgive anyone in the present, or from the past, I can live and labor more peacefully and more compassionately. I can be more hopeful and remain connected.

A CURRICULUM FOR SELF-KNOWLEDGE, RESPECT, AND LOVE

In addition to forgiving children in a more consistent and heartfelt way, it seems increasingly apparent that we have come to a critical time in civilization when we need to take on the task of explicitly teaching children about emotional awareness.

Offering a new curriculum of emotional awareness, part of which would be exploring the principles of forgiveness, would naturally nurture self-discovery, self-awareness, and self-esteem. Teaching about emotional awareness and forgiveness in explicit, forthright ways would give children the means to be aware of the richness and value that is always within them. It would help them to understand, and empower them to deal with fear, anger, rejection, and loss. It would teach them about listening, cooperation, respect, and caring.

As children become more aware of who they truly are, the innate wisdom of their hearts will instinctively play a greater role in guiding them in their actions and in their relationship with themselves, others, and the planet.

Every heart has a profound intelligence, and only when we learn to pay attention, listen, and recognize this intelligence can we be happy, experience satisfaction, and develop our mental intellect to its highest potential. Rather than being an end in itself, our mind can be a means to truly serve us and lead us to being happy, caring, productive citizens. Just think of how many "brilliant" academicians, doctors, lawyers, or writers you know (or know of) who are miserable and deeply dissatisfied with life. As

Robert Ornstein and Paul Erlich state in their book *New World, New Mind*, "We need to be 'literate' in entirely new disciplines, such as the structure of thought, rather than just learning more about the sequences of English monarchs." It is time to teach emotional-literacy skills. Facts, of course, are necessary, but as a culture we need to be responsible that our children don't learn them in a spiritual desert with quietly despairing souls that are starving for something more nourishing and meaningful.

We owe children a curriculum that teaches them that they are terrific people, that they all have unique and important gifts to give, that they are always worth respecting, loving, and caring—and that all the other children in their class, school, community, and the world are worthy of that same respect, love, and care, too.

FORGIVING YOURSELF

III

CHAPTER NINE

SELF-FORGIVENESS:
A GREAT BIRTH

Forgiving yourself is probably the greatest challenge that you will ever meet. It is, in essence, the process of learning to love and accept yourself *no matter what*. In Chapter Six, *love* was defined as no more or no less than the simple, honest, and natural expression of our own wholeness, our full self-acceptance. *It is the state of being that arises from our willingness to accept, without judgment, all of who we are, our seeming shortcomings as well as our innate glory.* Love and self-forgiveness are essentially the same thing.

There is often great resistance to self-forgiveness, for like any significant change, it is a death. It is dying to the habit of keeping ourselves small and unworthy, dying to shame, guilt, and self-criticism: "I'm ashamed of myself for having gained all that weight." "I'll always feel guilty for not saying good-bye." "I'll stop feeling guilty if things turn out okay." "I'll forgive myself when she forgives me." How many times has your willingness to love and accept yourself been contingent on circumstances being other than the way they are? What self-criticism would you have to let go of in order to forgive yourself?

The purpose of self-forgiveness is to shine light on the illusions, fears, and self-judgments that have held us captive in the role as our own jailer. It is to discover the option of retiring from this merciless job so that we can nurture the whole truth of who and what we are.

Self-forgiveness is a great birth. It is inherent in those moments when the compassion, love, and glory of the greater Self is born within our direct experience and known beyond old definitions.

LEVELS OF SELF-FORGIVENESS

There are many levels of self-forgiveness: existential, cultural, ethical, historical, physical, and spiritual.

EXISTENTIAL SELF-FORGIVENESS

On an existential level, forgiving yourself requires you to (re)examine beliefs about the nature of your very being. Did you grow up believing that being good was contrary to your true nature, and something you had to work at? Were you taught, according to Christian tradition, that we are born into the world as sinners, heirs to original sin, guilty until our efforts at repentance have redeemed us? Guilty until proven innocent.

For some, the concept of original sin is taken for granted, but consider that rather than an original sin, there may have been an original blessing. As theologian Matthew Fox points out in his book *Original Blessing*, the concept of "original sin" goes back to St. Augustine, about A.D. 354. "Nineteen billion years before there was any sin on earth, there was blessing." According to Fox, spiritual teachings throughout the ages point to the idea that "the sin behind all sin is dualism. Separation. Subject/object relationships." "Take any sin," he writes, "war, burglary, rape. Every such action is treating another as an object outside oneself . . . This is behind all sin." This separation from our Self results in a separation from our creative intelligence and our loving will.

If we are separate from our Self, habitually lost in fear, the instinctive survival mechanism will be to project this separation outward, trying to manipulate circumstances in an attempt to feel secure, in control, and powerful. The more active the search to find these states outside ourself, the more powerless, separate, and guilty we feel.

"According to a Jain maxim," writes Fox, "he who conquers this sin [this separation from Self] conquers all others." If we are not separate from the Self, we experience the blessing that life is, and the fundamental innocence and holiness that is our very nature—regardless of what we have done in the past.

PERSONAL-CULTURAL SELF-FORGIVENESS

On a personal-cultural level, one experiences guilt in accordance with prevailing values, beliefs, and norms. They may vary according to your environment, gender, class, race, religious training, family, and ethnic background. If you are Catholic, you may feel guilty for choosing divorce, even though at the time you know it is the most loving and honest choice. If you were raised in a country where starvation was common, or you were frequently reminded that "children are starving," you may feel guilty for not always eating all the food on your plate. If you were raised with a Puritan work ethic, you may be unable to relax and enjoy leisure time. If you were taught that sex is merely functional, you may feel guilty about experiencing great sensory pleasure while making love. For survivors of the Holocaust, there may be a chronic, underlying sense of guilt for having survived.

Many poor people often go through life feeling guilty for their poverty, thinking, "There must be something wrong with me for being poor." Many wealthy people also suffer from class guilt, feeling guilty and uncomfortable for having more than others.

You may feel guilty because "you haven't made it yet." Here social standards foster the belief that you should be achieving more and doing better. No matter how much you succeed, it doesn't feel like enough. "I should have written a book by now." "I should be the vice president of the company by now." "I should be earning $100,000." "I should be married with two children by now." Self-forgiveness extricates you from buying into arbitrary cultural standards that diminish the validity of your unique life.

All these "levels" have, so to speak, porous boundaries that merge into one another.

PERSONAL-HISTORICAL SELF-FORGIVENESS

The personal-historical level of forgiveness is probably the most difficult. It is simultaneously the most subtle and the grossest, the most concealed, while the most obvious. Forgiveness at this level requires that you examine beliefs about yourself that were established long ago, and that today undermine your experience of, and belief in, your fundamental lovableness, innocence, goodness, intelligence, respectability, and worthiness. Self-forgiveness at this historical level has its roots in childhood and has to do with healing unhealthy guilt and shame.

PERSONAL-ETHICAL SELF-FORGIVENESS

On a personal-ethical level, you may need to forgive yourself for having done something that you feel is wrong, such as cheating, lying, or stealing; something that your conscience or deeper knowing tells you lacks honesty and integrity.

FEELING GUILTY

Guilt can be very healthy. If you shirked responsibility for something that negatively affected others, guilt can be a valuable signal to wake up and pay attention. It is healthy if it is used as an opportunity to recover your power and responsibility to act with integrity. Healthy guilt posts boundaries indicating that our behaviors and motivations are appropriate or inappropriate, caring or insensitive, have integrity or lack integrity. According to personality theorist Erik Erickson, healthy guilt is developed at around three years old. Healthy guilt guides our conscience. When there is no internalized moral code, when healthy guilt and shame are undeveloped and totally repressed, this state is identified as sociopathy or psychopathy.

When you feel healthy guilt but this guilt is indulged—if months or years later you are steeped in guilt for choices you made long ago—this very same guilt becomes unhealthy. This is when the ego, in the form of the self-critic, acts like a robber who steals the present, has you tied to the past, and frightened about the future. There is still the judgment that you are wrong or bad visited upon yourself by yourself, again and again. It is the sure death of self-esteem. If you are dominated by guilt, it is impossible to feel compassion for yourself, even though gentleness and compassion always lie dormant within. It is by forgiving yourself that they are awakened and the bullying grip of the ego is released. It is by forgiving yourself that you come to accept your mistakes as fearful reactions and confused attempts to get the power or love you felt you lacked.

If we don't participate in the process of forgiving ourselves, and we stay indentured to these internal warlords, the guilt will play itself out in some way. An insidious aspect of unhealthy guilt is that rather than spurring us on to heal and change in a positive way, it can create a vicious cycle. The "guilty" self unconsciously demands punishment for what was done, and then doles out the sentence in the form of unhappiness, depression, a chronic sense of unworthiness, or even physical and mental illness. For instance, convicts who have not been rehabilitated—and self-forgiveness is a critical aspect of rehabilitation—will often commit another crime shortly after being released. This is a way of unconsciously punishing themselves for the profound guilt they still feel.

In addition to turning inward, guilt can also be projected outward as chronic anger and resentment toward others. The chronic projection of guilt paints a static view of the world as a hostile and unfair place. As theologian Paul Tillich so eloquently stated, "In metaphorical language I would like to say to those who feel deeply their hostility toward life: Life accepts you; life loves you as a separated part of itself; life wants to reunite you with itself, even when it seems to destroy you."

As with forgiving others, self-forgiveness doesn't imply condoning behavior that was lacking in integrity and hurtful to yourself or others. It also doesn't imply that you won't feel remorse for the past. In fact, feeling deep remorse for pain that you have inflicted is part of the healing process. Feelings of remorse may stay with you for a lifetime when you think of a certain person or incident. Yet if you are to move on, this remorse can't remain a predominant emotional force. If it predominates your life long after the incident that precipitated the remorse is over, you must find a way to help it float free in a sea of mercy and compassion.

GEORGE'S STORY

George has been a prisoner in a medium-security prison for the past thirteen years.

> I am a person who committed a crime against another person. I don't have bitter or angry feelings about being locked up for what I did, because I know I was guilty, and I deserve punishment. I not only felt guilt, but I felt remorse, shame, and embarrassment for hurting another person. I became aware that my behavior had affected a lot of other people, not just the victim, but that person's family and friends as well as my own family and friends, not to mention my own life. For the first time in my life, I felt suicidal. I felt that I didn't deserve to live. I was a nothing. I didn't even have the courage to commit suicide, so I had to struggle with my feelings of self-worth. At the time, I considered it courage, but now I realize that suicide would have been a coward's way out of having to deal with feelings.
>
> I tried working hard to take care of the people who loved me. This gave me a feeling of value and self-respect. It was a starting point for rebuilding my low self-esteem. During this time, I was involved with various forms of psychotherapy. In my therapy, I dealt with my relationships and my feelings. I sifted through every aspect of my life. I did this over and over again to try to find the answers that would help the feeling of unsettledness inside.
>
> A person I had met through a business transaction while incarcerated started to visit me on a regular basis. This turned into a friendship that I cherish to this day. A few years later, I was out on a visit with my friend. We were discussing and sharing thoughts and feelings when suddenly my friend said to me, "You've done so much and have made so many changes in your life. You're a good person, and you are my friend, so I need to say this to you: 'Forgive yourself.' " My friend repeated it again to make sure I heard what she had said.

Hearing those words was truly the beginning of my life. It was the beginning of a kind of change I never believed possible. As I write this, tears of happiness and love flow from my eyes in gratitude for two words no one had ever said to me before. "Forgive yourself." These were the two words I needed to hear and feel and put into practice in my life along with all the other therapeutic work to feel settled inside.

THE WHOLE TRUTH

As with forgiving others, true self-forgiveness requires complete honesty with oneself. Just as we can repress anger and seem to have forgiven someone when we really haven't, we can also deny our guilt, deceiving ourself into believing that all is well. Denial keeps parts of ourself in the dark, and in order to fully heal and experience the peace and liberation that self-forgiveness offers, each darkened corner of our psyche must have the light of truth and compassion shone upon it.

Acknowledging the entire truth of our experience takes courage. It is the courage to accept the fear, humiliation, shame, sadness, self-disdain, self-hatred, and the actions, inner thoughts, and feelings that a part of us would rather repress and avoid. If, in the process of allowing the entire truth of your actions, feelings, and thoughts to come to the light of awareness, the belittling ego is given a chance to dominate center-stage, it is apt to hinder this process. You may be left feeling pained, scared, and humiliated. The ego can act like a presiding inner judge who sees you as bad, stupid, or guilty before you have even stated your case. If, however, the Self is allowed to take its right place on center-stage, the truth of your fundamental innocence will be the verdict. Your past actions, feelings, self-judgments, terrors, and fears will be met with compassion, and you will learn and grow from these experiences while feeling the strength and inspiration you need in order to keep the process of self-forgiveness and self-healing on sure footing. It is the nonjudging acceptance of your inner thoughts and feelings that will lead the way to self-knowledge and self-love.

~~~~~~

P A U S E   A N D   R E F L E C T

Recall a situation when you felt guilty. Reflect for a few minutes on what motivated your behavior. What did you (or can you presently) learn about yourself from that experience? With this new awareness, how might you behave differently if you encounter a similar situation in the future?

~~~~~~

Self-forgiveness is the process of (1) acknowledging the truth, (2) taking responsibility for what you have done, (3) learning from the experience by acknowledging the deeper feelings that motivated the behaviors and thoughts for which you now feel guilty and hold yourself in judgment, (4) opening your heart to yourself and compassionately listening to the fears and calls for help and acknowledgment that are within, (5) healing emotional wounds by heeding these calls in healthy, loving, and responsible ways, and (6) aligning with your Self and affirming your fundamental innocence. You may be guilty of a particular behavior, yet your essential Self is always guiltless and lovable.

Remind yourself again and again of the golden rule of forgiveness: *Be gentle with yourself.* Even if for the first thousand times you remind yourself to be gentle with yourself it feels like mere empty words, make this choice again and again. Trust that its meaning will take root and know that its fruit will be splendid.

PAUL'S LETTER
Paul was incarcerated for sexually molesting his daughter. He wrote this letter to his ex-wife after a great deal of self-reflection, aided by individual and group-therapy sessions he had been attending in the prison. It is a poignant example of how forgiveness is not just a superficial process of saying, "Ya, I did such and such, now I'll forgive myself." True self-forgiveness requires a depth of honest looking that not everyone is ready or willing to do—and that not everyone has the needed safety and guidance to do.

Dear Mary,
    The letter you are about to read is my personal history. I

have mixed feelings about letting you into my deep dark past. I value you highly—your opinion, your friendship and love. I am so afraid! I feel so ashamed of my own past and so vulnerable but I know that if I am to help you understand why I acted the way I did I *must* tell you.

As you know, my family was not deprived—not of material things. Sure I had plenty of clothes and toys, but I was deprived of one major aspect of life . . . love. Mary, you have seen how my folks are. They don't express love. They try to buy it. Well, they have been like this as long as I've known them.

I have a few memories of growing up and most of them cause nothing but pain. My earliest memories are of being tied to a tree in the backyard while mom cleaned the house. The house *had* to be clean—it was more important than I was. When I was 7 or 8 dad was chasing me and I crawled under his truck. I cut the shit out of my back, I was bleeding like a stuck pig. I went running to mom who was hanging laundry, and she said to me, "Don't come crying to me." She had absolutely no sympathy.

I remember another time, thinking she would forgive me for swearing so I told her I had swore and I was sorry. She dropped my pants right there and gave me a good beating. The thing that made it so hard was that I was outside with some of the kids from the neighborhood when I told her. She beat me in front of them. I was the joke of the neighborhood for months.

Then I was about 8 or 9, like most kids I was playing with matches. Me and David got caught lighting matches. David's mom yelled at him. Mine turned on the electric stove and kept my fingertips on the coils until my fingers *smoked*. I hated David for getting off so easy.

Then there are the memories of not going to school because I had been beaten and was all swollen. One time, the Sunday after Thanksgiving, mom and dad went up to see nana and grampa. I was babysitting. When they came home the phone rang. The operator said that someone at this number was making obscene phone calls. My dad asked us if we had done it and for some reason I laughed. That's all it took. I can remember me trying to run. He caught me by the hair and literally threw me *over* the dining room table. Needless to say I was out of school a couple of days. To this day I don't know if one of the kids had been making those phone calls.

The whole time I was in school the only time I was out sick was once for the mumps the other times were for *stankings* as they used to call them.

The only thing I can remember about living at home was pain. When I was about 9 this guy who lived a few houses away started to make friends with me. He was in high school. He would have me sexually perform for him. He molested me, but I didn't think of it as bad because he gave me attention, which I thought was love.

Mare, now comes the hardest part yet. When I was young about 11 my cousin who I won't name used to baby sit me. She was older, maybe 19. She was my first lover. At first she had me fondle her breasts and she would get me to suckle on her. I remember her patting my head as I lay in her lap suckling. This relationship went on for almost four years. Mare, we ended up having a full sexual relationship. She lived next door which made it quite easy. Along with a sexual relationship we also had a mother and son relationship. She became the mother I had never had. She knew when I was being punished and she would come visit me during the night.

I see now that whenever I had a girlfriend I tried to get adopted by her family. I also can see how I had to get physical to feel that I was communicating my feelings. Mare, you remember how much I hung around. That was because your family meant so much to me. I can't really describe the depth of my feelings towards your family, but I can honestly say I felt closer to your family in the short time I was a part of it than the life time I was with my own family.

As you know one of us got pregnant and both of us got scared! I remember your mother guessing you were pregnant and although she blew off steam she tried to be understanding. I also remember how my family reacted. Needless to say I never got any support from them and I hated them for that. We got a truck load of gifts but not an ounce of support.

I wanted our marriage to work *soo* bad!! I wanted to be a good husband and I wanted my child to have the best. Most of all I wanted her to *know* she was *loved*. Now that I look

back I wanted to give her something I knew nothing about—
love.

As our marriage went on you know how I got violent and
beat you up. Then I said I was sorry. I was in so much turmoil.
I didn't know how to communicate the anger or disappointment of the particular situation, so I struck out physically. I
did realize I was converting to the violent attitude of my
parents. *I was not going to let that happen!* I started saying I
was sorry for everything even though down inside I wasn't
sorry. I just didn't know how to talk about it.

Now comes the really scary part—scary for me. Please
understand this has been ripping me apart for years.

When we moved to your mother's I was living in a world
of depression. I saw the only world I felt like I fit into slowly
decaying. Then came the night that started the downfall. I
can't remember where you were, but Joann [Paul's daughter]
did something that made me snap. *I hit her!*

In a matter of seconds I felt my whole world had crumbled.
The family I was part of no longer accepted me. I couldn't
handle the realization of the rejection, of losing or admitting
I had lost you and the family. After I hit her I didn't know
what to do to tell her *I love you.* Mare, I fell back on what I
had been taught—to love is to touch. So I took Jo out back
and tried to show her I loved her and I was sorry by the only
means I understood. After I had assaulted her I took her to
McDonalds to buy her something, to *buy* her love like my
folks had always done.

I can't tell you how ashamed I am. It wasn't until I saw
how others perceived me that I realized how dirty and filthy
I had acted. What I did was try to show the love of my life
the purest sense of love I knew. I didn't mean it to be anything
disgusting or filthy, to me I was saying *Joann, I love you.*
Believe me!

It took me almost two years just to be able to face myself—
to be able to say it wasn't *all* my fault and that someone had
helped me be this way. I don't know if I will ever forgive
myself for what I did to Joann. I realize I am taking a big
gamble telling you all about me. I don't know how you will
react, will this help you understand me? Will this help you
to see me as a man who loves you and Joann very much

and is trying to find a way to be understood or (possibly) be forgiven?

Mare, I'm scared. I don't know if I will ever hear from you after reading this. I feel like I have ripped open my chest and are showing you all my scars and ugliness, and I'm standing here waiting to see if you scream at the ugliness, or will you possibly see me, the man trying to heal. I am a man who loves you two but didn't know how to express it. Please hear how sorry I am for all the pain I have caused. All I want is a chance to repair the damage.

Since I have been incarcerated I have learned more about myself. I admit to what I feel. I don't ignore it, I am honest to myself. I have developed this strange feeling called self-esteem. Before I didn't believe myself. My own opinion didn't mean a thing. Now I care about me. I am not afraid to say what I think. I have found *ME*. I have found and destroyed the animal and saved the man. It's up to you whether or not you see that man . . . It's up to you.

Paul's story demonstrates the boldness that is required to be honest, to ask for forgiveness and to forgive. And as he asks, "How does the story of a person making these choices end?"—"with saving the man." Each act of forgiving ourselves or others comes down to a choice that each of us must individually make. The bottom line is . . . It's up to you.

COMPLETION AND CLOSURE

When we align with our Self and discover the basic guiltlessness of our own true nature, our consistent inclination will be to live with honesty and integrity. We will want to create closure or completion with any unfinished business from the past and actively make amends when it is possible and appropriate to do so.

All forgiveness implies some completion. Completion is coming to closure with issues. It is a healing or letting go. If you have unfinished business, inner conflict and uneasiness arise each time you think about particular people or circumstances. Do you automatically feel angry or guilty when you think of certain people or circumstances? This is a sure way to know that unresolved issues remain.

There are many ways to foster completion in relationships; these include apologizing, asking for forgiveness, confessing or telling the truth about what has transpired, or doing some sort of penance. Sometimes completion happens just by seeing yourself and others in the light of a new understanding—then what felt bothersome before may not bother you anymore.

Forgiving yourself and others may not require that you do or say something beyond your own inner process of letting go. There may be times when you think, "I need to talk with X in order to clear the air." But the other person may not be interested in talking. In order not to get stuck in the past, what you need to do must be tempered by what is possible to do. There are times when things may be better left unsaid. An issue to be aware of, however, is not choosing silence as an escape from facing the truth with another because it feels frightening, if being directly honest is the choice that is likely to be most healing.

Apologizing In many cases the best way to deal with someone you have wronged, or been insensitive to, is to acknowledge the truth straightforwardly and apologize. Some people may be relieved, and welcome this opportunity to heal the relationship. This doesn't mean that you or they will necessarily resume an active relationship. But it does mean that you can begin to disencumber yourself from the painful past.

Apologizing can be very freeing, *but* it is freeing *only* if it is done from the heart without any expectations. If you assume that your apology will be gladly accepted, you set yourself up for getting angry if your apology isn't accepted. Remember that despite apologies, genuine remorse and positive changes in your behavior, such as ceasing to do the things that evoked anger in the past, other people may still not be ready or willing to forgive. It is important that you are careful not to impose your need for completion on another person who doesn't want to engage. It is also important that you don't allow another's anger and fear to fan the fire of your own guilt. Don't allow your self-forgiveness to be contingent on somebody else's readiness or willingness to forgive you. They may get something out of holding on to anger that they aren't ready to let go of. They may be too frightened or wounded to let go of their anger. Feeling angry may be an important part of their process of healing at this time.

Allow others to be where they are. Respect their right to feel the way they feel. Only in accepting another's right to be where they are can you maintain self-forgiveness for yourself. You may certainly have a desire for them to forgive you and respond differently, but recognize that you have the desire and let it be. When you get caught in wanting another person to change, you separate yourself from your Self, and necessarily experience guilt and anger again.

Writing Another useful way to support the completion process is to write a letter of apology or a letter simply sharing what the truth is for you. There may be many things you want to say to someone. Writing is a powerful way to clarify your thoughts and feelings. You may write it intending to send the letter. You may choose not to send it, even if this person is alive and available, if you sense they aren't open to hearing you at this time. Or, there may be times when you feel guilty and remorseful, but sending the letter might compromise a third party—for instance, writing to someone's husband and telling him you are sorry you slept with his wife once, even when the wife has chosen not to tell her husband about it. Even if you throw the letter away or never send it, putting your feelings and thoughts into words on paper can move you further on the path of your own healing.

Visualization Completion can also be aided by visualization. You can stop for a few minutes a day, holding that person in your heart with love and asking for their forgiveness. Allow yourself to experience self-forgiveness even if you feel the person to whom you are apologizing is still angry.

Penance Another way to achieve completion is penance—an act of giving with a sincere desire to amend that arises from caring and love. Here penance does not imply doing or giving because you feel that you are a horrible sinner, and that by giving you may be able to work off your sins and become worthy of getting others to love and forgive you. You already are worthy of love and forgiveness. Penance can be useful when you feel the desire to make amends and the other person will not be actively engaged in the healing.

My friend Sue realized that as a child she drove her sister Gina crazy. Gina was very sensitive and emotionally vulnerable; this was something Sue didn't understand while growing up. She had no intention of distressing her sister as she did, but Gina felt threatened and abused by her behavior. As an adult, Sue tried to explain to her sister that she was sorry, that she hadn't intended to hurt her. But her apologies had no effect on Gina, who tended to be emotionally unstable as an adult. At first, her sister's inability to respond to her apology frustrated Sue. What Sue chose to do, which was a form of penance, was to be very aware of giving her sister extra gentleness, extra understanding, and extra compassion. By doing this Sue eventually forgave herself and let go of her guilt. Even though Gina hadn't forgiven, Sue no longer felt that she was stuck. By offering her sister love, compassion, and gentleness, Sue was able to offer these to herself as well.

Another example is that of Gary. He was feeling very guilty for having treated his wife insensitively in recent months. He genuinely apologized, but his wife wouldn't hear or accept the apology in a way that made him feel more complete. His therapist suggested that perhaps there was something he might do for his wife, an act or gesture that would demonstrate his love and caring. When Gary acted upon this suggestion by being very helpful around the house and sincerely offering more acknowledgment and affection, he was more able to let go of his self-judgments even though his wife chose not to acknowledge his actions.

Giving from your heart is always healing even when you don't get an overt response from somebody else.

Confessing Confessing to someone about the things you feel guilty about can be an extremely important part of the process of completion and self-forgiveness. The Fifth Step in the Twelve Step program of Alcoholics Anonymous is ''We admitted to God, to ourselves, and to another human being the exact nature of our wrongs." By acknowledging your mistakes and transgressions to another, you actively support the process of letting go. By sharing the things about which you feel badly with a loving, compassionate person, you help lift the heavy burden of guilt. Telling the whole truth to another can be a terrifying process, making you feel very vulnerable and open to rejection. Yet often the fear around sharing your darkest truth with another dissolves as telling it brings relief in its place. As you allow yourself to share your pain, guilt, and shame with a trusted person, you give up sole possession of these feelings. You find you are still acceptable, and you create more room in your heart for yourself.

EXPERIENCING TOXIC SHAME

Forgiving yourself requires that you step back and take an honest, objective look at the people and circumstances that influenced your thoughts and feelings about yourself. It requires that you recognize that some of the people who most influenced your emotional and mental development may not have known the reality of their own forgiven state. Out of their own fear, separation, and ignorance, they may have conveyed fundamentally false and neurotic messages about who you are, what you are capable of, and what you deserve.

In order to heal, these influences need to be recognized so that you are not left rejecting yourself and feeling you should be better, more, different, or, worse yet, that you shouldn't be at all. There may be the insidious and deep-rooted confusion between "I made a mistake" as distinct from "I am a mistake," "I am wrong" as distinct from "I did something wrong." This way of feeling and this type of thinking results in what John Bradshaw in his book *Healing the Shame that Binds You* refers to as "toxic shame."

Toxic shame is distinctly different from the passing shame we all feel if we are temporarily embarrassed or suddenly lose face in a situation. Toxic shame is not a quickly passing state but rather a fixed identity that is the result of rejection, abuse, and abandonment at a very young age. Here, primary caretakers are so emotionally distressed and needy that there is no reliable warmth, love, and emotional safety to extend, and there is little or no room for the emotional needs of the child. The child senses she can never be enough to satisfy the needs and expectations of the adult and unconsciously concludes, as Bradshaw points out, "I am flawed and defective as a human being." Dr. Joan Borysenko characterizes this shame and unhealthy guilt as a case of "mistaken identity."

For a child, unhealthy shame and unhealthy guilt are intertwined. If one's primary needs for acceptance, approval, and caring are not met, one experiences life with an undercurrent of feeling basic inadequacy.

P A U S E   A N D   R E F L E C T

Do any of the following messages sound or feel like familiar messages from your past?

Don't express your real feelings . . . I don't care what you feel— or think . . . Do as I say . . . Are you stupid? . . . You can't be trusted . . . Don't bother me . . . Get out of the way . . . What's wrong with you? That's not good enough . . . Can't you do anything right? . . . You can always do better . . . Don't disappoint me . . . I only love you when _____ . . .

Do you remember repeatedly feeling guilty for being inadequate . . . guilty for relaxing . . . guilty for doing what you genuinely felt was right . . . guilty for enjoying life and being happy . . . guilty for not being happy?

Reflect on your childhood. What did you have to do or be in order to be loved and accepted by the important people in your life? What were the "do's" and "don'ts" that were prerequisites for love and acceptance?

Becoming aware of the messages that created guilt and shame is essential to freeing yourself from the emotional and behavioral reactions they now elicit. Dr. Borysenko lists some of the adult signs of unhealthy shame and guilt in her outstanding book *Guilt*

Is the Teacher, Love Is the Lesson. Among them are: I'm overcommitted. I really know how to worry. I'm a compulsive helper. I'm always apologizing for myself. I often wake up feeling anxious or have periods when I am anxious for days or weeks. I'm always blaming myself. I worry about what other people think of me. I'm not as good as other people think. I'm a perfectionist. I hate to take any assistance or ask for help. I can't say no.

Once you are aware of what messages from your past instilled fear, inner conflict, guilt, and shame, you are better able to recognize when you react in old guilt-ridden ways to similar messages in the present. Forgiving yourself at this level is a process of uncovering, acknowledging, and healing what you learned about yourself in relation to these basic truths:

The truth is: you were and are lovable. Perhaps some of your actions weren't or aren't lovable, but *you* are. Pause and reflect: What did you learn about how lovable you were when you were growing up? What do you believe now?

The truth is: you are innocent. Perhaps you are guilty of certain acts. Yet, you are, at your core, fundamentally innocent, fundamentally good. Perhaps you learned to feel guilty and ashamed for things that weren't even within your control. Perhaps as a child you encountered sexual or physical abuse, alcoholism, or other such situations—which even as a child you instinctively knew were somehow "not right"—yet, being a child, you were powerless to change. Any child who has been abused and who has grown up in a dysfunctional home has experienced feeling responsible for things he or she could not be responsible for, and has known the resulting powerlessness, shame, and guilt.

Did you—or do you—go through life feeling bad, wrong, or guilty because of things that happened to you and around you as a child?

The truth is: you are always worthy of love, respect, and acceptance. Did you grow up believing you were worthy of love, respect, and acceptance from others—even when you didn't "do" anything special? Or did you learn that basic respect and acceptance were conditional, dependent on how you acted and behaved?

The truth about you may have been unknown and therefore unacknowledged by at least some of the people who most influenced your emotional and mental development. If this was so, the experience of your lovableness, innocence, and beauty were dampened in you by those you believed in and depended on most. And, as mentioned earlier, to confound things even more, these truths were, and are, lost to this culture at large.

The truth is: you are forgiven already. You are already innocent and worthy of love and respect. "We are forgiven whether we like it or not," states theologian Father Thomas Hopko. We are forgiven by virtue of the fact that our very being is rooted in the Self—in love, wisdom, beauty, innocence, and the divine. But because we have been conditioned by personal history and collective consciousness, *and* because we have free will, we have the ability to reject our very nature, reject our Self, reject our potential for happiness, and, as a result, live our life captive to the past and the small, separated selves upon which our experience of fear, unworthiness, shame, blame, and guilt are based. Self-forgiveness is realized by unraveling the very thought system upon which this self-rejection and self-deception is based and aligning with the fundamental innocence and beauty of who we are now and have always been.

It is the innocence, beauty, and strength of our essential nature, and the spiritual reality that it awakens, that greets us as we give ourself the gift of self-forgiveness.

It can be very useful to work with an affirmation like "I am now willing to be more aware of when I feel guilty or ashamed." Then, when you notice yourself feeling this way, pause. Pay close attention to what you are feeling and thinking. Follow the feeling back to where you learned to feel that way. Breathe, and remind yourself, "I now have a choice to respond to this current situation with insight and new clarity." Also remind yourself, "I can choose self-acceptance and self-love instead."

HEALING EMOTIONAL WOUNDS
FROM THE PAST

If you grew up getting negative messages and still feel a lack of self-acceptance and emotional safety, there are several powerful things you can do to facilitate healing. Some of these were mentioned in Chapter Four, where the importance of accessing, accepting, and releasing emotional pain was discussed. In addition to this, developing healthy relationships with others and developing a relationship with the child within you are important ways for healing emotional wounds.

REACHING OUT TO ESTABLISH
HEALTHY RELATIONSHIPS

If you learned to feel ashamed and guilty as a child, you undoubtedly formed an emotional barrier to protect yourself. It is likely that interpersonal connections based on physical and emotional safety, which are crucial for healthy development, were broken. If this was true for you, establishing relationships that can offer the emotional safety of empathetic acceptance is vital to your process of healing as an adult. If your current relationships with your spouse, family, or friends don't offer that kind of reassurance, make an effort to seek out and develop such relationships. Many people find the Twelve Step recovery programs such as Alcoholics Anonymous offer this kind of empathic acceptance, as do compassionate, nonjudgmental therapists and clergy.

Reaching out in this way takes courage and the willingness to risk rejection again. But if you are willing to establish such a relationship, here, perhaps for the first time, you will experience forgiveness. You will experience forgiveness in the sense that you can finally feel respected and accepted regardless of how you feel, what you need, what you "do," or the story of your life. As your implicit worthiness and acceptability is affirmed, you learn that you are truly worthy of caring and loving, and that there is safety in vulnerability. It offers the context to discover that it is safe to have needs, to be intimate, and to feel. As you gradually build an interpersonal bridge with another human being, founded on respect, you will develop what was missing from your childhood—feelings of self-worth, self-esteem, and self-love.

HEALING THE CHILD WITHIN

The importance of "inner child" work has been recently embraced in many psychological disciplines as a powerful tool for healing old emotional wounds. In addition to seeking relationships that are affirming and nurturing, you can also look inward and access your own wisdom and power to nurture yourself.

The child within each of us—our "inner child"—needs to know that she or he is and was worthy of unconditional love and respect even if that wasn't what she or he experienced before.

KATIE'S LETTER

Katie wrote to her brother Ben while he was in a drug rehabilitation center for cocaine addiction.

Dear Ben,

This letter is about me, but I'm writing it for you. . . .

I am a 41 year old woman who has a very little girl inside who hurts a lot. She's hidden away, often not consciously present even to myself, but has been forever hurting, hurting and hurting.

The hurt started when this little girl was a real little girl. She craved love, she craved to be held, and she craved to be special. But this little girl grew up with a mother who also had a very hurt little girl inside, a mother who couldn't show love, especially in any physical way, like hugging her child, because the hurt little girl inside her had probably never been held herself. Thus, the little girl inside me learned to believe she was unlovable.

As a child, the little girl longed to be accepted, valued, and appreciated. But this little girl grew up with a father who had a hurt little boy inside himself who believed he was stupid and not good enough. He tried to teach his little girl to be good enough by trying to create a "thinking mind" by challenging and debating everything that the child said. Instead, the little girl learned that whatever she said, thought or believed was wrong. The little girl learned she was stupid.

The real little girl wanted to do things "right," wanted to be "good enough," wanted to be the best she could be, but because her parents had children inside them who believed they weren't good enough, everything their child did was also not good enough. They were very critical of their child, stressing the shortfalls in accomplishments and the neglect (stupidity!) in the failures. The child learned she could never be good enough.

The real little girl would get angry because she was hurt and couldn't get her needs met. But, anger was very destructive and painful in her house. Both parents had very angry children inside them and expressed that anger in unhealthy ways. Anger became very dangerous and hurtful, sometimes physically, but more so emotionally. Sarcastic comments, terrible fights, loud noises that smashed against the child's innermost feelings leaving behind an aftershock that has survived a lifetime. The child learned to become invisible. The child learned it was never safe to express her angry feelings. The child learned to be a sponge that soaks up anger and keeps it from spreading.

The real little girl "knew" instinctively that love was vital but had no way to feel love and no way to express love because love was lost in the hurt and pain of generations. This little girl learned she was trapped in hopelessness . . . a life without love.

This little girl learned to cope with the hurt by "stuffing" it deeper and deeper inside . . . and taking her very self with it. She kept very busy . . . Working too much, trying to do too much and never relaxing or daring to, because then the pain would rise up and hurt too much to bear. But the pain turned to a constant ache and she learned to try to cope with it by planning her death—not to kill herself as much as to kill the pain. She tried to find ways to numb the ache . . . tranquilizers, anti-depressants, and always knowing the ultimate relief would be alcohol. But, the little girl grew up with her alcoholic parents and feared alcoholism more than the pain, so she forced herself (most of the time) not to drink. The little girl became exhausted.

Ben, as I said, this letter is about me but it is for you. You grew up with the same hurting parents that I had and inside you there is a hurting little boy. Maybe that little boy "learned" different things than the little girl in this letter but I'm sure that the things the little boy learned are not true. Ben, I want so much for you to feel the love that I have for you. I want to comfort you, to hold you and to help you carry your pain until it's not so heavy. The only way that I can think of to do that right now is to write you this letter in the hopes that sharing what I've come to realize might help you see that there are very real reasons why you hurt inside. It is understandable that you have been looking all your life for ways to cope and ease the pain. I hope that you will continue with therapy after your discharge. Maybe it would be helpful if you show this letter to your counselor as a way to begin (or continue) looking at what untruths the little boy inside you learned and as a start toward healing that little boy.

I have a very clear image of the little boy inside you (he's adorable by the way! big blue eyes with a wonderfully impish twinkle in them!) and I'm holding that little boy with all the love in my heart.

I love you Ben no matter where you are or what is happening in your life. I'll keep in touch and please call me anytime.

Love,
Katie

BEN'S REPLY
Dear Katie,

Well, I've been debating with myself whether to write or to call. This debate has been raging for a week. This is my last day here [drug rehab. center] and I've decided to write.

I have not been able to read your letter a second time, but I will when I get the nerve. This letter is taking about 15 minutes per sentence—I can't seem to find the words.

Prior to coming here the ideas in your letter would have meant nothing. However, as a result of being just slightly more receptive, I was allowed to have the most profound revelation as to who and why I am. For the first time in my life I felt that I might understand me, and I knew that at least someone else did. One reason why I need to read the letter again is because I cried through most of it—in fact I was still crying 45 minutes later while running around the track. When I cried it was like a tremendous release of pressure.

I've been looking back at all the major decisions of my life and now have some insight as to why I always went the wrong way. Even the decisions that appear to have been right were made for the wrong reasons.

I could write on and on—but for now, Katie, know that I love you very much and I can't put into words what your letter meant to me.

Love,
Ben

As with Katie and Ben, recognizing and reconnecting with your inner child can be crucial for healing and self-understanding.

Many adults feel ashamed of the innocent feelings of their inner child. Often there is great embarrassment and inhibition to exposing and sharing the loneliness, terror, and hurt of that child with another human being. Many adults criticize themselves for having these feelings—i.e., "What am I, a little baby? I'm supposed to be a grown man!" "I feel foolish—what do I have to be afraid of?" In the process of healing the hurt, guilt, and shame of our wounded inner child we must meet their truest feelings with gentleness and compassion, letting them know that, yes, now there is really someone with whom they can share their pain. This is the work of the healthy inner adult.

As an adult you may feel so wounded that it seems difficult, if not impossible, for you to offer your inner child the love, forgiveness, and safety that she or he needs. You may even find yourself feeling contempt for or fear of your inner child. In this situation it can be most helpful to evoke in your imagination a universal symbol—such as the Great Mother, the Wise Man, the Crone, the Great Protector—that embodies for you all the qualities that your inner child needs at this time. Any of these universal symbols evoke a powerful psychic energy within your consciousness which can serve as a dynamic source of inspiration and healing. These are part of humanity's collective memory, what Carl Jung referred to as archetypes from the collective unconscious. In times of need or stress it is possible to evoke these archetypes and actually feel and utilize their strength and wisdom.

An example of one archetype that would provide safety for the inner child is that of the Great Mother, the feminine as the source of life and nurturance. When the Great Mother is evoked in one's imagination she embodies the attributes of a being who is un-questionably present to protect, nurture, love, and guide you. If you relax and let go of inhibitions and invite and allow yourself to relate with the reality of such a presence, you begin to heal and internalize her attributes for yourself.

Visualization: Calling on the Great Mother

Imagine for a few moments the presence of the Great Mother . . . a being who is loving, nurturing, powerful, and committed to your well-being . . . Allow yourself to open to the presence of such a being into your life now. Imagine she is there for your inner child and will never abandon you when you're in need. Sense for a moment her qualities of wisdom and decisiveness that empower her with the fierceness to protect your inner child if ever her/his Selfhood is being threatened, much like a lioness would protect her endangered cub. She is always available to your inner child. Imagine how your inner child feels knowing such a loving, strong, and committed being is now there for her or him.

· · ·

In addition to evoking the nurturing archetype, you, as an adult, can go back in time and offer the frightened child within the respect, love, safety, and comfort that was denied. With time, the child within will begin to feel comfortable enough to open and reunite with the creative, spontaneous, accepting part of his or her nature. This kind of process provides an opportunity to go back into your personal history and re-parent, protect, comfort, and befriend yourself.

In addition to the exercises and visualizations below, it may be useful to just take some time each day to remember the child within. Listen to her/him and take the time to nurture her/him in whatever ways feel most natural and loving. Occasionally looking at a photo or film of yourself at the age when you felt you could have used the most love and support can be useful.

This kind of inner work can elicit powerful emotions, especially if you had a traumatic childhood. Actively participate in the visualizations only if you feel inclined to do so at this time. If you had a traumatic childhood, old feelings may get stirred up that you may not wish to deal with now. You may decide to just skim over the visualizations and wait to fully participate in them at a later date when a friend or therapist is there for support. Do what feels comfortable and safe for you.

Inner Child Visualization #1

Set aside a time to reconnect with your inner child each day. First take some time to breathe deeply and relax . . . Allow yourself to go within and get in touch with feelings of gentleness, kindness, compassion, strength and love . . . Then allow yourself to return to a time in your childhood when you felt judged, emotionally abandoned, insensitively treated, guilty, ashamed, unworthy, frightened, or unlovable . . . Now let the adult within you who is strong, kind, compassionate, and loving meet your inner child who is in need of comfort and love . . . Let the "adult you" be fully there for the child, offering her/him the unconditional respect and safety that was once denied . . . Allow your inner child to share her/his experience, just the way she/he felt it. Assure the child that you will not abandon her/him, no matter what . . .

Go through each prior year of your life, lovingly assuring the child within that she or he is lovable and beautiful, and worthy of respect and adoration.

Listen to your inner child's experience of birth. Did she or he feel wanted and loved? Whatever the feelings, let your inner child know that she or he has a right to be here, and that she or he is loved now . . . Welcome yourself into the world . . . Find the place within you that is infinitely loving, gentle, and generous, and treat yourself as if you were your only child . . .

Now, listen to the experience of the one-year-old within you. Honor her or him fully. Let her or him know that she or he is safe . . . Share joy . . . See and acknowledge the inner child's light . . . When you are ready, continue through the years until you reach your current age.

If going through each year of your life up until the present is more than you're willing to do now or more than you feel you need, choose only the times when you felt disrespected, confused, or frightened. Perhaps your greatest need was to have a loving ally in school. If so, go back in your imagination and be a loving teacher or friend to yourself. Champion your abilities . . . Let your inner child know that she or he is bright, creative, and a great pleasure to be with . . .

Taking the time you need, when you are ready, go on with your day.

·   ·   ·

Inner Child Visualization #2

First, take some time to breathe slowly and fully and allow yourself to deeply relax. Follow your breathing in and out . . . After doing this for a minute or so, count back from three to zero on the next four exhalations. When you reach zero, imagine seeing a door. On the other side of the door is you as a child, at a time when you needed the safety and comfort of a loving, gentle, and trustworthy adult.

Open the door and allow your inner child to come out to be with you. Remember to breathe. Allow your heart to be open to this child. Let her or him know she or he is safe now . . . Call upon your infinite patience if your inner child is somewhat reluctant to respond at first. Let her or him know that you are there, you understand, and you won't abandon her or him even if it takes a while for her or him to respond. Offer the inner child love and safety . . . Listen as she or he tells you—verbally or nonverbally—about her or his experiences. Open your heart and comfort her or him. Take her or him by the hand. Let her or him know that you will always be there with her or him and for her or him.

Imagine giving your inner child a special gift to remind her or him that you will always be there . . . Imagine your inner child giving you a gift . . . Imagine both of you allowing yourselves to experience a new bond, founded on love, understanding, and compassion . . . Place your inner child in your heart.

Taking the time you need, when you are ready, return to a normal, waking state. From time to time, remember to assure your inner child that the unsafe past is over and that you will always be there for her or him now.

Inner Child Visualization #3

First, take some time to breathe slowly and fully, and allow yourself to deeply relax. Follow your breathing in and out. Then imagine yourself as you are today and allow yourself to open to compassion, warmth, love, and gentleness . . . Now imagine a recent time in your life when you felt "not good enough," or "unloved," "guilty," or "ashamed." Just notice what was going on for you . . . where you were . . . what you were doing . . . what thoughts were in your mind . . . what you were feeling . . . Now take a deep, gentle breath, and as you breathe out, let go of this experience and relax . . .

Now go back to an earlier time when you felt this way. Remember what was going on for you . . . where you were . . . what you were doing . . . what you were thinking . . . what you were feeling . . . Now take another deep relaxing breath, and as you exhale let go of this experience and relax . . .

Now go back to the earliest time when you felt not good enough, unloved, unworthy, guilty, or frightened. (Just take whatever comes to mind.) Notice what was going on for you . . . where you were . . . what you were doing . . . what thoughts you were thinking . . . what you were feeling . . . Now imagine that child being with the warm, compassionate, loving, gentle person you are right now . . . Imagine offering this child unconditional love and support in whatever way feels most natural. Listen as this child tells you the truth of her or his experience . . . Imagine opening your heart to this child and telling her or him what she or he really needs to hear . . . Allow this child into your heart, surrounding her or him with love and light.

Now allow yourself to identify with this child, feeling totally supported and nurtured by this love, accepting the love totally, absorbing its nourishment . . . Now gently release this child into the world. Watch as she or he grows into a more confident, happy, whole, loving adult . . . Imagine being that adult now, secure in your feelings of self-worth, feeling strong and radiant . . . accepting your own personal power and love . . .

Whenever you're ready, open your eyes, ready to go on with your day.

· · ·

When the inner child feels safe, the heart of the child *and* the adult opens. "There is not a heart that exists that, if it were assured of safety, would not open instantly," wrote Pat Rodegast in the book *Emmanuel*. When your heart opens, you can feel without pushing parts of yourself away. You can feel fear, anger, and pain so that you can open the door to emotional healing. You can feel love, so at last you can know the greatest healing power and the purest joy of being alive. Only when your heart is open can you experience your deepest essence, your core Self. And only then do you know the truth of your innocence.

FAILING YOURSELF

"I'll never forgive myself for _____."
"I should have _____."
"I never should have _____."
"If only I had _____."

Guilt and chronic regret and remorse are familiar to most of us. We wish we had done it differently and we think, "If only I had it to do over again." Author and psychiatrist Alan McGlashin refers to blame and guilt as "the great twin monsters." Many of us live with these monsters as our personal and constant companions. Some people have an exaggerated sense of guilt and feel guilty for things they don't even have anything to do with. Mark Twain captured the essence of exaggerated guilt in Huck Finn: "But that's always the way; it don't make no difference whether you do right or wrong, a person's conscience ain't got no sense, and it just goes for him anyway."

Some of the things for which we blame ourselves may not be things that we think of as ethically wrong, but rather we judge them as stupid, thoughtless, impulsive, or weak. "I can't believe I did that! I must have been spineless." "I must have been blind." "What a fool I am." "I sold out on myself again." Actions and decisions that might provoke that kind of reaction may include having been part of an abusive relationship, having worked for an employer who was greedy and took advantage of you, never doing things that you've always wanted to do or doing things you didn't want to do, being addicted to something or someone you know is hurtful. You may even resent yourself for being afraid to make a change and hate yourself for feeling helpless and hurt.

You may feel, "Of course I blame myself—who else am I going to blame?" You live with one of the core thoughts of the guilty person, which is, "It's my fault." You may think that blaming yourself will motivate you to change or live up to your true potential. Like anger that is projected outward, guilt, self-disdain, and self-blame can be ways of diverting your attention from deeper feelings and fears, buffering you from feeling hopeless, helpless, or powerless. Just as anger and being judgmental can serve as a protection, ultimately such feelings deprive us of our genuine strength. In the same way, chronic guilt and self-blame can seem to serve as the constant nagging that we need to wake ourselves up, yet they actually lull us to sleep keeping the power to heal ourselves inactive.

You may wonder how we can trust ourselves to make thoughtful, judicious, loving, and appropriate choices if we don't judge ourselves and others. We have been conditioned to believe that our judgments are necessary, that they have value, and that if we didn't always judge ourselves, we would never change, we would be unethical, and we would act like lazy slobs. Our egos assure us that our judgments will keep us in line. But quite to the contrary, it is the undermining nature of our chronic self-judgments that keep us stuck in an often-vicious cycle of act and remorse. What these judgments really do is keep us out of our own heart and separate from the clarity, love, and natural integrity that is our deepest inclination and highest need to express.

Exercise: Becoming Your Own Friend
Imagine what it would be like to live with someone who constantly judges you as wrong, bad, weak, or stupid for the things you have done and do. This would, in all likelihood, undermine the confidence and/or motivation to make the changes you want.

Now imagine instead that you make choices that are not what you really want for yourself, and that you live with a kind, wise, and insightful person who can clearly see when you make those choices, but instead of emotionally and mentally beating you down for them, she or

he offers you love and acceptance. At the same time, this person helps
you to look at your choices with a new clarity, compassion, and wisdom.
Imagine that this kind person supports you in seeing the fears and
conditioning that motivate you. She or he understands that your choices,
even self-destructive ones, were or are attempts to find relief, peace, and
happiness. She or he knows, and wants you to know, that coming from
the degree of fear and separation from yourSelf that you were coming
from, you were doing the best you could. She or he assures you that
there are other choices you can make now. She or he says to start by
being gentle with yourself. She or he encourages you to open to and
accept support from a higher power, and from others. She or he tells
you that there is truly grace in your life and that only you can let it
in . . .
Go back over the last two paragraphs and imagine what it would be
like if you befriended yourself in this same way. Repeat this suggestion
many times in the days ahead. Become a true friend to yourself.

When we use insight and look at ourselves with discriminating
wisdom, rather than judging ourselves as bad, stupid, or wrong,
we begin to see clearly what motivated us to make the choices
that we may or may not consider desirable now. With this clarity
comes a growing compassion and love for yourself. In order to
stop the cycle of self-blame and self-judgment, and the self-pun-
ishment that follows, you must offer yourself greater gentleness
and compassion, even though you still feel guilt, shame, anger,
blame, grief, and pain. Rather than beating yourself up for where
you are or what you have done, you can begin, even for only a
moment at a time at first, to see that you made the choices that
felt the safest and the most secure at the time, although they might
have been self-defeating.

Throughout your day consider:

The past is over.
I will open my heart and forgive myself today.

~~~~~~

P A U S E   A N D   R E F L E C T

If you find that you are unwilling to forgive yourself now, complete and contemplate the following:
* I am not willing to forgive myself for _____.
* What I get out of holding on to this self-condemnation is __
  _____.
* What I give up by holding on to this self-condemnation is __
  _____.

Notice your responses with a gentle nonjudging awareness.

~~~~~~

WAYNE'S STORY

Years ago a woman I loved was going to fly to another city to meet me for a week of loving exploration. We had been seeing each other off and on for several weeks and this was the time we chose to see if we wanted to make a deeper commitment. The night before, she called to say she wasn't sure she should come. She wasn't feeling well and she had bad feelings about the outcome of the trip. I had my doubts too, but I pushed them all aside and said, "Please come, I want you to get on that plane and come." She laughed and said, "I was hoping you'd say that," and agreed. We made plans for a romantic dinner the next night with renewed excitement.

The next day while I waited for her someone told me of a terrible plane crash. It was her flight.

I went into deep shock and disbelief and could not accept the reality of what had happened. I went through a gamut of feelings, but above all I could hear my voice saying, "I want you to get on that plane and come." That night I watched the news and there were filmed excerpts of the fragments of the plane strewn across the screen. I watched in vain hope that her name wouldn't be there. When I saw it, I still could not take it in. I finally fell into bed staring at the ceiling wondering if I would ever sleep again. Most of all I feared closing my eyes, because each time I did I saw visions of fragments of body parts. After a long time a part of my mind said, "Accept this vision; if you don't, you will never be able to close your eyes again." So, saying her name,

I closed my eyes and allowed the images to come. They were horrible and revolting, but I took them in with all the love I felt for her, and eventually I slept.

For months I was angry and guilt-ridden. I could not forgive myself even though my mind knew she had made her own choice to get on that plane. I was haunted by visions of the fragments of the plane and her body broken and burned. When the investigation revealed faulty mechanical maintenance I had a new source for my rage. Some mechanic had not made the right adjustment—someone was careless, in a hurry to get off the boring repetitive job and have a beer or play cards or whatever. In some part of myself I made a vow never to be like that. I would always be thorough and responsible. I would never be careless—never be like the man who was responsible for that plane crash and the death of my lover. I drove myself in my work to be as perfect as possible. I was scornful of people who made mistakes and unwilling to allow myself any slack. Then as time went on, I became more tolerant of small mistakes in others. I became aware of my cruel perfectionism and worked on it in therapy. I even began to let myself off the hook a little. But some part of me was always ready to flare up in violent judgment when someone was careless or showed disregard for responsibility. I also developed the feeling that if I wanted something done right, I had to do it myself, and then I could only blame myself if it went wrong. I knew I could forgive others, but the real, serious responsibilities were mine and mine alone. And I wouldn't make mistakes when the stakes were high, because I knew deep in my being what the consequences could be.

One day in therapy I was feeling very judgmental and the therapist asked why I was so fierce and unforgiving. The reply in grim tones was, "Because this is life and death. Mistakes can be fatal. People can die." "Who can die?" the therapist asked. I burst into tears and said the name of my dead lover over and over. The therapist asked me how I thought she would feel if she saw me like this. I suddenly had the image of her face looking at me with love and compassion and forgiveness. I heard her voice saying, "It's not your fault. Please stop punishing yourself. I got on the plane because I loved you. Remember my love, not my death. Please forgive yourself." Hearing her voice set something loose in me. I cried for a long time—something I had not allowed myself to do. The anger and the judgment melted and I felt deep waves of loss. Over many weeks I began to feel my layers of armor slowly coming down, and as I forgave myself I was able to let more love in.

I still get angry and upset when people are careless and when I make mistakes. I still have moments of severe self-judgment, and when things get really rough I sometimes feel that I can never really forgive myself. But sooner or later I return to center and breathe and sometimes I remember my lover's voice saying "remember my love, not my death." And I realize I do have a choice in how I react to things. And if I'm really doing well, I can even manage to forgive myself for falling back into the old habits of judgment and self-cruelty.

PERFECTION AND GUILT

One way to ensure guilt is to constantly demand perfection from yourself. The demand for perfection can be our harshest enemy. We go into battle with a saboteur that we can never really defeat. Even if we manage to achieve our goals, we will have forfeited pleasure in the process of achieving. And there will always be something else that hasn't met our standards.

There is a significant distinction between doing things really well because you genuinely want to, and being run by a "perfectionist" subpersonality. For the perfectionist, true vitality and pleasure is usually missing, because the foundation of one's self-worth is at stake when things threaten not to be "perfect." If you always expect perfection, when you experience the "imperfect" side of human nature, or experience failure in projects or personal endeavors, you feel fundamentally diminished. If it isn't "perfect" then "I am, at some fundamental level, a failure and not good enough." We are blinded to the truth of being a worthwhile, good person even if our project fails, even if our marriage ends in divorce, even if our skin is flabby, even if we flunk that course, even if we are unemployed, and even if we think we're not good enough. A person addicted to perfection, like all actively addicted people, is cut off from his or her true Self. Thinking that they always have to do better, they reject who they are now. As a result, they are blinded to the potential perfection in many situations. For instance, being unemployed could be an opportunity to work on self-development or make a career change that will ultimately be more rewarding. Every circumstance and situation offers us the opportunity to rediscover our Self.

Chronic perfectionism is self-abusive. It keeps our heart closed to ourselves and robs us of our aliveness. Charles Johnston, M.D., in *The Creative Imperative*, refers to aliveness as "the degree an act or situation is creatively vital, ultimately enhancing life." Aliveness determines the quality of life and can only be experienced when we can accept the common dualities within us: mind/body, masculine/feminine, joy/sadness, perfection/imperfection. When we are willing to accept only our ego's definition of "perfection" (and only the ego demands perfection), we smother our aliveness by rejecting a part of ourself that is an integral part of the whole.

From time to time reflect:

Would I rather be "perfect" or would I rather be alive?

HOW LONG DOES IT TAKE TO FORGIVE YOURSELF?

Like all forgiveness, self-forgiveness is a process. It's a path you travel, not a permanent state you reach. Sometimes people wonder, "When will I ever let myself off the hook and forgive myself for things that are over and done? Will I ever really love myself?" Even when it comes to healing the more glaring guilt and shame, there is no prescribed time that healing takes. Even a few minutes here and there when you feel more compassionate and loving toward yourself indicate there is healing and health. It is important to remember that growth happens in a spiral. The more you heal, the more you love and accept yourself, the more the subtler feelings of guilt, shame, and unworthiness can come to your awareness, to be owned and healed.

For some people, it takes many years for certain wounds to fully heal. For others, certain healing may take but a moment in time. There will be times when you can see or sense great progress—when you feel self-accepting, peaceful, and optimistic. There will also be times when you feel guilty, ashamed, embarrassed, self-critical, and discouraged. The important thing to remember is that if you are willing to be more compassionate and more self-affirming, even though the connection to your Self will be lost and found again, and lost and found again, and lost and found again—it will be lost less and less. It will be found more and more.

JONAS'S STORY

All my life I had dreamed of achieving fame and fortune as an author. I had been groomed for it in a very achievement-oriented family, and had adopted it as a major personal goal.

In 1980 I wrote a book on compulsive eating. I sent the book to a well-known New York literary agent, who called me back within the week, *very* impressed with the book and agreeing to try to sell it to a publisher. Within two weeks, two major New York publishers expressed interest in it, and my agent held an "auction," and one of the publishers bought the book, sending me a rather sizable advance for a first-time author. Both my agent and my editor indicated that this would probably be a very big book, possibly a best-seller, and, as my agent said, "the *Jonathan Livingston Seagull* of diet books." I was totally psyched. I began watching all the TV talk shows, practicing for the time when Phil Donahue or Johnny Carson would be asking *me* questions. I began having fantasies of great wealth. This was it! All my dreams were coming true. I would achieve what my father and mother had wanted me to achieve all my life! I felt great about myself and about life!

The book was published in May, 1981. Although it got some pretty good reviews, it got one terrible review in *Pub-*

lisher's Weekly, and it was obvious within a month that the book was going nowhere at all. It was a bomb, a bust, a dud. It went out of print within a year, and now, ten years later, the only remaining copies that I know about are in a cardboard box in my basement.

I actually was on a talk show, though. It was a local talk show in Boston called *Five All-Night Live.* I was on at 2:37 A.M. for about seven minutes, answering shallow questions that missed the point of the book entirely, and the act that I followed (this is true!) were two parrots and a cockatoo. I went into a depression for about a year after the failure of my book, mixed with self-hate and a prevailing sense of shame.

Even to this day I still have periodic "attacks" of these feelings which last anywhere from a couple of seconds to a couple of days, but they are few and far between now, and I don't pay them much attention. I have done a lot of inner work on myself in the last ten years, mainly through a spiritual path, plus some therapy and a lot of love and support from my wife, and the whole event has lightened up for me to the point where I can joke about it, and I now understand the larger (karmic) context in which it happened and it makes perfect sense.

Have I forgiven myself? Not completely. I still feel shame that I'm not rich and famous. Have I forgiven my parents for "setting me up" to believe that my self-worth depended on my achievements? Not completely. They should have done better parenting. Have I forgiven my agent and editor? Not completely. They should have been smart enough to package the book better and then to stand behind it much, much longer. Have I forgiven God? Not completely. God should not have tantalized me so cruelly by dangling the Desired Object so close to me and then pulling it away at the last moment.

But there *are* moments when I forgive us all. Those are the moments when I know that what happens on the outside is the sideshow and what happens on the inside of us is the real show. Those are the moments when I *trust.* I trust that things are happening as they're supposed to happen, as they must necessarily happen, for my spiritual unfoldment. Within that understanding there is no one at fault and no one to forgive.

SELF-FORGIVENESS AND
SPIRITUAL GROWTH

Self-forgiveness, in its crowning stead, moves us beyond forgiveness's function as the means for healing apparent guilt, shame, and unworthiness, to self-forgiveness as a means for nurturing self-realization or spiritual growth. To integrate this level of self-forgiveness most completely, basic developmental needs for safety and acceptance must first be met. Then self-forgiveness is embraced as the means for aligning with and accepting the beauty, magnificence, and innate glory of our true Self with greater and greater certainty and consistency. From this comes the experience of the deepest sense of fulfillment, belonging, joy, and participation.

Self-forgiveness serves as a continual means for experiencing the deepest truth of who we are. It is the way for realizing that our most essential nature is love, and it is the means for remembering this truth as an unalterable reality.

As self-forgiveness roots itself in your consciousness, even when outer circumstances don't ensure safety and people around you aren't accepting, you come to know an abiding inner safety and acceptance nonetheless. You become clearer and more powerful, finding your source of strength in a growing trust and faith in something infinitely greater than the sum of your small selves. There is the growing reliance on an aspect of your Self that includes, but is not bound by, the rational, linear mind for direction and assurance. There is a deepening awareness of inner guidance and grace. Regardless of the circumstances, you see that every trial and every situation is another opportunity for surrender, not to defeat, but rather to love that knows neither judgment nor rejection.

CHAPTER TEN

FORGIVING YOUR BODY:
IN SICKNESS AND IN HEALTH

The concept of forgiving your body may seem strange at first; however, take a moment to consider the following. Do you know one individual who truly loves and accepts his or her body? Do you love and accept yours?

For most people the body is the object of ridicule, rejection, hatred, neglect, and abuse. If you are like most, the judgments you hold are likely to defy the natural inclinations of your unique body type. Facial features, body shape, and hair texture or color may be but a few aspects of your appearance that you are unhappy with. There may even be parts of your body that you reject just by virtue of their existence. Were you taught, for instance, that your genitals were "not nice" or "dirty"? Are you embarrassed by or do you ignore certain parts of your body, putting them down as objects of disdain?

THE FIRST STEP

To heal and bring peace to your relationship with your body, you
first need to forgive yourself for being human, for to be human is
to have a body. And our bodies rarely look and do as we would
ideally like them to. We have needs and drives that are sometimes
powerful, such as the sexual drive, that can be distressing, confusing, and compelling. We don't always feel comfortable in our
body, and it is certain to age and die. Forgiving yourself for being
human means accepting that this is so. Again, acceptance doesn't
imply defeat or resignation. Rather, it implies the choice to not
reject and resist the way things are, the things you can't change
right now, or the things that are not changing as quickly as you
would like. Acceptance also doesn't imply that you should be
passive and neglect your body. Rather, as you let go of chronic
judgment and resistance toward the condition of your body *as it
is*, you will release energy that will help healing to occur and you
will undoubtedly feel better about being you.

TEN (OR, FORGIVING YOUR APPEARANCE IN AN OBSESSED CULTURE)

~~~~~~

P A U S E   A N D   R E F L E C T

What's the first word or thought that comes into your mind
when you think of the following?
- wrinkles _____
- cellulite _____
- body fat _____
- potbelly _____
- fat legs _____
- skinny body _____
- pimples _____
- sagging breasts _____

- small penis _____
- large buttocks _____
- thinning hair/bald head _____

Think of any of the above that apply to you. How do you feel about yours? When you think of your overall appearance how do you feel? What does your mind tell you about yourself? Does it accept you? Do you have many negative judgments?

~~~~~~

Do you remember the 1980 movie *10*, with Bo Derek?—Young. Tall. Long, thin legs. No cellulite. Flat stomach. Voluptuous breasts. Long flowing hair. Stereotypically pretty face. No wrinkles. On a scale from one to ten, it's no surprise that in this culture, Bo scored a solid ten.

Very few of us grow up in this culture without being instilled with very specific images of "the" acceptable body and face. These images are relatively inflexible, especially for women. The stereotypes for men are perhaps not as rigid. But men, too, are easily made to feel inferior if they lack the standard handsome attributes. If you look at popular magazines and movies, it's easy to see that we are a culture obsessed with the myth of glamour. This artificial and unrealistic ideal is the standard against which we first learn to compare and measure ourselves, and sadly, it is also the standard against which our aging and elderly are held. The natural changes that inevitably occur—lines, wrinkles, sagging, hair loss—are often viewed with disdain and distaste. In a society that has directed its psychic energy into idolizing youth, there is scant recognition of the great physical beauty in our elders. Consciously forgiving one's body for aging initiates the process of re-assessing fundamental values. It initiates one into living with the grace and poise that comes from living in the moment and not resisting what is perfectly natural.

Can you imagine being at peace with your physical appearance *as it is*? If you answered "no" to this question, *are you willing to open to the possibility* that you could be at peace with your appearance as it is? If you are at peace with your appearance and more self-accepting, the desire to change your appearance will not necessarily alter, but rather than being motivated by self-loathing and self-condemnation, your motivation for change will be inspired by self-respect and the desire to care and nurture yourself.

THE GREAT WEIGHT DEBATE

In addition to aging and body type, people are particularly merciless with themselves about their body weight and shape. Frequently, being overweight becomes a primary focus in life. Everything not conforming to the illusion of the ideal image is fuel for judgment and confirmation that "the way I am is not lovable or acceptable." Whether you are constantly worrying about those ten "extra" pounds, or you are bulemic or anorexic—starving yourself in the pursuit of thinness—calories and fat are often seen as "the problem." The deeper issues that result in overeating, compulsive dieting, or body fat may be completely repressed and overlooked. Sometimes people overeat as a form of self-nurturance, or are overweight as an unconscious form of protection. Like all addictions, food can be a way of feeding the hungry heart, an attempt to fill an emotional and spiritual void. When people chastise themselves for being overweight, they divert their attention from the real issues and deny themselves the emotional nurturance and safety that may have led to the feelings of emptiness and hunger in the first place.

To begin the process of forgiving your body for being the weight and shape it is, be gentle with yourself just as you are. Being gentle with yourself doesn't mean being lazy or self-indulgent. It means being a loving friend to yourself and your body; when you feel loved and accepted, you will be far less likely to eat when you're not really hungry for food. It means giving yourself permission to enjoy your body *now*. What if you never lose those extra pounds? You deserve to enjoy your body anyway! You deserve your love anyway! Being gentle with yourself means being willing not to chastise yourself for things that are already done. If you are constantly judging yourself, you are starving for the only things that will fill you. You are starving for self-acceptance. You are starving for your love.

As you heed the inner callings of your emotional and spiritual life, you may find that feeling more balanced will naturally lead to losing weight. Or perhaps you'll decide you are fine the way you are. What may change instead is the longtime struggle with yourself. If your attempts at change have been fueled by your fears and self-hatred, the changes you have managed to make until now may have been unreliable, unsustained, and demoralizing. If you are changing because you are addicted to an image you believe will finally make you acceptable and lovable, rather than because you truly want to, you will be engaged in a struggle forever. Are you willing to participate in a cease-fire? Are you willing to open to the possibility that you can love and accept your body even if it isn't your ideal? Here "love" doesn't imply egoistic self-indulgence or narcissism, but rather an accepting, respectful, and appreciative attitude for the functions your body serves and the relationship with life it allows.

Exercise: Affirmations for Healing Your Relationship with Your Body

A very helpful technique for healing your relationship with your body is working with affirmations. One way to work with affirmations is: Write a statement that affirms a loving, accepting relationship with your body. After writing the statement, allow a reaction to this affirmation to come to mind. Don't censor your reactions. For instance, if you made the affirmation "I am willing to accept my body as it is," the first spontaneous reaction to your affirmation might be something like "not a chance." Then write this reaction next to your affirmation. Then write the same affirmation many more times, writing your spontaneous reactions next to each one. For example:

I am willing to accept my body as it is.
  Not a chance.
I am willing to accept my body as it is.
  I don't think so.
I am willing to accept my body as it is.
  Then I'd never change.
I am willing to accept my body as it is.
  Ha!
I am willing to accept my body as it is.
  I don't like my legs.

I am willing to accept my body as it is.
   What a relief.

Notice how your reactions change as you keep working with the affirmation. Allowing negative responses from your unconscious to surface and be recognized gives you the opportunity to see the beliefs and attitudes that stand between you and self-acceptance. Create affirmations that express your desired goals and keep working with the same affirmation until your reactions are neutral or positive, then start working with new affirmations. If a reaction doesn't come to mind, repeat the same affirmation again. As your feelings, attitudes, and beliefs are revealed, you will discover the transformational potential of affirmation work.

The following is part of a journey through one workshop participant's process of healing her relationship with her body using affirmations.

NANCY'S AFFIRMATIONS
   I am willing to see my physical beauty.
      I can't.
   I am willing to see my physical beauty.
      Where is it?
   I am willing to see my physical beauty.
      It's not good enough.
   I am willing to see my physical beauty.
      But it's not good enough.
   I am willing to see my physical beauty.
      I'd have to let go.
   I am willing to let go of others' standards.
      It's all I've ever measured myself against.
   I am willing to stop judging my body.
      Death.
   I am willing to stop judging my body.
      I can't imagine.
   I am willing to stop judging my body.
      I'll try.
   I am willing to stop judging my body.
      Poor baby.

I am willing to let my body into my heart.
I am willing to let my body into my heart.
  How scary.
I am willing to let my body into my heart.
I am willing to let my body into my heart.
  It's so yukky.
I am willing to let my body into my heart.
  It's so messy.
I am willing to let my body into my heart.
I am willing to see that my body is part of me.
  Of course.
I am willing to see that my body is me, too.
I am willing to see that my body is me, too.
I am willing to see that my body is me, too.
  Oh no, please, please. Hold out your arms to your body. Hold out my arms to my body. Hold my body. Hold me. Let go of the revulsion, just hold me. Let go of the revulsion, just hold me. Accept me, I am part of you, of me. Oh, my poor baby. Why have I turned on you for so long? Why have I hated you so long, so hard? I feel such pain, your pain. What an innocent body. Where would I be without you? I guess like always I needed to be ahead of the pack. If I say I hate you before everyone else does, it won't hurt so much. Bullshit. I'm lovable, you're lovable. It hurts not to be loved. And you deserve to be loved not only by me but by others.
My body deserves love.
  It needs love.
My body deserves love.
  It wants love.
My body deserves love.
  It craves love.
My body deserves love.
  My body does deserve love!
My body deserves love.
  Where have I been?
My body deserves love.
  Sadness.
My body deserves love.
  I'll stop abandoning you.

I am willing to forgive my body.
For the first time.
I am willing to forgive my body.
For moments, anyway.
I am willing to forgive my body.
It craves my forgiveness.
I am willing to forgive my body.
I am. I am. I am.
I am willing to forgive my body.
I'll forget.
I forgive my body completely.
Moments, moments at a time.
I forgive my body completely.
It'll take some getting used to.
I forgive my body completely.
It'll take some getting used to.
I love my body.
I love my body.
I love my body.
What a lovely home.
I love my body.
I love my body.

Following her conscious work with affirmations, Nancy shared the following dream that illustrates her healing work on an unconscious level.

    I am crouched in a corner, maybe scrubbing or looking for something, when I sense a presence above me. I look up and the man who is standing there says, "My God! You're beautiful! Were you born beautiful?" I am a little surprised, and in attempting to answer him I skim back over thirty years of ugly moments. Finally, however, I return to the present and my newfound view of things and decide to affirm that truth. I tell him firmly that I was born beautiful, and he nods and says, "Oh yes, I could tell!"

The possibility of actually loving your body can elicit a range of feelings. You may feel sadness from the awareness of the self-rejection and self-hatred that have come before. You may feel grief from letting go of an old ideal that you sense will never be. You may also feel relief, peace, and a growing sense of acceptance and self-love. Actually, only through self-acceptance can you stop compromising self-love. The more you accept, appreciate, love, and listen to your body, the more integrated this self-love becomes. The more self-acceptance and self-love grow, the more at ease you are in your body and the more physically attractive and beautiful you become. Self-forgiveness always activates an inner radiance that is essential to anyone's attractiveness. Self-judgments always rob you of the natural glow and the sparkle that instantly say *beautiful* to anyone who truly looks—regardless of the shape of your body and the features on your face. True beauty always comes from within.

A powerful way to start cultivating self-love and acceptance for your body is by expressing gratitude.

Exercise: Welcoming Your Body Back Home
Pause and breathe. Now bring your awareness to a part of your body that you feel good about and accept. Allow yourself to experience appreciation for this part of your body. Express your gratitude to it . . . Reflect on what a marvel your body is . . . Now bring your awareness to some area of your body that you have rejected and judged as unacceptable or unattractive. Breathe into it . . . Welcome awareness and feeling back into this part of your body . . . Allow a dialogue between yourSelf and this area. Imagine that this part of you had a voice and could tell you how it feels and what it needs from you to be happy . . . Breathe a gentle peaceful energy into this area. Allow yourSelf to send acceptance into it. Open your heart and offer that part some loving kindness and compassion . . . Go to other areas of your body, inside and out, and offer them kindness, gratitude, acceptance, and compassion . . . Breathe deeply. As you breathe out, allow yourself to release the fear of your past conditioning. As you breathe in, imagine a healing light permeating this area . . . Take the time to dialogue with all the areas of your body—asking how they feel and how you can serve them. Allow yourself to offer them gratitude, compassion, and loving kindness.

Remember to breathe . . . Allow yourself to feel whatever you feel—and remember to be gentle with yourself.

Repeat this exercise (or parts of it) frequently until your attitude toward your body becomes more friendly, accepting, and appreciative.

As you go through your day affirm:

I give myself permission to enjoy my body now.

FORGIVING YOUR BODY FOR BEING SICK

Good health, if we're fortunate enough to have it, is one of those things that most of us take for granted. If we lose it, even temporarily, it's usually a major disruption, requiring significant adjustment. Suddenly we're forced to deal with unwelcome changes, and the unknown.

With serious or chronic illness may come some or all of the stages that Elisabeth Kübler-Ross speaks of when people face death. Even if we're not at risk of physical death from a particular illness or impairment, we are faced with a passing of life as we have known it before. With certain illnesses and symptoms may come a sense of isolation, shock, and denial. You may ask, "Why me?" You may feel depressed, helpless, and victimized. You may feel betrayed by your body, and angry at it for being this way. You may make bargains with God and yourself ("If my emphysema goes away, I swear I'll never smoke again"). As your body or lifestyle change, there will be sadness and grief, mourning the loss of what was.

If you give these feelings a safe place to be allowed and acknowledged, you can begin to relate to the changes and symptoms in a healing way. Accepting your symptoms isn't a passive resignation to things not improving. It doesn't imply letting go of hope of physical recovery or not using all available medical, spiritual, and personal resources. You can accept your condition while doing what you can to heal it. Acceptance is an *active* choice. If we can be with our illness and listen to it, there are often important lessons to be learned. Even pain or illness can be purposeful. This is a perspective we are rarely taught.

The way we respond to physical pain is a metaphor of how we're taught to deal with emotional pain and suffering: run away, cover it up, numb it. Whether it's alcohol for personal problems or over-the-counter drugs for minor problems, we are trained to run from discomfort and pain. An interesting cultural commentary can be found in the large percentage of the commercials on TV that offer instant pain relief. The message is essentially that no matter what discomfort you have, get rid of it immediately. Don't look at it. Don't try to understand it. Don't see it as a potential teacher. Don't allow for life to have pain or slow you down. So, when pain does arise, we often feel hatred or scorn for the pain and for our body.

Acceptance implies that we gently and compassionately accept the weakness and frailty that comes at times with being human. Acceptance is acknowledging that, for example, "Like it or not, I have pain (or cancer, or arthritis). Now how can I most lovingly respond?" *You may not always have the power to change the circumstances, but you do have the power to change the way you respond to them.*

Forgiving the body—responding to it with kindness, listening to its message, honoring its frailties and strength—enables you to summon inner emotional and spiritual resources for healing that are always closed off by the tension created by contempt for your body. When we forgive the body for being in pain, for physical distress, for not doing what we want, the change of mind affects the body in that it will always be more relaxed. In turn, the mind becomes more at ease. The balance and harmony that ensue may even have a powerful and positive healing effect on the physical symptoms. Even if it doesn't affect the symptoms or illness, it will help you cope with the other aspects of your life.

C. INTERRUPTING A NEGATIVE FEEDBACK LOOP

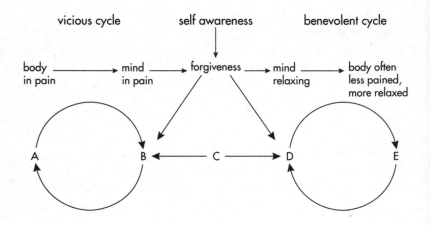

Diagram C above illustrates how the negative body/mind feed-back loop can be intercepted by awareness and transformed through forgiveness. Without awareness, A and B continue to reinforce each other and form a vicious cycle. We lose sight of how this cycle perpetuates itself. With awareness and the choice of an alternative and expanded response (C), we change the pattern: By allowing ourselves to consciously relate to the pain or illness, the mind directs the body and emotions to a healing response, such as relaxation and surrender. The stress response (B) is transformed into the healing response (D), which in turn activates the body's healing response (E). Thus the vicious cycle is replaced by a more adaptive and healthy dynamic (D/E). As the benevolent cycle from D to E gets activated, a shift in one acts to reinforce healing in the other. Even if relaxing the body and mind does not help alleviate physical pain, it will probably enable you to live with greater love, awareness, and effectiveness.

ILLNESS AS OPPORTUNITY

If you are ill and your body and physical symptoms are always seen as the problem, you lose the opportunity to gain insight into deeper personal issues that may be at the root of some symptoms. The body can become the scapegoat for unhappiness and emotional pain. This awareness is not intended to suggest that all disease has a psychological origin, nor is it intended to "blame the victim." This awareness can, however, when used with kindness and compassion, help us recognize whether some greater learning may be gained from the circumstances. When looked at in this way, certain symptoms can be an opportunity and a new beginning.

The various reactions to illness are not stages with a clear hierarchy or distinct boundaries. One is likely to move in and out of them, feeling acceptance in certain moments, victimization and anger in another, and perhaps more alive and joyful than ever before at other times. With chronic and/or degenerative symptoms, forgiving the body takes great intention, patience, and perseverance. Even if you've been a very disciplined meditator for years and live with a very high degree of awareness, it's unlikely that even then you could maintain a clear, forgiving awareness all of the time. With serious illness, fearful emotional patterns are likely to reassert themselves frequently.

As people learn to use their illness as an opportunity to grow— as any stressful life event can be—it sometimes becomes a turning point for developing a more loving and gentle relationship with oneself. Under the pressures of dealing with illness, we can discover a wellspring of inner strength and love that we were unaware of before. The initial chaos of an illness can become a healing crisis. Even though given the choice you may certainly prefer not to have a certain symptom or disease, by your willingness to work with the situation, you may discover a silver lining. The more one consciously opens to forgiving oneself and the body, the greater the possibility of going beyond even acceptance to more and more moments of personal power, peace, joy, and aliveness, regardless of whether the symptoms are there or not. As one spiritual teacher said, "No matter what kind of body it is, healthy or sick, it can be the vehicle for a great life."

This was illustrated by the contrast of two men I know with AIDS. Frank, after being diagnosed, became angry and resentful toward his body and toward life. He complained bitterly to doctors and nurses and isolated himself from his closest friends who sought to offer him love and support. Essentially he stopped "living" when he got his diagnosis, and went on to die within six months.

Joe, in contrast, decided to start living when he was diagnosed with AIDS. Before his diagnosis he had been an angry, resentful person who abused his body and frequently complained and blamed others for everything that didn't go as he thought it should. After his diagnosis he got involved in the popular work of Louise Hay and Dr. Bernie Siegel. He began taking care of his body and paying attention to his emotional needs. He made up his mind to really live for whatever time he had left. He also began reaching out to others who had AIDS. He organized healing groups and decided to live each day to the fullest, caring and loving everyone he came in contact with. For whatever reason, five years later he is still energetic and working full-time. He is helping in the AIDS community and living life to the fullest.

YOU ARE MORE THAN YOUR BODY

The part of you that can have a body, physical sensations, thoughts, and feelings without *being* them is the Self that does the forgiving. The Self is sometimes referred to as the witness, the observer, or simply as consciousness or awareness. The following exercise offers the opportunity for you to strengthen your identity with this objective aspect of the Self.

Exercise: Who/What Is Aware?
Pause and take about five minutes to do the following: Take a minute and just notice your breathing . . . Then ask yourself, Who/what is aware? . . . Now, sit quietly and simply observe your thoughts for a minute . . . Then ask yourself, Who/what is aware? . . . Then, for a minute, notice how you're feeling. Notice if your emotions and moods change . . . Then ask yourself, Who/what is aware? . . . Then become

aware of the changing sensations in your body for a few min-
utes . . . Then ask yourself, Who/what is aware of the changing sen-
sations? . . . Notice that there is a part of you that can witness and
observe your changing thoughts, feelings, and sensations . . . You can
be the observer at the same time you are experiencing the sensations,
thoughts and feelings.

You need to be in touch with yourSelf in order to forgive your
body. Like any other offering of forgiveness, the process of forgiving
your body—especially in times of pain and physical distress—must
be a conscious and deliberate choice. When you're hating your
body, it isn't until you become aware of this, and choose to relate
to your body differently, that you facilitate healing of the suffering
that has its roots in this adversarial relationship. Becoming the
witness as you did in the *Who/What Is Aware?* exercise strengthens
your ability to have anger or resistance without having it dominate
you. Then, rather than treating your body as an enemy, you can
consciously befriend it, relating to it with renewed caring and
gentleness. Anger can be a mobilizing force for healing, yet if it
persists, at a certain point it follows the law of diminishing returns.
After a while the emotional conflict may inhibit physical healing
and will certainly inhibit emotional and spiritual healing. Try to
suspend your anger, be kind toward yourself, and listen to what
your body has to say.

Exercise: Dialoging with Your Body
Take in a few deep relaxing breaths. Gently breathe into an area of your
body where there has been some pain or distress.
    With an open heart, dialogue with this area of your body or your
body as a whole. There is a tremendous intelligence within. Ask your
body: Is there something you are trying to tell me? How can I be more
helpful and loving to you? What is it you need from me? Listen to your
deepest needs as they are expressed through your body. Treat yourself
with kindness . . . and respect . . . Allow your mind to let go of judg-
ments.

Just as we have learned to identify with emotions, roles, and
beliefs as being "me," so we have identified with the body as being
"me." It is understandable that when we get sick, our primary

identification is with the illness and our body. Yet try to remember that there is also an aspect of your being that is separate and greater than just your physical body.

PAIN AND SUFFERING

Pain and suffering are not the same. Pain is the result of physical and emotional injury. Pain is felt in varying degrees by everyone. Suffering is the reaction to pain. It results from the way we relate to our pain. It is an attitudinally determined experience. It is an experience that can be negotiated and reframed. For example, menstrual cramps may be experienced as a minor discomfort. But for an infertile woman who wants to conceive, each menstrual cramp may be a reminder that she has not conceived; her cramps may be experienced as incapacitating and the source of great suffering. Similarly, the pain of labor may be experienced as manageable, even exhilarating, if one is prepared and eager for childbirth.

When you are feeling physical discomfort and pain, it may be extremely difficult to remember that you can influence your experience of suffering. Our instinctual reaction to pain is to resist, to hold our breath, and constrict our muscles. This, in turn, increases the fear and discomfort which contribute to the experience of suffering. Once again we get into the vicious cycle demonstrated in Diagram C (see page 184). The next time you experience physical discomfort, try the following:

Exercise: Working with Physical Discomfort
Remember to keep breathing. Breathe slowly, fully, and gently. On each exhalation give yourself the suggestion to ''relax.'' When you notice the physical sensations that are uncomfortable, keep breathing, instead of constricting your breath. Consciously remind yourself to relax. Rather than labeling your discomfort as pain, try to notice the different qualities of sensations: Can you feel heat? cold? tingling? stiffness? burning? Are the sensations sharp or dull? Does the sensation expand or contract? Does it move or stand still? Does it call you to respond physically?—to embrace it? Stretch away from it? Do you want to move or sit still? Does it remind you of something? Does it evoke familiar or unfamiliar emotions?
Now that you've experienced yourself in the role of objective observer,

you are invited to allow yourself to go one step further. Keep breathing gently and fully and yield into the discomfort by softening around the sensations . . . Gently let go of resistance . . . Keep releasing resistance . . . Yielding into the discomfort by softening into the sensations . . . Send kindness and love into that area. Do this for five or ten minutes at a time, if possible . . . If you can't sustain it for that long, try it for a minute. Even a brief moment of relating to the discomfort in this way will be helpful and healing.

As teacher and author Steven Levine put it, "You are responsible *to* your body, *to* your cancer, *to* your heart." Levine, who has worked extensively with people with chronic and life-threatening illnesses, says, "We suggest that people treat their illness as though it were their only child, with that same mercy and loving kindness. If that was in your child's body, you'd caress it, you'd hold it, you'd do all you could to make it well. But somehow when it's in our own body we wall it off, we send hatred into it and anger into it. We treat ourselves with so little kindness, so little softness."

Forgiving allows you to let go of repetitive comparisons to the way it used to be and to the (healthy) condition of others. "I used to be able to do so much more. Others have so much more energy than me." Comparing your body to the past and to others will keep you locked in chronic dissatisfaction, separate from the vitality that is available for you *right now*. Feeling frustrated with yourself and envious of others is normal, particularly if your symptoms or illness limits you in your work, diet, activities, sexuality, or relationships. Yet try to be aware so that your feelings don't chain you to the past, to fear, and to chronic discontent. Remember to be kind to your body and gentle with yourself, and try to focus on what you can do.

Reflect on the exercise, *Who Is Aware?* Even when symptoms are most pronounced and uncomfortable, we can sometimes experience a certain detachment from them. As one person described it, "I was not any of these experiences. I was the point of awareness watching it all." This is the incredible healing and freedom that forgiving the body can offer. It is the freedom to know that despite the fact we have an illness, it is not all of who we are. We need not be totally identified with it. You can have cancer, hypertension, colitis, asthma, muscular sclerosis, etc., yet there is a dimension to you that can simultaneously be vibrant and healthy. You can be healed while your physical body is not cured. Your body can be diseased, yet you can be at peace. It is also possible that your physical symptoms may be gone, yet you may feel fragmented, fearful, and angry. Your physical body can be cured and you may not be healed, for if most of your emotional and physical energy is invested in anger, resistance, and fear, there is little energy left to mobilize for healing.

The process of healing is much more than a change in physical symptoms. Healing occurs in those moments when we let go of fear and allow a deeper peace, as Levine says, "when we allow our minds to sink into our hearts"—in other words, when we surround our pain with love. When we consciously allow ourselves to contact our essential core, we are most able to reconnect with our innate healing capacity.

FORGIVING YOUR MORTALITY

Unless we are truly at peace with ourselves, it is difficult to forgive ourself or our body for dying. Culturally we are conditioned to fear and deny death. We live in a country where the vast majority of people die in institutions where death is feared, denied, and considered the enemy. Even dying becomes a reason for guilt, self-judgment, and self-rejection. When death is held in contempt, it is impossible to fully forgive the body, since, inevitably, all bodies will die. Forgiving your mortality doesn't imply that you will "want" to die. It does, however, help to offer peace, assurance, and courage to accept physical death when it comes. Through forgiveness we can learn that even death doesn't need to be avoided or feared.

"One can experience an unconditional affirmation of life only when one has accepted death, not as contrary to life, but as part of life" noted Joseph Campbell during his PBS *Power of Myth* series.

Forgiving yourself or others for dying raises the most fundamental questions of human existence: Who and what am I? What is death? Who and what is it that dies? As Campbell asked, "What am I? Am I the bulb that carries the light, or am I the light for which the bulb is a vehicle?" Forgiveness is a key to knowing which of these is true. In aligning with the Self, we come to know we are the light and the body is the magnificent vehicle that temporarily houses the miracle of our existence as we know it.

All major religions, despite their many differences, share the belief that within our physical body is a nonphysical, energetic reality that lives on even after the body dies. Some call it the soul, others call it the spirit. Here it has been referred to as the Self. Forgiveness teaches us that our truest and most essential identity is the Self, and the Self exists beyond death.

The apprehensions and terror that death—or thinking about death—evokes can come from guilt, "unfinished business" with loved ones, the fear of punishment after death, and the fear of letting go. Anger at oneself or others for dying can be a resistance and defense against fear, grief, and love. As we consciously let go and die to the small fearful selves in life, we heal the terror of physical death as well. Each time we forgive, we affirm life to the fullest. It is then that we discover the utter safety in letting go— letting go of the past, of constricting perceptions, of outdated concepts of who we are, of limiting ideas of what is important. When we let go of our fears of life, we can let go of our fears of death.

Every time we let go of our anger, judgments, and fears, we die to our attachment to our ego, and a little more of the boundless reality of the Self gets rooted in our conscious experience. The illusions and fears that result in constriction and that demand control and permanence are diminished or transcended.

If we can summon the wisdom and gentleness within our hearts to forgive ourselves and others for our humanity and human imperfections, it opens up the great possibility that death will be at the very least bearable and, at best, like birth, a profoundly loving, mysterious, and grace-filled transition. If we die to our restrictive small selves while living, we are given the great grace to trust even death. This doesn't mean we will want ourselves or others to die; it doesn't mean we will welcome death; it doesn't mean we won't use all available inner and outer resources to live; it doesn't mean we will not grieve, for if we love, we most certainly will grieve.

It does mean that despite all these actions and feelings, when death of the physical body calls, we will surrender to the moment at hand, letting go and trusting what comes next.

> I am not I.
>   I am this one
> Walking beside me, whom I do not see,
> Whom at times I manage to visit,
> And at other times I forget.
> The one who forgives, sweet, when I hate,
> The one who remains silent when I talk,
> The one who takes a walk when I am indoors,
> The one who will remain standing when I die.
>
> by Juan Ramon Jimenez
> translated by Robert Bly

THE BODY AS A TEMPLE FOR THE SPIRIT

Imagine the body is a vessel. If that vessel is filled with the dense, constricted energy of fear, shame, anger, resentment, and guilt, there is little room for more expansive and luminous energy such as that of compassion and love to ground within us. Forgiving ourselves and others is a way of emptying our vessel so that this radiant energy can enter and shine forth. We forgive to invite the Spirit into our being (body and mind) to fan the light of the Self within. The qualities that are an expression of the Spirit incarnate are those of the higher Self: love, compassion, faith, trust, joy, inner strength, kindness, generosity, integrity, and the like.

When we are aligned with ourSelf, our body is free to fulfill its highest and natural function as a home or temple to the Self (or soul), radiant with spirit. In moments of alignment we can experience a powerful and flowing aliveness. Gracefulness and integrity are restored. The bodymind—when in this expansive state—engages in a broader energetic relationship with life that is open and flowing while secure, present, and powerful. Whether we are anxious and constricted or loving and radiant, the body is the vehicle through which our energy is experienced and expressed in the world. Through our bodymind we express not only our less evolved human instincts but also what Abraham Maslow described as our "most species-like" qualities. Probably no other species lives with the yearning and inner urge to love, serve, and merge with something greater than itself. A body congested and constricted in anger and guilt thwarts this inner urge.

Without such aliveness at an energetic level in our body we are numbed, inhibited from a cellular, immediate, and intuitive response to the world. A cellular response understands more directly and honestly than the mind our true relationship to ourselves, others, and the universe. The more unrestricted the bodymind, the more it serves as a natural biofeedback loop, as a sensing element for truth. The Spirit thus grounded and at home in the body inspires clarity and grace.

When fear reigns and the Self is not realized with some consistency, according to the founder of Bioenergetics, Alexander Lowen, we tend to experience our body most fully below the pelvic area and above the neck. He suggests that when energy is repressed and stagnates, the body becomes a storehouse for chronic muscular tension. This tension cuts us off from the authentic experience of our emotions, power, and love. In other words, at a bodily level, we are cut off from our gut, our solar plexus, and our heart. Being out of touch with these, our reactions and actions tend to be primitive and unenlightened.

Separate from our true source of personal power, there is the tendency to relate to life passively and/or aggressively. As a result, our mind serves our fears rather than serving our heart. We become cut off from the center of our physical body and isolated from what in Eastern philosophies is referred to as the Hara—the source of power and universal energy. It is also from the Hara that we experience harmony and deep peace in the body. The energetic pulsations from the Hara become dampened by suppression of emotions and separation from the Self. Thinking we can compensate for this lack of aliveness and energy, we turn to compulsive activity and/or stimulants in the form of drugs, alcohol, coffee, etc. This is always a thwarted attempt to rebalance and compensate for the depression of the life force from which we are alienated.

Here also our sexuality, when separated from our heart, is reduced to being at the service of a primal level of gratification and release rather than a vehicle for true sharing and communion with another.

When we align with the Self we inhabit the body with an ever new aliveness. All babies have this aliveness, this rhythm, gracefulness, and spontaneity. This is often lost as the ego is developed, especially when there is a lack of dependable emotional support. The body becomes more rigid, and emotional holding patterns and armoring find static residence in different areas of the body. We shut down emotionally, mentally, physically, and spiritually. Our heart closes in the need for self-protection.

As we consciously grow and heal, there is a release from rigid constriction and armoring in the bodymind. The Spirit has room to inhabit and expand in the body, and the incredible power of gentleness, compassion, self-acceptance, love, and forgiveness is rooted or grounded in our direct experience. Faith in our fundamental goodness, worthiness, and safety are known in the body. The body armor is more porous or it dissolves, pulsations of passion and compassion flow through our heart, and we lose the fear of loving ourselves and others. Being grounded in the Spirit, we regain our innocence while growing in joy and strength. As we feel the dynamic energy of these qualities within, healing at a cellular level occurs. Simultaneously this state of expanded awareness allows us to experience a bigger, more loving reality than our small selves ever imagined.

CHAPTER ELEVEN

FORGIVENESS AND PHYSICAL
HEALING

When my friend Jack told his co-workers that he had ulcers, no one was surprised. For years Jack had been the "worry-wart" in his office, and the relationship between high anxiety and stomach ulcers is common knowledge.

What isn't as commonly recognized, however, is that anger, resentment, hostility, shame, and guilt also affect our physical well-being. Like any fear-based human reaction, feelings such as guilt and anger influence not only our mood but our physiological functioning as well. If the inner conflicts that gave rise to the anger and guilt are resolved, the body, being very resilient, will usually return to balance. If the inner conflicts aren't resolved, the body suffers.

In the last ten years or so, more and more medical research has shown that chronic anger, resentment, hostility, shame, and guilt correlate significantly with physical breakdown. However, not everyone who is habitually angry or guilty will necessarily get physically sick. Some people somaticize their emotional stress and some do not.

There is also increasing scientific evidence, primarily from the new discipline of psychoneuroimmunology, that peace of mind, joy, optimism, and love translate into measurable biochemical responses that activate an innate healing system in the body. These positive feelings always bear the fruit of emotional health, and they often nurture the healing of physical symptoms as well.

THE PHYSIOLOGY OF FEAR AND LOVE

In a highly stressful situation, have you ever felt nauseated or had diarrhea, or experienced a pounding heart or a throbbing headache? Have you ever felt your pulse racing? Have you felt that, if necessary, you could physically fight off a giant? These are some signs of the hyperarousal brought on by the fight-or-flight response first identified by Dr. Walter Cannon in 1914. The mechanism of the fight-or-flight response gives us insight into how fear, which is at the foundation of hostility, anger, resentment, shame, and guilt, affects the body.

When the fight-or-flight response is triggered, normal digestion, assimilation, and elimination functioning is altered as blood vessels to the stomach and intestines shut down. Blood flow increases to large muscle groups, the brain, heart, and lungs. Blood pressure rises, the pulse races, and heart rate increases. The biochemistry of the blood changes. There is an outpouring of stress hormones, adrenaline, and noradrenaline, and sugar and fatty acids are released into the blood, serving as fuel for muscular activity.

All these changes are healthy responses to prepare the body to take quick action for emergencies, and to fight or run away. For primitive people, this fight-or-flight response was essential for surviving the perils of living in nature among wild animals and other predators. The fight-or-flight response is still necessary today when we are required to react to short-term emergencies such as jumping out of the way of an oncoming bus. In day-to-day lives, however, we rarely need the fight-or-flight response for actual physical survival. Yet many of us still experience this physical reaction quite frequently, whether we are aware of it or not. The same changes occur in the body when we feel threatened by a remark by our boss, when we want to run the driver in front of us off the road, or punch someone out for how they look, or for what they said or did. People in routine daily encounters are often experienced as the threat, enemy, or predator.

The person or circumstance we are angry at, or threatened by, doesn't even have to be present for this response to be triggered. Because the nervous system cannot distinguish between events that are actually occurring, and ones that we relive in our mind, not only do we experience emotional and physical stress each time we get angry, but until we have resolved the anger, we experience emotional and physical stress each time we recall it.

Take a moment and see if you can recall a time when you were safe at home and awoke from a frightening dream. Recall how you felt. Perhaps your heart was racing, your shoulders and jaw muscles were tense. Perhaps you were sweating, scared, exhausted, or revved up, even though you had just been asleep.

Your nervous system didn't know that you were safe in your own bed. As far as it knew, you were in actual danger. As a result, your body was prepared to fight or escape. In the same way, when you carry resentment, reliving the fight with your boss in your mind after leaving the office, or the anger of being treated insensitively as a child, or you go over an incident where you felt victimized, feeling like a victim again and again, your nervous system doesn't know that the actual event is over. Just dwelling on an upsetting encounter from the past or an imagined conflict in the future is enough to trigger the fight-or-flight response. When we hold on to anger, the nervous system gets the signal to ready itself to fight or flee over and over again, even when there's no one to fight and no place to flee.

The damaging effects of the fight-or-flight mechanism occur when the physiological changes, designed for short-term emergencies, become a routine reflex for daily encounters. A human always revved up for the fight-or-flight response is like a car with its motor left idling at 30 or 40 mph. It's certain to run hot, wear out, and break down more frequently than the car that has a chance to rest its engine. To be healthy we all need those times of letting go of inner conflict so that the body and psyche can rest and be renewed.

How and where the body breaks down is highly individual. Of course, environment, social support, genes, and other variables are important factors, but when faced with chronic stress that we aren't skillfully coping with, each of us has a propensity to weaken or become devitalized in some way. Some of us are more vulnerable to emotional breakdown during times of stress—perhaps feeling depressed, lethargic, indecisive, or hostile. Some of us are more vulnerable to physical breakdown. Our area of vulnerability might be the joints, muscles, the respiratory system, particular internal organs, or depression in immune functioning. Symptoms might include chronic headaches, skin irritations, gastrointestinal ailments, cancer, herpes, high blood pressure, coronary heart disease, etc. Some of us are vulnerable to both emotional and physical breakdown.

In his landmark study, *Adaptation to Life,* Dr. George Vaillant of Harvard Medical School observed that the most important predictor of physical health was mental health. After analyzing the data of Harvard University alumni over thirty years, he found that men who had immature coping styles (this includes dwelling repetitively on emotional preoccupations and seeking reassurance that personal change is not necessary), had four times the incidence of illness as those who could handle the stress of daily living more maturely. When we recognize and transform potentially damaging stress reactions by working through anger, guilt, hostility, and fear, we significantly reduce our chances of becoming physically ill.

Deepak Chopra, M.D., author of *Quantum Healing: Exploring the Frontiers of Mind/Body Medicine,* writes that "when we think, we are practicing brain chemistry . . . there is no twisted thought without a twisted molecule." Chronic resentment and hostility, unhealthy guilt, and shame are all "twisted thoughts," producing physiological stress reactions. When we are stressed, peptide messenger molecules are manufactured by the brain. These transform our feelings into chemical reactions, affecting the link between the body and mind. There is a feedback loop within the body/mind that goes from one's thoughts or perceptions to one's feelings and emotions, to messages transmitted to the brain, to hormonal secretions, to cellular action in the body, back to the mind and brain. The chain reactions activated by the manufacture of peptide molecules affect the body positively or negatively, depending on the nature of the thoughts, perceptions, and feelings that initiate the process.

The use of placebos exemplifies how a hopeful, positive, optimistic emotional outlook affects the production of peptides in a positive way and activates the healing system. Hundreds of studies measuring the effects of placebos have shown that when a positive, hopeful feeling arises from an expectation that a pain or symptom will be lessened or disappear, the body responds. Positive expectations stimulate the production of peptide molecules in the form of endorphins, the body's natural pain reliever. The pain relief is real but its source is your perception and brain where the peptide molecules and endorphins are generated. Peptide molecules also have a direct effect on the immune system.

EMOTIONS AND THE IMMUNE SYSTEM

A suppressed immune system can affect our susceptibility to the common cold and the flu. It can be a factor in autoimmune diseases such as rheumatoid arthritis and lupus. It can also affect our bodies' ability to rid itself of cancer cells.

The relationship between stress and malignancy has been addressed in hundreds of articles in medical literature. Dr. O. Carl Simonton and Stephanie Matthews-Simonton, pioneers in bringing to public attention the relationship between emotional factors and cancer, first identified a key psychological trait of those prone to cancer as "a tendency to hold resentment and a marked inability to forgive." This psychological trait is certainly not present in everyone who has cancer. Yet for some, chronic resentment, especially chronically suppressed resentment, may be the most significant contributing factor in suppressing the immune system.

According to the Simontons, the healthy immune system has a natural surveillance function. When cancer cells form, as they do in everyone, the healthy immune system disposes of them and inhibits them from proliferating. Stress hormones that are triggered by anger and resentment play a part in affecting the body's normal process of ridding itself of the cancer cells. When anger is maintained and suppressed over time, the immune system becomes depressed and can't function effectively. If the immune system is where one's physical vulnerability lies, then it is here that breakdown may occur. As part of their program for healing, the Simontons encouraged finding creative outlets for expressing and healing anger and fear.

Dr. Sandra Levy, Director of Behavioral Medicine in Oncology at the Pittsburgh Cancer Institute, found that a sense of joy was the most important predictor of positive outcome of breast cancer among women. A sense of joy was even more powerful than the number and location of metastatic sites. The women's relationships with their physician and significant other were also of primary importance. The healing power of love, forgiveness, and joy can be our most potent medicine.

HOSTILITY AND HEART DISEASE

More recent reports in the medical literature recognize that the stress resulting from chronic hostility significantly impacts the incidence of heart attacks. Redford Williams, M.D., of Duke University Medical School, has brought the relationship between hostility and health to the attention of the general public in his recent book, *The Trusting Heart*. Williams writes that "scientific evidence shows that trusting hearts live longer, healthier lives." He studied the Type A personality first identified by cardiologists Meyer Friedman and Ray Rosenman.

The Type A personality has been characterized as being keenly ambitious and competitive, always in a hurry, and easily moved to hostility and anger by everyday annoyances. It was thought that the people with Type A personalities were much more prone to heart attacks and coronary heart disease than those with the Type B personality, who are more patient, less competitive, and less hostile. Williams writes, "It now seems clear that being in a hurry and being ambitious are not, taken alone, putting you at risk of having a heart attack or dying from coronary disease. . . . Hostility, anger and their biological consequences are the toxic part of Type A behavior. . . . It follows, therefore, that the most important thing you can do to decrease your coronary risk if you are a Type A person is to learn to reduce your hostility and anger." It is the quality of cynical mistrust that results in hostile conclusions about others' motivations, that sets a negative, fear-based thinking in motion.

In a study of 1,000 men with a history of heart attacks ("The Recurrent Coronary Prevention Project," conducted by Meyer Friedman), it was found that the men who learned ways to effectively reduce time urgency and hostility had a significant reduction in heart problems and a reduced mortality rate. Williams points out that reducing hostility should be beneficial in preventing a first heart attack as well.

Even though cancer and heart disease have been highlighted here, guilt and anger can impact on physical symptoms in any one of hundreds of ways. Many times the body speaks to us in metaphors in its attempt to get us to pay attention. It may be chest pains that are calling us to heed the emotional pain of a heart that won't let love in or out. Or, it may take the form of the two stories that follow: one where the muscles of a hand cripple, projecting into the body the crippling effects of guilt and dishonesty; another that tells of a woman's menstrual bleeding that won't stop because of unacknowledged guilt resulting from not wanting to have a baby out of obligation to her husband.

MICHAEL'S STORY
Michael is a thirty-six-year-old composer and musician who does competitive pistol shooting for a hobby.

About a year ago I was heavily involved in pistol shooting competitions. I had gone undefeated for about six months and was breaking all of the standing records, when one day after a match, I noticed that my wrist was hurting. The pain continued to worsen match after match until it began to affect my piano playing as well. I could no longer play octaves with my left hand, and then, after a while, I couldn't even play scales. Finally, I had to abandon both shooting and piano playing due to the pain.

At that point, I went on a search for a cure. First I went to a sports medicine orthopedic doctor, who essentially picked up my hand and said, "Oh, you've got tendinitis. Here." He threw a generic splint at me and prescribed an anti-inflammatory drug. I tried that for months, but it didn't even touch the pain. Then I went to a hand surgeon who felt I had damaged the collagen in my wrist. He in turn referred me to a hand therapist, who rediagnosed me as having tendinitis and made a custom-made, Plexiglas splint for my arm. She told me to continue taking the anti-inflammatory drugs and not to use my wrist or hand for four to six weeks. Although I was a very good patient and never so much as tried to use my wrist, the pain was untouched.

One night, I happened to go to a talk by Dr. Joan Borysenko, the noted mind-body specialist, on the topic of guilt and forgiveness. After listening to some of the case histories that she reported, I began to reflect on the circumstances surrounding the onset of the pain in my wrist. It occurred to me that around the time the pain started, I had been feeling very guilty about my shooting. I had been winning competitions so consistently that I had begun to feel a lot of pressure to stay on top. In order to do that, I had started cheating. After I started the cheating, shooting wasn't fun for me anymore, but I was stuck in a bind and couldn't seem to give it up. Right around that time, the pain began.

It occurred to me that there might be a connection here, so that night I decided to go back to shooting, sore hand and all. Only this time I would shoot very conservatively, following the letter of the rules exactly, and I would accept whatever the outcome was. Well, I was surprised to find that first of all, my scores didn't suffer at all when I went back. I won easily, which was very nice. But more surprisingly, from that night on, my hand and wrist began to feel better.

I think my body had been sending up a red flag trying to let me know that cheating was unacceptable to myself on a very deep level. Once I recognized the signal, forgave myself for falling into a trap, and rectified my behavior, my wrist healed. My wrist has now been pain free for over six months. Once again I play the piano and shoot at the pistol range with no discomfort.

For me, what was required was forgiving myself and offering myself permission to come in last in the competition if need be. Now, I feel vindicated. I feel that I'm on the right side of the competition and of my own morality.

LISA'S LETTER
My friend Lisa describes another powerful physical expression of emotional pain.

Dear Robin,
    Seeing you and reading your manuscript on forgiveness has had a profound and helpful effect on our lives.
    Lee and I have been together now for six years in relative bliss, the "relative" referring to the predictable ups and downs in a relationship, and I think we have finally come to a healthy and happy point also, in terms of Lee's relationship with my two boys. The only factor that never seems to be resolved is Lee's desire to have a child and my physical inability to get pregnant. At the point of dissolution of my first marriage, I had my tubes tied, being thirty-five and never contemplating wanting to have another child. Now, at forty-three, I am unwilling to go through the major surgery that would be required to give us the small chance of my being able to conceive again. At this late date and with a bad back and some other health complications it just doesn't seem reasonable.
    Lee accepts this but still yearns for a child. Adoption does not seem the answer for him. So sometimes the "pressure rises" and it is not always on an expressed level.
    In the two months or so before your visit, I could feel Lee moving away from me but neither of us said anything. About a month before you came I got my period and it never stopped. I thought perhaps it was the beginning of "change of life" or something, and I just went from day to day expecting the bleeding to stop.

Reading your manuscript made me realize that I had been trying in some irrational place in my soul to create a baby, despite the physical impossibility. I felt that I had to make it all right and give Lee the baby he wanted. What you wrote on forgiveness allowed me to accept myself and clearly realize that I cannot do this for Lee and that is the way it is and it's o.k. I'm o.k.! I had an open talk with him and he confirmed that wanting a baby had been on his mind a lot. I was able to say to him that I cannot do it and that I forgive myself.

The remarkable thing is that immediately after we had this conversation, I stopped bleeding, I don't mean the next day, I mean within the hour! I haven't had the problem since. We are now talking about realistic options, perhaps adoption. . . .

Knowing that your emotional state influences your physical well-being offers you the opportunity to take a look at your life when symptoms occur. With a gentle, nonjudging awareness, look to see if there are repetitive fearful thoughts, perceptions, and emotions that may be contributing to physical breakdown. Reflect on these questions: Do you feel guilty a lot? Are you bound to someone by resentment? Could you benefit from forgiving someone in your life? Is there something you need to accept or let go of? Are there old emotional wounds calling out to be healed? Is your body telling you that it's time to say "no" to certain things in your life and "yes" to others?

Rather than being a passive victim to illness, you have the opportunity to participate in the process of your healing. This includes not only getting the most effective medical attention, but it also includes getting the emotional and spiritual support that will help you to heal the pain and fear that block your awareness to your inner strength, and the faith, joy, compassion, and love that are always the ultimate healing.

BLAMING THE VICTIM

Psychological factors are not always a precipitating factor in the onset of physical symptoms—yet when they are, we are given the opportunity and signal to pay attention. The onset of illness is not always a cause and effect relationship, and the issue at hand is never a matter of blame.

Writer and philosopher Ken Wilbur has addressed the phenomenon of what he calls "new age guilt." Someone suffering from new age guilt immediately wonders, when faced with illness or misfortune, "What did I do to get this illness?" or "What did I do for this to be happening to me?" Looking to see if there is a way that you contributed to the onset of an illness can be a powerful way to blame yourself and make yourself wrong and guilty; or, it can be a powerful way to take responsibility when there is a way that you can help yourself heal. Self-inquiry should encourage self-discovery and self-renewal and a more loving, nurturing, wholesome relationship with yourself and others. Again, to truly heal, you need to look neither from a vantage point of blame and guilt, nor from the assumption that you necessarily "did anything" that caused the symptom to occur.

Self-inquiry needs to be done, as Dr. Borysenko suggests, "in the service of awareness." And pure awareness, nonjudgmentalness, and love are all ultimately the same thing. It is this spirit of awareness and self-inquiry that is the agent of healing. If you open with gentleness and love into this self-inquiry, it will always be healing, although the healing that occurs may or may not manifest in the body. True healing is first and foremost a coming to peace with yourself. By healing fear-based patterns of thinking and feeling, some people do heal physically. Some people, however, do whatever they can do to heal emotionally and physically—change their diet, take medication, exercise, visualize, meditate—and their physical symptoms remain. As Dr. Borysenko notes, "Many great spiritual teachers die from cancer and other diseases. Your emotional life can be sane and you can still get sick."

Whether or not you have physical symptoms, ill-will and sustained grievances toward yourself, others, or toward life in general are always toxic. If you look at yourself and see that certain attitudes and actions lead to animosity, separation, and fear, be gentle with yourself. Look for ways to relinquish these feelings and let them go. Know that you have the choice to work toward forgiving yourself and others. Take a leap into trusting the extraordinary capacity of your heart.

Whether or not you have physical symptoms, good will and love toward yourself and others is always healing. They heal the emotions and help to create an optimal climate for healing to occur in the body. Regardless of your physical health, love always enhances the quality of life. It helps to give us the inner strength and faith to deal with whatever life brings.

FORGIVING THE WORLD

IV

CHAPTER TWELVE

FORGIVING GROUPS:
THE MASS SCAPEGOAT REVEALED

How do you feel about Hispanics? . . . Asians? . . . Blacks? . . . Whites? . . . Jews? . . . Arabs? . . . Russians? . . . The Irish? . . . Catholics? . . . The church? . . . Men? . . . Women? . . . Doctors? . . . Lawyers? . . . Homosexuals? . . . The physically handicapped? . . . Drug addicts? . . . Ex-convicts? . . . Children? . . . The elderly? . . . Politicians? . . . Psychiatrists? . . . Marines? . . . Multimillionaires? . . . People on welfare? . . . Professional athletes? . . . French women? . . . Italian men? . . . People who are pro-life? . . . People who are pro-choice? . . . The police? . . . NYC cab drivers? . . . The homeless? . . . Feminists? . . . Chauvinists? . . .

If someone asked, "Who do you need to forgive to be at peace?" you might respond with an answer like "I need to forgive my sister, Bob, and myself." Individuals rather than entire groups would probably first come to mind. Yet just the thought of certain groups of people might activate a burning desire for retribution and revenge, make your blood pressure soar, or, on a quieter note, evoke some subtler prejudice.

~~~~~~

PAUSE   AND   REFLECT

As you look over the groups named above, do you have immediate negative reactions to any of them? Is there a particular group that you blanketly dislike? How do you feel when you interact with people from this group? Do you let past experiences determine your level of peace and goodwill? What groups, not noted above, trigger anger, hostility, or prejudice in you?

~~~~~~

Hostility, resentment, and prejudice toward entire groups of people can become such an integral part of our thinking that just bringing them to mind reflexively activates fear and separation. Even if we've never met an individual from that group, we have certain beliefs about who they are, how much we can trust them, and what we can expect from them. The identity of the group blinds us to their light.

NICOLE'S STORY

Until I was well into my thirties I didn't realize how angry I was at men. Since adolescence there had almost always been a man in my life. I *loved* men—I needed men—or so I thought. Through my own therapeutic process I discovered the many ways I had been used and abused by men since childhood. I had been sexually molested, humiliated, ridiculed, ignored, abandoned, and lied to by men since I could remember. Then I realized how many of my women friends had experienced the same fate, and my shock quickly turned to rage. I *hated* men: I hated their arrogance; their dominance in the world. I hated their limited version of human history. I hated their emotional unavailability. I hated their frequent abuse of women. While all this venom was arising I found myself married—to a man. I'm sure that he became the target for my anger—he became all men to me. I expected that his behavior would be exemplary for men; that he would transcend all sexism and cultural programming. I demanded that his behavior be so above reproach that he would make up for all the wrong done to me by men in the past.

Of course he fell short of my expectations. He was still a man. And yet as I allowed myself to soften, I was able to see more and more that inside the man was a human being; underneath the programming was another soul—and as I looked to the soul I gradually began to forgive the man. I then started feeling compassion toward other men as well.

What allowed me to begin to forgive men was seeing how isolated and alone men are in their pain. I became aware of how women support and nurture each other while men are so often in competition with each other. I saw how few men could rely on their male friends for comfort and caring when in pain.

I began to see that behind their abusive behavior was a great unspoken fear of women. I saw how many men felt helpless without a woman, and resented women as a result. I saw how insecure most men really were; how fragile their delicate egos were. I saw that hiding behind all the macho bravado were many small, frightened little boys. As I saw that more and more, I realized how insane it was to be angry at them. I started to relate to each man as an individual. And my behavior toward men began to lighten up. I realized that women only had half the accurate view of reality and that men had the other 50 percent—and that we had a great deal of healing and learning to do from each other.

SUBTLE PREJUDICE: BLATANT BLIND SPOTS

Forgiving groups, like forgiving individuals, can be done on many levels. We may hold subtle prejudices toward people of certain nationalities or professions, or feel more blatant hostility or hatred toward perceived national, ethnic, racial, ideological, or political "enemies." As with our more personal enemies, when we are hostile or prejudiced toward a particular group, fear and projection dictate our perceptions and we are blinded from seeing who and what the "enemies" really are. The true motivation for enmity isn't seen, and as a result, the potential for peace is thwarted.

The most subtle level of forgiving groups occurs when we transform prejudice that doesn't necessarily engender overt anger; nonetheless, this prejudice steals away the moment at hand—and with it the possibility for seeing clearly or relating with an open heart. Prejudice determines our expectations and experiences, because we assume each person of a particular group will behave in a certain way. We relate to an abstraction rather than to an individual human being. For instance, if you are planning a trip to Paris and a friend says, "Watch out for the French. They're so rude and they hate Americans," you might feel suspicious and defensive of all French people. You make foregone conclusions and assume the worst.

This kind of stereotype often comes from someone's actual experiences. If you see numerous people belonging to a particular group behave in a way that you perceive as negative, you're likely to make negative generalizations about everyone in that group. If these generalizations or prejudgments aren't held up to the light of awareness, they're sure to foster an uneasy, defensive posture in all future interactions. This psychological posture keeps us separate from ourSelf and nurtures a self-fulfilling prophecy. What we think and project is what we help to create. Sometimes the fear and anxiety we feel in an interaction is a sound and relevant signal to pay attention. Yet in everyday circumstances, more often than not, it is a defense against the truth of who We are and who the other individuals are.

As with individuals, once we have decided the shortcomings and faults of another group, we unconsciously adopt a process of selective perception. We only see what is consistent with the judgments we have already made. Because "they" are all like this, we can assign blame, rationalize, and justify our position. This dynamic often plays itself out among hostile nations. As Sam Keen, author of *Faces of the Enemy: Reflections of the Hostile Imagination*, wrote, "The problem [of resolving conflict and stabilizing peace] seems to lie not in our reason or our technology, but in the hardness of our hearts. Generation after generation, we find excuses to hate and dehumanize each other, and we always justify ourselves with the most mature-sounding political rhetoric . . . We are driven to fabricate an enemy as a scapegoat to bear the burden of our denied enmity. From the unconscious residue of our hostility, we create a target; from our private demons, we conjure a public enemy."

P A U S E   A N D   R E F L E C T

Once again bring a group to mind toward whom you have adverse feelings. Reflect on what it is about this group that scares you. Do you imagine that every individual in this group embodies the qualities you fear? For the next week, if you see a person from this group, remind yourself that this person has a unique self. Try to imagine what this person might feel and what their life might be like.

Forgiving groups requires the willingness to see beyond preconceptions; to see each individual in a particular group anew. In the example of going to France, it would mean giving each French person with whom you interact the gift of acknowledging their potential for kindness, rather than assuming they would greet you with a less-than-helpful response. It means that you put aside your prejudice in order to discover the good feelings and goodwill that can come from creating the relationship freshly. In forgiving, prejudice stops with you.

Hating, blaming, and rejecting a group of people ensures that we don't have to take the risk or responsibility of looking more honestly at the individuals who make up the group, and at our deeper feelings. It makes it easier to carry on a story line that proves that our past perceptions about the group are currently accurate and that they will be accurate for the future as well. Hostility toward a whole group depersonalizes everyone in it. There are no eyes to look into. There are no individual souls to relate to. There is just a collective blank face and no heart pulsing with life and possibility.

Exercise: Heart to Heart
*Take a minute and listen to what the beating of your heart sounds
like . . . Now think of a group toward whom you hold some prejudice
or hostility. Take a minute and allow the actual face of someone from
that group to come to mind. Imagine what the beating of their heart
sounds like . . .*
  *Now imagine you are in a place where you feel safe with this person.
Imagine looking into their eyes . . . Imagine that you are looking into
each other's eyes. Remember to breathe . . . Imagine that at least for a
few minutes you are both willing to see beyond each other's appearances . . . Listen as they tell you their fears . . . Imagine they really
want to understand you . . . Tell them why you fear them . . . Once
again, listen to the beating of your hearts . . .*

  If you are willing to forgive, you first need to remember that
every group is made up of individuals. They are individuals who
have a heart and who have their own fears and conditioning that
have fueled their motivations and actions. Like you, each has his
or her wounded parts and an instinct for healing and caring—
even though some may be too unconscious, too scared, too hurt,
or too pained, and therefore too shut down, to access their Self at
a particular time.
  Some individuals may substitute a personal identity with an
aggressive group ego out of fear and for a sense of belonging. Some
may lack the awareness, self-love, and courage that it takes to
break away from their group identity even when it is one that lacks
integrity.
  Forgiving groups, like other kinds of forgiveness, doesn't mean
that we don't take specific action to change a course of events. For
instance, because we forgive a nation, it doesn't mean that we, as
a nation, eliminate all existing weapons and dismantle the military
as a show of good faith—for, in reality, there are obviously peoples
and leaders of nations who, disowning their own anger and inner
conflicts, have a need to project it outward, often in the form of
military might. With groups, as with individuals, forgiving is not
about what we do; it is about where we come from in thought
and action. By forgiving, we participate in ways that contribute to
positive and peaceful outcomes.

DICK'S STORY

For many years, especially during the Cold War era, Americans and Soviets held each other in contempt, fearful of the other by virtue of their country of origin. The following account was shared by Dick, an American physician who volunteered his medical expertise in Armenia a few days after the earthquake in December 1989.

Here we were, Michael and I, in a town named Spitak in northern Armenia shortly after the devastating earthquake. We were in the "land of the enemy." Soldiers in gray coats were patrolling. Army vehicles were everywhere. The day before in Yerevan we had seen tanks in the main square. We recalled the images of the Red Army, the intercontinental ballistic missiles, and of Nikita Khrushchev threatening to bury America. We found that in the Red Cross tent we had been working with members of the Communist party.

Late that night we were talking with our new colleagues in bits of Russian, French, and English. The temperature outside was well below freezing and the mountain winds were fierce as they tore at the flaps of our tent. As we huddled around a small stove, we became aware that the images we had held of one another as children evaporated almost instantaneously. We realized that the stereotypes had melted away. We had begun to depend on one another. We had begun to trust one another. One of our new friends reflected, "If our leaders should ever ask us to hate one another again, it would simply be impossible."

MASS OPPRESSION AND GENOCIDE: CAN ONE EVER REALLY FORGIVE?

What is forgivable for one person may be unforgivable for another. There are some circumstances, such as genocide (the systematic destruction of one people by another) or oppression (the institutionalized denial of basic rights and freedoms), where one may be unwilling to consider forgiving, much less choose it. Groups who have been victimizers and victims, oppressors and oppressed, offer another challenge of forgiveness work. This would include groups like blacks forgiving whites; Tibetans forgiving the Chinese; Jews forgiving the Nazis. Here it may feel much, much tougher, if not impossible, to forgive.

Imagine you are a member of a particular group whose people have been the object of genocide, oppression, brutality, harassment, and/or discrimination. (Perhaps this has been your experience and you don't have to make it up.) The idea of forgiving the "enemy" group may trigger enormous resistance. You may think, "If I forgave, I would be betraying myself, my culture, friends, ancestors, and family. If I forgave, I would be part of the problem. If I forgave, I would be condoning all that is against human dignity. If I forgave, I would be condoning evil. If I forgave, I would be letting history repeat itself; nothing would ever change. If I forgave, I would forget."

These are clearly extremely powerful reasons not to forgive. If we believe any of these are true, with good reason, we would hold firm to anger and a position of maintaining the enemy. Paradoxically, however, *if we don't learn to forgive, then history will continue to repeat itself.* It's *not* forgetting that causes us to relive the inhumanities and atrocities of the past. We haven't forgotten anything, and we continue to have the atrocities throughout the world that we have had for centuries. There continues to be apartheid, genocide, and war. There continues to be incest, child beating, rapes, and murders. Until we learn to forgive—not condone, not turn our back on, not go numb on, not forget—but forgive, we will be run by our pain and anger. We will attack and defend. And what's most insidious is that our anger will make attack appear reasonable and righteous. We will be in pain and project our pain outward. We will be the initiators of more pain, the perpetrators of more separation; more us and them; more subject and object. We will not learn the lessons that history has to teach.

Forgiving groups, as with forgiving anyone, doesn't imply that you shouldn't feel angry, or whatever you're feeling. It doesn't imply that groups should not be held accountable for their actions. To do otherwise would often be neglecting the highest interest of everyone. During the week of April 15, 1990, the newly elected

East German government made international headlines with one of its first official acts: The government of East Germany acknowledged the responsibility for the Nazi Holocaust and asked forgiveness of all the world's Jewish people and specifically of the nation of Israel. Accepting an invitation of this nature may be a very, very bold choice, but one of its rewards is that it helps one heal from perpetually being emotionally victimized by a past one has not chosen.

The possibility of forgiving Nazis or other blatant oppressors who would be considered evil by many brings us to look at how we understand evil. As scientist and philosopher Gary Zukav in his best-selling book, *The Seat of the Soul,* explains:

> Evil needs to be understood for what it is: the dynamic of the absence of Light. Understanding that evil is the absence of Light doesn't mean that it is inappropriate to respond to evil.
> What is the appropriate response to evil?
> The remedy for an absence is a presence. Evil is an absence and therefore, it cannot be healed with an absence. By hating evil, or one who is engaged in evil, you contribute to an absence of Light and not to its presence. Hatred of evil does not diminish evil, it increases it . . . A compassionate heart is more effective against evil than an army. An army can engage another army, but it cannot engage evil. A compassionate heart can engage evil directly—it can bring light where there was no light . . .

Forgiving groups, Zukav points out, doesn't imply passivity, shirking social responsibility, or hesitating to come to another's aid. As we view evil in this way we see that we don't have to be hateful to be passionate about changing forms and structures. It was not the hatred of evil but the love for truth and justice that fueled Gandhi and the Reverend Martin Luther King. Tensin Gyatso, the Dalai Lama exiled from Tibet, and Desmond Tutu, archbishop of Cape Town, South Africa, are present-day social activists and spiritual leaders whose peoples are the victim of severe oppression, yet who are deeply committed to change and deeply committed, despite the daily abuse and oppression of their people, to letting love and nonviolence guide their social and political action.

Catherine Ingram, author of *In the Footsteps of Gandhi: Conversations with Spiritual Social Activists*, interviewed both the Dalai Lama and Desmond Tutu.

The Dalai Lama is head of the Tibetan people, who since 1948 have suffered genocide, religious persecution, forced labor, political imprisonment, and torture at the hands of the Chinese government. Despite the suffering and atrocities that his people have been and are subjected to, the Dalai Lama holds no anger toward the Chinese, believing they are "misguided people." Ingram describes the Dalai Lama's attitude as "one of incredible kindness, even toward the Chinese government, who would like him dead." He describes the Chinese as "my friends, the enemy."

Desmond Tutu prays every day for the leaders of the white South African government that maintains the injustice and oppression of apartheid. He has committed his life to working to end apartheid, yet, as Ingram points out, "he counsels forgiveness and understands that 'oppression dehumanizes the oppressor as well as the oppressed.' "

People like the Dalai Lama and Desmond Tutu who have lived through the horrors of genocide and oppression have as much justification as anyone would need to hate and harbor ill-will forever. In situations like these, one may never forgive certain *behaviors* or *acts*—while being willing to forgive *people*.

To forgive in situations like these is a remarkably bold choice, one that may initially be far more difficult for many than the obvious choice to hate. Yet a decision to forgive diminishes the aggressors' power to completely make one their victim. Forgiving is, paradoxically, a way of "fighting back" because it is refusing to accept hatred as any solution.

If you are identified with a group whose general attitude is angry, your own anger may ensure your allegiance and acceptance into that group—be it with your family, a particular community, or a larger political or national group. Because anger sometimes buffers us from feelings of despair or hopelessness, and because it may motivate us for needed action, perpetual anger may be perceived as natural and necessary. As a result, members of a group may be invested in staying angry. If you take the risk of forgiving, it may mean that you lose the acceptance of that group. Or, on the brighter side, your forgiveness could awaken new awareness and compassion in others in your group as well.

Forgiving frees us from the bane of hating and spiritual oppression. As an ancient book of Chinese wisdom counsels, "hatred is a form of subjective involvement by which we are bound to the hated object." Hate ultimately cripples. It fuels a sense of threat, which in turn creates a cycle of defense, attack, and revenge that the ego always sees as justified.

Forgiveness offers the way out of this vicious cycle. It emancipates us from being fear's slave. Forgiveness teaches us that under behavior that appears heartless, there is a heart; beyond actions that do not have an iota of redeemable value, there is a soul of value. Yet again, at a personality level, some may be so constricted and fearful as to be starkly disconnected from these realities.

Forgiving requires that we acknowledge the personal and collective fear that motivates destructive action. Forgiveness is an act of true seeing. It is exercising the vision that we are given to see beyond even the sickest of appearances. It is the knowledge that the essential Self of everyone, however buried, has not exceptions. It allows us to go forth strong in this knowledge, armed with the power of clarity, strength, and dignity. Forgiveness allows the weapons of attack to be laid down and the walls of defensiveness to be dismantled. Forgiveness gives us the clarity to differentiate the past from the present while offering us hope for the future.

CHAPTER THIRTEEN

FORGIVENESS, GOD, AND GRACE

People have long pondered the nature of God: Is there a power greater than ourselves? Does God exist? Who and what is God? Can we know God? Is God only external to us or does God live within us as well? Are we all made in the image of God? Is God benevolent? Is God punitive? Is God omniscient? Is God all-sustaining? Does God create famine and war? Why does God let children suffer and die? If there is a God, what kind of God would permit the seemingly senseless evil and violence that exists in the world?

How we come to our relationship with God, and what our expectations are in this relationship, are very personal matters. For some, this relationship may be a continuation and projection of childhood experiences with parents. God may be thought of as the "Super-parent." If your parents were critical, harsh, and communicated a lot of "shoulds" and "should nots," God may be perceived as a judge who watches every move while keeping score.

My friend Susan grew up in a very religious household. She

was taught to memorize Bible passages before she could even read. One of the first that she memorized was the twenty-third Psalm— the one that starts out with "The Lord is my Shepherd . . ." When she got to the verse that reads "Surely goodness and mercy will follow me all the days of my life," she thought it meant "Shirley Goodness and her friend Mercy will follow me all the days of my life." As Susan described it, "The prospect of two wizened hooded women following me around and telling God everything I did wrong loomed over me long after I learned what the verse truly meant. My God was a suspicious tyrant who had spies out following innocent people around and reporting on them to Him!" Even as an adult, it is difficult for Susan to think of God as benevolent or loving.

Depending on your religious training, God may be perceived as critical, wrathful, or loving and sustaining. Your experience of God may be intellectual, or it may be a spiritual sense that by its very nature cannot be wholly defined.

ANGER AND BETRAYAL

If your notion of God is that of someone in the heavens who is all-powerful, all-knowing, all-merciful, *and* always in control, you may be among those who have tremendous difficulty reconciling some of the horrific things that happen in life with your concept of God. How do you forgive a God who allows us to despair? Where is the bestower of mercy when bad things happen to good people?

If you consider yourself an agnostic, your feeling about God may pose no dilemmas. If you believe there is no convincing evidence for or against the existence of God, you are likely to be in neither a dependent nor an expectant position. Without expectations, there will be no anger. Similarly, if you consider yourself an atheist you would not feel anger toward something or someone that doesn't exist.

You may believe "God is dead," having set the world in motion and then abandoned us to an irrational, chaotic human destiny. In this case you may feel very angry at God. There is also a subset of atheists who may rage at God while repudiating God's existence. A believer whose young child dies, for example, may not be able to reconcile this event with a loving God. Feeling angry and devastated, he or she decides there is no God. This sudden denial and rejection of God might also happen when illness strikes, natural catastrophes occur, or when we are confronted with difficult and frightening circumstances that are beyond our control. There are those who have an ongoing adversarial relationship with their God. Picasso, for instance, was tormented because he perceived God as malicious and cruel. For a few, like Picasso, there is a degree of anger projected onto God that becomes emotionally and spiritually devastating.

If we believe God exists and is a benevolent force who will take control of outer circumstances, guard us from the trials of human existence, shield us from death, loss, sickness, and pain, and fulfill all our hopes, then conflict in our relationship with God is inevitable. When we encounter difficulties or when life seems to lose its meaning and purpose, we will certainly feel betrayed and angry.

"To be angry at God means we have a false God. We are worshiping an idol. To be angry with God implies we have placed God in a position that God never intended to be. This is the all-powerful superman," says the Reverend Dajad Davidian, pastor of St. James Armenian Church in Watertown, Massachusetts. However, he continues, "to be angry can be good, it can be creative in that it can be the thing that helps us to demolish our false images of God. These moments of anger and suffering can destroy our preconceptions. They can force us to go deeper into our faith to seek to understand, to question, to quest. In these moments of anger at God are potential moments of breakthrough and growth."

Many of the dynamics involved in forgiving God are the same as those involving family and friends. As long as we are angry at God, the source of unhappiness and strife is always outside ourselves. Anger puts the blame on God and places the ultimate responsibility for our peace and happiness elsewhere. It absolves us of the responsibility of coming to an acceptance of what is or what was and moving on with our life.

If you are angry and unwilling to let go of anger toward God, you are getting something from holding on. If this is the case, it may be useful to review the section on secondary gains in Chapter One.

After many weeks of working with the issues of forgiving, one of the forgiveness-class participants came to the conclusion that she was angry at God. Several weeks after the class ended she wrote, "We are not really angry at God. We are angry at ourselves because we have not mastered our divinity yet. Impatience and anger are the same. Our divinity is realized through forgiveness. It is the unconditional love for ourselves that we are seeking. Forgive self = Forgive God. They are the same."

As with anger projected toward anyone else, there are many inner feelings that we can avoid acknowledging and responding to if we keep our focus on blaming God. Like the class participant just mentioned, we can avoid dealing with the impatience and self-condemnation that we may feel toward ourselves. We can avoid dealing directly with sadness, disappointment, loss, and the fear that can come from not having control over our circumstances.

Perhaps our perception of God can be expanded by the following perspective: As the Reverend Davidian sees it, "God is not a noun, but a verb. God is not only love but the active evolutionary process, and like any evolutionary process, it is not measured. It happens sometimes in quantum leaps and sometimes these leaps are experienced as very chaotic."

FORGIVING GOD

Implicit in forgiving God is an acceptance of forces in the universe that are part of the great mystery of life, which we cannot ultimately understand, control, or predict. In order to forgive God we must go beyond the image of God as Big Daddy and ourselves as helpless children.

We can forgive God when we let go of our rigid ideas of what life is "supposed to be" and enter into a relationship with God that is both accepting *and* co-creative. Then we look for ways to embrace life in its totality and to make the most of every situation.

When we are co-creators we become conscious of living the questions: How do I undermine love and peace in my life? How can I bring love and integrity to my relationship with myself, others, and all of nature? How can I summon my loving will? Out of our willingness to live these questions, our will and Divine Will become one. The philosopher Heidegger wrote, "A person is not a thing or a process but an opening through which the Absolute can manifest."

When we can trust in the midst of hardship and chaos, there lies our healing. All humans have an innate need, conscious or not, to connect with something greater than themselves. An integral aspect of spiritual growth involves responding to this innate need. Biblical scholar Walter Brueggemann writes about how this issue of trust in God is a reciprocal one. In his essay "The Trusted Creature," Brueggemann wrote, "What God does first and best and most is to trust His people with their moment in history. He trusts his people to do what must be done for the sake of his whole community."

To forgive God is ultimately to forgive ourselves—to accept that we don't have the power to alter some circumstances, as well as to accept that part of us that does have the love, strength, wisdom, vision, and courage to work with what is. Clearly the nature of reality is such that our outer security will be shaken again and again. There are often no absolute answers to our specific dilemmas, yet there is an absolute love; God is perfect in this way. If we open to this love and let it into our hearts, it will illuminate the way for us and give us the strength for whatever happens.

We are here to love and to bring love into every area of our lives. Love is our nature, and when we live from the fullness of ourSelf we forgive and know that we are forgiven. The more we let go of the reality that we have made up where we have created enemies, and the more we live from who we truly are, the more we move beyond even the need for forgiving.

Choosing love and choosing forgiveness, be it toward God, ourselves, or others, is the choice for living in heaven now—on earth now.

THE GRACE TO FORGIVE

To this point we have viewed forgiveness as a conscious choice, an intentional decision to see things differently—and in most day-to-day situations, it is. There are, however, situations when the ability to forgive is unmistakably given to us. In these moments of grace we are enabled to do what we may feel unable to do through personal volition or conscious choice.

When forgiving happens as a result of grace, we experience the power of something greater than our small selves directing and working through us. The source of this grace and power may be experienced as coming from a manifestation of a higher power (one's higher Self, God, Goddess, the Holy Spirit, Jesus, a guru, a spiritual teacher, etc.). Whatever the name of the source, when it happens there is no question that one feels the power and presence of some higher or divine intervention.

Even if we feel we can't forgive, if we are sincerely open to healing, we attract grace into our life. Praying can help us to open to grace. If you want to forgive and find yourself unable to, try asking for help. Grace often comes when we have prepared the way, when there is this conscious desire to grow and be receptive to love's voice.

AMY'S STORY

Amy is a forty-three-year-old woman who after years of anger and turmoil in her relationship with her husband, emotionally hit bottom. To Amy, there seemed no place to turn at that point except to God. In her despair, she sought forgiveness and prayed for the strength to forgive.

The first incident of infidelity (that I knew of) was only a year after we were married. I was devastated. I'd never felt such deep loss, sadness, betrayal, and abandonment. Then came my anger and disgust, I was as afraid of my own emotions as I was of losing my husband. So I did the only thing that I knew how to do at the time, we "made up" and I went dead inside. Emotional deadness was my main defense against future betrayals, my protection, and, at the same time, a way that I could get even with him. I would control the love and affection I had so innocently given before, and give only when he had proven that he deserved it.

What followed was many years of extramarital affairs and relationships, mostly on his part, but on mine as well. And we continued to live with it and avoid it at the same time. Through all of this, however, my emotional deadness became more and more intense, yet I tried desperately to save the marriage.

Eventually I woke up. I realized how bad it had become. He had settled in with one woman as his "other wife." He would not leave her, despite my threats to leave him. Finally, all my rationales for trying to make an impossible situation work no longer made sense. "For the sake of the business"— the business was almost bankrupt. "For the sake of the marriage"—it had become public knowledge and a source of extreme humiliation and embarrassment to me that our relationship was a threesome. "For the sake of the children"— I finally realized that what my children were seeing most from me in this relationship with their father was a cold and unfeeling woman who occasionally exploded into hysterical rage. They would see him verbally degrade and berate me, sometimes becoming physically violent.

I finally had to admit that I was powerless to change this situation, to change him, to adjust my behavior to accommodate his emotional demands, to make it all better. I couldn't do it. I gave up. I truly gave up. It was so bad it couldn't have gotten any worse, and I had reached my limit. I remember vividly sitting in my bedroom after another terrible incident and saying to myself that "I give up." And then I prayed, I asked God to help me because I couldn't stand it anymore. My words spoken alone and out loud were a tearful and cathartic admission of my own failure and my own accountability for my part in the entangled mess that was our relationship. It was an admission that my spirit had died along the way. A confession that I had somewhere lost my loving and capable self into the morass of confusion.

It was at this point that I asked for forgiveness. I asked for God's forgiveness and for me to be able to forgive myself. It came immediately, like a calming presence brought on by a gentle wind that swept through me. Somehow, I was lifted out of myself to a different and new perspective on the years of struggling I'd been through to make an impossible situation work. In this moment it felt possible to love myself and forgive myself for my countless failures.

My next thoughts were toward my husband, whom I had blamed and resented for all these years. Somehow my forgiving perspective gave me eyes to see his life and struggles and his own helplessness in dealing with me and all the conditions of his life. I was filled with compassion and understanding. My heart felt full and open and I was able to say "I forgive you." He didn't have to be there. I knew I forgave him completely and felt tremendous love for him in that moment.

From this point in time and experience, I felt that I was standing on different ground. I knew that I was free from reacting to the events and failures of the past. This was the beginning of my own healing process and the end of the destructive influence of the relationship. The deadness I had experienced for years was replaced with a full range of feelings and emotions. I felt alive again.

Over the next months and years, from this growing awareness, I was able to discern and communicate what I needed and wanted out of our relationship and that which was unacceptable to me. I was able to define limits and propose options. I was, in time, able to face the fact that our marriage was over and all the emotions that accompanied the separation, divorce, and re-creating family life with our children out of brokenness. For the first time in years I felt positive about the future. By forgiving him I've realized that I became free within myself. It's a simple practice, but not always easy. But I've learned that as I forgive, I am forgiven, and in this practice I find the peace, compassion, and gratitude that always bring me home to myself.

When we are aligned with ourSelf, we touch an enduring source of love and wise counsel. Yet whenever we find ourselves mired in conflict, despair, and frustration, like Amy, we may be temporarily out of touch with this source. By acknowledging our present limitations and sincerely seeking guidance, we create the openness to reconnect once again. For Amy, "giving up," "feeling powerless," and admitting that she had lost herself along the way were steps on the path to surrendering to grace. She prayed out loud asking for God to help her, and in her surrender she took responsibility for her part in "the tangled mess."

Even in our surrender, we may not get an answer immediately. Delay is not denial. Sometimes to feel the working of grace, faith and patience are required. If we ask with an open heart and a sincere desire to receive, grace will come in some form to further our healing.

CORRIE'S STORY

The following story of Corrie Ten Boom offers another powerful demonstration of how forgiveness can be given even when we feel we cannot forgive of our own free will. Her heart assured her that everyone is forgivable, yet she couldn't seem to access what was needed for forgiving to be authentic.

The story of Corrie Ten Boom and her family is told in her book *The Hiding Place*. Corrie, her sister Betsy, and the rest of her family played a key role in the Nazi resistance in Holland. The Ten Booms were devout Christians who, because of their loving spirit, provided care, food, strength, and a place to hide for as many Jews fleeing Hitler's forces as they possibly could. Discovered by the Nazis, the entire Ten Boom family was sent to the concentration camps for years. Like others, they were subjected to the most inhumane conditions. Corrie's father and sister died in the camps. Corrie survived and, despite having lived through the most horrendous of circumstances, went on to teach the message of faith in God's abiding love—as she and Betsy had done in the camps whenever they got the chance.

It was at a church service in Munich that I saw him, the former S.S. man who had stood guard at the shower room door in the processing center at Ravensbruck. He was the first of our actual jailers that I had seen since that time. And suddenly it was all there—the roomful of mocking men, the heaps of clothing, Betsy's pain-blanched face.

He came up to me as the church was emptying, beaming and bowing. "How grateful I am for your message, *Fraulein*," he said. "To think that, as you say, He has washed my sins away!"

His hand was thrust out to shake mine. And I, who had preached so often to the people in Bloemendaal the need to forgive, kept my hand at my side.

Even as the angry, vengeful thoughts boiled through me, I saw the sin of them. Jesus Christ had died for this man; was I going to ask for more? Lord Jesus, I prayed, forgive me and help me to forgive him.

I tried to smile, I struggled to raise my hand. I could not. I felt nothing, not the slightest spark of warmth or charity. And so again I breathed a silent prayer. Jesus, I cannot forgive him. Give me Your forgiveness.

As I took his hand the most incredible thing happened. From my shoulder along my arm and through my hand a current seemed to pass from me to him, while into my heart sprang a love for this stranger that almost overwhelmed me.

And so I discovered that it is not on our forgiveness any more than on our goodness that world's healing hinges, but on His. When He tells us to love our enemies, He gives, along with the command, the love itself.

A Course in Miracles states that we live in a perpetual state of grace—an aspect of the love of God. Grace is experienced when judgment and hatred are lifted from our experience. It is the acceptance of love within a world that has much fear. Grace lifts us up, shows us the truth, and, as these personal stories demonstrate, puts us back down on solid ground.

ALYSIA'S STORY
There are times when we may not consciously ask for help to forgive, yet the grace of the power to forgive spontaneously arises anyway.

I was fifteen when I first experienced the incredible power of forgiveness. Every night my dad would come home and bend my ear over a couple of beers, telling me stories about his youthful sexual exploits. I dreaded it. I feigned interest when what I really wanted to say was, "You're a dirty old man and you have no business telling a young girl these kinds of stories." His first sin was having lived such a raucous life. The second was enjoying the telling of it, especially to me. I had the dreams of every young girl. I wanted to fall in love and have sex be part of the sweetness and foreverness I envisioned. I didn't tell him this. I didn't know how to formulate my thoughts into words, and he was not asking my opinions anyway.

One night as we sat down for our ritual, and he began his spiel, I had my usual reaction of "Oh no! Do I really have to listen to this again?" Then there came a thought. I call it the little voice or nowadays the Holy Spirit. Whatever you call it, it works. The thought said, "Try listening this time." Huh? Hadn't I been doing that?

So I listened and this time the listening was different. I stopped resisting, and listened. There was an opening up in my mind as judgment was placed aside. All of a sudden I wasn't a young girl having her dreams trampled on. I was a rake and a rogue, an alley cat on the prowl, a love 'em and leave 'em Romeo, dashing about, falling into dark places where I had no business being, reaping the consequences nonplussed. Through it all a sense of adventure prevailed. I was full of charm and wit and the ladies loved me, one and all. Dad was yucking it up, and for the first time, I found myself laughing with him. Then he looked into my eyes and there was a great silence. He stared at me. I stared at him. For the first time he saw a real person looking back at him. For the first time, I saw a real person looking back at me. He wasn't just a dad anymore. He glanced away, but not before I caught a glimpse of guilt laced with fear. I don't think he'd ever been admired for being a rogue before. We had joined for the first time and nothing would be the same again. When he glanced away I was still staring transfixed in wonder about my inner journey with him. He met my eyes again. I asked him to tell me another story. He said that was about it. He never told me another sexual story.

I don't think I was alone that night. I think a young girl needed help and received it without making any real efforts to get it.

In Alysia's story, grace removed the barrier that had separated her heart and mind from her father's. As grace intervened, Alysia found herself spontaneously sharing her father's experiences and the aliveness these experiences had given him. Her father no longer was experienced as a contemptible "other." For a few amazing moments, Alysia and her father were truly connected, and in that connection was their healing.

LINDA'S STORY
Linda Mark's story comes from her book *Living with Vision: Reclaiming the Power of the Heart.*

When I was sixteen, a violent experience turned my life around . . . I was attacked in my own neighborhood at night as I walked home from work. The experience was surrealistic, as though I was in the audience in a comfortable seat watching myself play the starring role of victim in a drama.

The moment of truth occurred as my attacker attempted to strangle me. I had used up all my physical and mental ability to stop him. My life was on the line. I had to make a choice: Would it be to live? I didn't know. Then a voice inside of me screamed, "I want to live!" "Let go," another voice said. I let go. "All right, God. All right," I surrendered. "If I live, I'll own my purpose. I'll embrace it. I'll live. I'll really live!" Out of the silence came an inner voice. "Forgive him!" instructed the voice. Without a moment's hesitation, without thinking, I found myself telling the man, "I forgive you," speaking calmly, offering peace and love.

As soon as I spoke, my attacker burst into tears. "I don't want to do this," he moaned. "I don't have a choice." He told me I was not his first victim. He had been in jail for murder and rape. He'd escaped prison, but life had no escape. While strong and brutal, he was also delicate, fragile, broken. He had nowhere to turn.

For a moment there was silence, just silence, he was breathing deeper as he lightened his hold. I wondered if it was over. No sooner had I thought I might be free than his mood changed back to violent anger. As he prepared to beat me once more, I again let go inwardly. At that moment a car came driving down the alley where we were. My attacker ran off into the darkness. I had been given the gift of life a second time.

As with Amy, Corrie, Alysia, and Linda, grace appears to be augmented by a certain humility and surrender. If there are people whom you have great difficulty forgiving, even though you want to forgive them, praying and listening for guidance may be powerful ways to make the seemingly impossible real. Even though we already live in grace, we often need to invite an awareness of it into our lives to experience what is already given.

WAYS TO OPEN TO GRACE

Prayer There are many forms of prayer. One form entails dialoguing with a higher power by expressing your truths, fears, and concerns; asking for help; quieting yourself and listening with your whole being for guidance; and being receptive to healing in whatever form it comes.

Meditation As with prayer, there are many forms of meditation. All forms of meditation are a process of emptying of one's preconceptions, going beyond the chatter of the mind in order to center oneself. The following are two commonly used forms of meditation: (1) Find a time and place to be quiet. Then focus your attention on the movement of your breathing and simply be aware of the changing sensations in your body as you breathe in and out. Whenever your attention wanders from an awareness of the breath, simply note that your awareness has wandered, and gently escort your attention back to the moment-to-moment awareness of the changing sensations in your body once again. (2) Focus on the repetition of a spiritual or neutral phrase as you breathe in and out. Synchronize the word or phrase with your breathing—for example, on each out breath repeat the phrase, "I am calm and peace." Depending on your personal preference, examples of other words or phrases you can use for repetition are "Hail Mary, full of grace," "Shalom," "I Am," "Om," "May all beings be at peace."

Gratitude Using gratitude to invite grace into one's awareness is a process of identifying and expressing thanks for the blessings in our lives. You can do this directly to people or to a higher power.

Nature Spend time in nature and allow yourself to experience the awe and wonder of it.

Service Allow yourself to serve others selflessly—without seeking external reward or recognition. This is particularly useful when serving someone less fortunate than yourself.

Creative expression When you give yourself permission, without judgment, to be creative through any art form, you may open to what artists call inspiration, which is the inflow of grace.

When I reflect on the idea of grace, I am reminded of reading the story of twenty-nine-year-old Steven McDonald, a tall and athletic New York City policeman who was senselessly shot while on routine duty one day. At the time his wife was pregnant with their first child. He now lives as a quadriplegic who will breathe through a respirator for the rest of his life. Throughout his healing he called on his faith to pull him through, and lived, despite the horror of his situation, with gratitude for life and for the help and love of his family, friends, and community. At a press conference a number of months after the shooting, over the gurgling sounds of his respirator, his wife read a statement from him. In it he said, "I'm sometimes angry at the teenage boy who shot me, but more often I feel sorry for him. I only hope that he can turn his life to helping and not hurting people. I forgive him and hope that he can find peace and purpose in his life."

That one can honor the dignity of the perpetrator in the face of such pain and adversity is an incredible testimony to the beauty and generosity of the human spirit. Steven McDonald made a personal decision to respond this way, but the very fact that human beings have the capability to choose such a relationship with life is an affirmation that we do indeed live with grace.

O ver the years, I have heard the following story told at a number of workshops, each time in a slightly different version. But the essence remains the same.

For some years the philosopher and teacher, G. I. Gurdjieff ran a meditation center in the outskirts of Paris. It so happened that among the community of people who lived in his center was an older Russian man whom nobody liked. This man, called Anton, was dirty, boisterous, and irritating to most everyone. Because of their dislike for him, the other residents in the center treated him like an outcast. Sometimes they ignored him. Sometimes they were rude to him, and they always rejected him as part of the community.

One day Anton got fed up with his treatment and decided he had had enough. He packed his bag and left with the intention never to return again. This was seen as sure cause for relief and celebration by the remaining members in the community, who felt that they could finally live in greater harmony and peace. Gurdjieff, who had been abroad when Anton left, questioned the members as to Anton's whereabouts. With relief and pleasure they told him of Anton's decision to leave.

After attending to some business of the day, Gurdjieff drove to the Russian immigrant section of Paris looking for Anton on the streets. After riding around for a while he finally found him passing time on a street corner. Gurdjieff asked Anton to come back and live in the center once again. His response was a clear *no;* he didn't want anything to do with the center again. Gurdjieff asked him if he had a place to live. He didn't, so Gurdjieff told him that if he came back to the community he could live there for free. It was an enticing offer, but it was not enough to get Anton to return. So Gurdjieff asked him if he had any money or a job. He didn't. So Gurdjieff offered him free room and board *plus* a small stipend. After some thought he decided that this was an offer he couldn't refuse. They both got into the car and returned to the center.

To say the least, the other community members were not happy to see Anton's return. Not only was he returning to live there, he was getting free room, board, and a stipend while they were all paying to live there. How could this be?! Gurdjieff minced no words in telling the others that Anton was the most valuable member of the community. Gurdjieff told them that their reaction to Anton would show each of them where they held on to judgment. He would mirror back to them when they closed their hearts. He would show them when they shut down in fear. He told them that when they no longer reacted with judgment, when they could keep their hearts open and meet him with respect, only then would they have learned what they had come to the community to learn in the first place. Anton would be their most valuable teacher, at least for a while. When they were no longer reactivated by him, they would be ready to move on.

Most of us have Antons in our lives—people whom we blame for some present unhappiness. Who are the Antons in your life now? Which family members? Which co-workers? Which friends or acquaintances? Which groups? Gurdjieff knew that his students' growth and learning was to be found in their relationship with

Anton *if* they were open to the learning. This is true for all of us. As cosmologist Brian Swimme says, "The enemy has a secret. The secret is ourselves. Our destiny is working with this." Our growth is intimately tied up in our creative relationship with our perceived adversaries.

Certain aspects of this growth and learning will be different with different people. With some, the initial lessons may be about acknowledging and claiming repressed emotions. With others, it may be learning to be assertive and forthright, taking a clear and self-nurturing stand. Part of one's lesson may be to become more flexible and less critical. Regardless of the particulars of our unique learning, there are always the lessons of cultivating greater insight and compassion for ourselves. By forgiving we are able to reclaim the power that is genuinely ours—the power to risk change, speak the truth, extricate ourselves from ineffective patterns, heal, and love.

Forgiveness is a required course for all of us. There is no way for us to have world peace without it. Forgiveness gives each of us the immediate power to play a vital and necessary part in a planetary peacemaking and evolutionary process. If enough individuals choose to live from their heart for more and more moments, perhaps we will reach that critical mass when world healing is not only possible, but inevitable. As my colleague David Gay noted, "Every act of forgiveness unbinds us from a world of untruths. Every act of forgiveness pulls evolutionary light into the sphere of our personal and planetary healing."

Forgiveness moves us toward what Brian Swimme calls "the supreme moment of the universe—when each thing is recognized in its sacred depth by everything else." To live without forgiveness is to live separated from the sacred and from the most basic instincts of our heart. To live with forgiveness is to reveal in each moment the beauty and value of life. To live with forgiveness is to choose in each moment an active role in creating relationships, organizations, communities, and a world that works for everyone.

I don't think our learning ever ends. We are given opportunity after opportunity to learn the lessons of love. We are given the knowledge of forgiveness to assure our success. In a world where there is much fear, we are given all the boldness that is needed to live out our purpose as teachers of love.

ACKNOWLEDGMENTS

With profound gratitude, I thank my mother and father, Alice and George Casarjian, for teaching me so much about love and forgiveness.

I am enormously grateful to my clients and all the workshop participants who taught me and continue to teach me the positive meaning of boldness.

This book especially reflects the love and attention of my friend and colleague Naomi Raiselle. In addition to enthusiastically supporting me in this process, Naomi created The Stress Reducer with me in 1982. It was during our co-creative work nine years ago that my interest in the teaching of forgiveness came to be. Her keen creative input is woven throughout this book.

I am also deeply grateful to my friend and colleague Fella Cederbaum, who in addition to offering valuable creative input and editorial suggestions so generously gave her loving support.

I am most grateful to Joan Borysenko, my friend and colleague who planted the seed of this book at Bantam. This was one of the many expressions of Joan's unceasingly generous spirit.

Many thanks to my editor at Bantam, Toni Burbank, whose

solid support and astute creative direction were invaluable at crucial points along the way.

Many thanks to my agent, Ned Leavitt, who has been steadfastly supportive and a pleasure to work with.

My heartfelt thanks go to my dear friends Rick Ingrasci and Peggy Taylor for many years of loving support. Over the years Rick has encouraged my work and generously opened many professional doors to introduce it.

My thanks to Cyrisse Jaffe for her thorough editing of the first draft of this book.

My thanks to Matthew Budd for the personal and professional support he has offered me over the years.

A very special thanks to my godmother, Mary Brunton.

A special note of gratitude goes to many other people who have contributed directly or indirectly to this book. Thank you, Eileen Borris, Helen Bonny, the Reverend Dajad Davidian, Ilene Robinson, Stephen Walters, David Gay, Nancy Gray, Andrea and Chet Lyons, Roberta Colasanti, Sally Jackson, Myrin Borysenko, Karen Firmin, Betsy West, Robert Alter, Jack Brotman, Kathy Borelli, Geri Schumacher, Victor Mancini, Amanda and Bethany Casarjian, Rose and David Thorne, and Michelle Rapkin.

A special note of gratitude goes to my dear friend Tricia Stallman, who taught me by the way she lived and died so much about courage and dignity.

Very loving thanks to my siblings, Carol, Zaven, and Conrad, who all learned well the generosity of my parents.

My thanks to the fine men and women whom I worked with at the Massachusetts Correctional Institutes at Framingham and Gardner.

My heartfelt thanks go to the teachers at the Insight Meditation Society in Barre, Massachusetts, who so generously, gently, and skillfully help thousands of students awaken to love's presence.

With great gratitude I thank so many people who are not mentioned here—people who have taught me so much about forgiving by mirroring back to me both my fears and the light of love.

Profound recognition goes to *A Course in Miracles*. Had I not been introduced to *A Course in Miracles*, this book would not have been written.

REFERENCES

Chapter One
Paul Tillich. "To Whom Much Was Forgiven." *Parabola: The Magazine of Myth and Tradition*. Volume XII, number 3, 1987.

Chapter Two
Gerald Jampolsky. *Good-bye to Guilt: Releasing Fear Through Forgiveness*. New York: Bantam, 1985.
Terry Dobson. "A Kind Word Turneth Away Wrath." © 1981 by Terry Dobson. Reprinted by permission of the author.

Chapter Three
Gerald Jampolsky. *Good-bye to Guilt: Releasing Fear Through Forgiveness*. New York: Bantam, 1985.

Chapter Four
Eva Pierrakos. *The Pathwork of Self-Transformation*. New York: Bantam, 1990. © 1990 by The Pathwork Foundation.

Matthew Fox. *Original Blessing: A Primer in Creation Spirituality.* Santa Fe, NM: Bear & Co., 1983.

Chapter Six
Paul Pearsall. *The Power of the Family: Strength, Comfort and Healing.* New York: Doubleday, 1990.

Chapter Seven
Robert Johnson. *We: Understanding the Psychology of Romantic Love.* New York: Harper & Row, 1985.
Frank Pittman, M.D. *Private Lies: Infidelity and the Betrayal of Intimacy.* New York: Norton, 1989.

Chapter Eight
Matthew McKay, Peter D. Rogers, and Judith McKay. *When Anger Hurts: Quieting the Storm Within.* Oakland, CA: New Harbinger Publications, Inc., 1989.
Alice Miller. *The Drama of the Gifted Child.* New York: Basic Books, Inc., 1981.
Robert Rosenthal and Lenore Jacobson. *Pygmalion in the Classroom: Teacher Expectation and Pupils' Intellectual Development.* New York: Holt, Rinehart and Winston, 1968.
Robert Ornstein and Paul Erlich. *New World, New Mind: Moving Toward Conscious Evolution.* New York: Doubleday, 1989.

Chapter Nine
Matthew Fox. *Original Blessing: A Primer in Creation Spirituality.* Santa Fe, NM: Bear & Co., 1983.
Paul Tillich. "To Whom Much Was Forgiven." *Parabola: The Magazine of Myth and Tradition.* Volume XII, number 3, 1987.
John Bradshaw. *Healing the Shame that Binds You.* Deerfield Beach, FL: Health Communications, Inc., 1988.
Joan Borysenko. *Guilt Is the Teacher, Love Is the Lesson.* New York: Warner Books, 1990.
Father Thomas Hopko. "Living in Communion: An Interview with Father Thomas Hopko." *Parabola: The Magazine of Myth and Tradition.* Volume XII, number 3, 1987.
Pat Rodegast and Judith Stanton, eds. *Emmanuel's Book: A Manual*

for Living Comfortably in the Cosmos. New York: Bantam Books, 1985.

Charles Johnston, M.D. *The Creative Imperative.* Berkeley, CA: Celestial Arts, 1986.

Chapter Ten

Stephen Levine. Excerpt from the *Thinking Allowed* television program presented by the Institute for Noetic Sciences.

Juan Ramon Jimenez from *Lorca and Jimenez: Selected Poems,* translated by Robert Bly. Boston: Beacon Press, 1973. Reprinted by permission of Robert Bly.

Chapter Eleven

George Vaillant. *Adaptation to Life.* Boston: Little, Brown, 1978.

Deepak Chopra, M.D. *Quantum Healing: Exploring the Frontiers of Mind/Body Medicine.* New York: Bantam, 1989.

O. Carl Simonton and Stephanie Matthews-Simonton. *Getting Well Again.* New York: Bantam, 1982.

Redford Williams, M.D. *The Trusting Heart.* New York: Random House, 1989.

Chapter Twelve

Sam Keen. *Faces of the Enemy: Reflections of the Hostile Imagination.* New York: Harper & Row, 1988.

Gary Zukav. *The Seat of the Soul.* New York: Simon and Schuster (Firestone), 1989.

Catherine Ingram. *In the Footsteps of Gandhi: Conversations with Spiritual Social Activists.* Berkeley, CA: Parallax Press, 1990.

Chapter Thirteen

Corrie Ten Boom with John and Elizabeth Sherrill. *The Hiding Place: The Triumphant Story of Corrie Ten Boom.* Permission by John Sherrill.

Excerpt from *Living with Vision: Reclaiming the Power of the Heart* by Linda Marks. © 1989 by Linda Marks. Reprinted with permission by Knowledge Systems, Inc., 7777 W. Morris St., Indianapolis, IN 46231.

READING LIST

There are many books that open the way for personal insights and inner healing. The following are some of the books that I have found helpful. If you care to read further, I recommend any of them.

A Course in Miracles. Farmingdale, NY: The Foundation for Inner Peace, 1975.

Abrams, Jeremiah, ed., *Reclaiming the Inner Child*. Los Angeles: Jeremy P. Tarcher, Inc., 1990.

Borysenko, Joan. *Guilt Is the Teacher, Love Is the Lesson*. New York: Warner Books, 1990.

Borysenko, Joan. *Minding the Body, Mending the Mind*. New York: Bantam Books, 1988.

Bradshaw, John. *Healing the Shame that Binds You*. Deerfield Beach, FL: Health Communications Inc., 1988.

Bradshaw, John. *Homecoming: Reclaiming and Championing Your Inner Child*. New York: Bantam Books, 1990.

Dossey, Larry, M.D. *Recovering the Soul*. New York: Bantam Books, 1989.

Ferrucci, Piero. *What We May Be*. Los Angeles: Jeremy P. Tarcher, Inc., 1982.

Fields, Rick, with Peggy Taylor, Rex Weyler, and Rick Ingrasci. *Chop Wood, Carry Water: A Guide to Finding Spiritual Fulfillment in Everyday Life*. Los Angeles: Jeremy P. Tarcher, Inc., 1984.

Fox, Matthew. *Original Blessing: A Primer in Creation Spirituality*. Santa Fe, NM: Bear & Co., 1983.

Fox, Matthew. *The Coming of the Cosmic Christ*. San Francisco: Harper & Row, 1988.

Hunt, Terry, and Karen Paine-Gernee. *Emotional Healing: A Program for Emotional Sobriety*. New York: Warner Books, 1990.

Jampolsky, Gerald. *Love Is Letting Go of Fear*. New York: Bantam Books, 1981.

Jampolsky, Gerald. *Goodbye to Guilt: Releasing Fear Through Forgiveness*. New York: Bantam Books, 1985.

Johnson, Robert. *We: Understanding the Psychology of Romantic Love*. New York: Harper & Row, 1985.

Kabat-Zinn, Jon. *Full Catastrophe Living*. New York: Delacorte Press, 1990.

Keen, Sam. *Faces of the Enemy: Reflections of the Hostile Imagination.* New York: HarperCollins, 1991.

Lerner, Harriet Goldhor. *The Dance of Anger: A Woman's Guide to Changing the Patterns of Intimate Relationships.* New York: Harper & Row (Perennial Library), 1986.

Lerner, Harriet Goldhor. *The Dance of Intimacy.* New York: Harper & Row, 1989.

Levine, Stephen. *Healing Into Life and Death.* New York: Doubleday (Anchor Books), 1987.

Levine, Stephen. *A Gradual Awakening.* New York: Doubleday (Anchor Books), 1979.

Marks, Linda. *Living with Vision: Reclaiming the Power of the Heart.* Indianapolis, IN: Knowledge Systems, Inc., 1989.

Maslow, Abraham, *Toward a Psychology of Being* (2d ed.) New York: Van Nostrand, Reinhold, 1968.

Miller, Alice. *The Drama of the Gifted Child.* New York: Basic Books, Inc., 1981.

Miller, Alice. *For Your Own Good.* New York: Farrar, Straus & Giroux, 1983.

Parabola, volume XII, number 3, 1987: "Forgiveness"

Pelletier, Kenneth. *Mind As Healer, Mind As Slayer.* New York: Dell, 1977.

Prather, Hugh. *Notes on How to Live in the World and Still Be Happy.* New York: Doubleday, 1986.

Ram Dass and Stephen Levine. *Grist for the Mill.* Berkeley, CA: Celestial Arts, 1987.

Ram Dass and Paul Gorman. *How Can I Help?* New York: Alfred A. Knopf, 1987.

Rodegast, Pat, and Judith Stanton, eds. *Emmanuel's Book: A Manual for Living Comfortably in the Cosmos.* New York: Bantam Books, 1985.

Siegel, Bernie S., M.D. *Peace, Love and Healing.* New York: Harper & Row, 1989.

Siegel, Bernie S., M.D. *Love, Medicine and Miracles.* New York: Harper & Row, 1986.

Small, Jacquelyn. *Transformers: The Artists of Self-Creation.* New York: Bantam Books, 1992.

Ten Boom, Corrie, with John and Elizabeth Sherrill. *The Hiding Place.* New York: Bantam Books, 1971.

Williamson, Marianne. *A Return to Love: Reflections on the Principles of* A Course in Miracles. New York: HarperCollins, 1992.

Woodman, Marion. *Addiction to Perfection: The Still Unravaged Bride.* Toronto, Canada: Inner City Books, 1982.

Zukav, Gary. *The Seat of the Soul.* New York: Simon & Schuster (Firestone), 1989.

Request for personal stories:
I am continuing to study forgiveness as the basis of healing and am interested in receiving personal stories and experiences. If you would like to share your personal story of forgiveness, please send it to me:

Robin Casarjian
c/o Soundiscoveries
Box 194 Back Bay
Boston, MA 02117

Please indicate whether I may have permission to publicly share or reprint your story. Names and specific identifying information will be changed to ensure confidentiality.

Audiocasette tapes:
The Forgiveness Tapes is a five-tape set of guided visualizations with music designed to promote inner healing.

- *Love and Forgiveness*
- *Healing the Inner Child*
- *The Forgiveness Walk: Transforming Everyday Encounters*
- *Forgiving A Child: Nurturing Self-Esteem*
- *Forgiving Your Students: Nurturing Self-Esteem*

Individual tapes: $10.95 each.
Massachusetts residents add 5% sales tax.
Add 20% to total for shipping and handling. Please make out check or money order to Soundiscoveries.

Also available: *The Stress Reducer*® created and produced by Robin Casarjian and Naomi Raiselle.

Lectures, workshops, and trainings:
Robin provides programs on the subjects of forgiveness, self-esteem, and stress-management for private, community, educational, religious, health, business, and other organizations. Please send inquiries to Soundiscoveries.